PUBLIC RELATIONS FOR PUBLIC HEALTH AND SOCIAL GOOD

Foregrounding the work professional communicators do to support public health and social missions, this book examines how the principles and practices of public relations can be applied by nonprofit, government, and corporate entities working to understand and improve public health and social conditions.

Many organizations attempt to influence prosocial behaviors, such as donating one's time, money, or talents; participating in advocacy or activism; or otherwise working to protect public health or inspire social change. This book explores research and practice related to communication and other factors involved in motivating such efforts. Each chapter focuses on a different topic, providing definitions, summarizing research, and explaining how it has been or can be applied to practice and ends with discussion questions to consider and references for further reading.

Ideally placed for advanced undergraduate and graduate courses in public relations, health communication, or strategic communication as well as for communications professionals looking to apply research to their practice.

Brooke W. McKeever is Professor and Chair of the Department of Advertising & Public Relations in the College of Communication & Information Sciences at the University of Alabama, USA.

PUBLIC RELATIONS FOR PUBLIC HEALTH AND SOCIAL GOOD

Edited by Brooke W. McKeever

Routledge
Taylor & Francis Group

NEW YORK AND LONDON

Designed cover image: Macrovector / © Getty Images

First published 2025
by Routledge
605 Third Avenue, New York, NY 10158

and by Routledge
4 Park Square, Milton Park, Abingdon, Oxon, OX14 4RN

Routledge is an imprint of the Taylor & Francis Group, an informa business

Library of Congress Cataloging-in-Publication Data
Names: McKeever, Brooke W., editor.
Title: Public relations for public health and social good / [edited by]
    Brooke W. McKeever.
Description: New York, NY : Routledge, 2025. | Includes bibliographical
    references and index.
Identifiers: LCCN 2024005930 (print) | LCCN 2024005931 (ebook) |
    ISBN 9781032355092 (hardback) | ISBN 9781032355085
    (paperback) | ISBN 9781003327189 (ebook)
Subjects: LCSH: Communication in medicine. | Public health. |
    Public relations
Classification: LCC R118 .P83 2024 (print) | LCC R118 (ebook) |
    DDC 610.1/4—dc23/eng/20240412
LC record available at https://lccn.loc.gov/2024005930
LC ebook record available at https://lccn.loc.gov/2024005931

ISBN: 978-1-032-35509-2 (hbk)
ISBN: 978-1-032-35508-5 (pbk)
ISBN: 978-1-003-32718-9 (ebk)

DOI: 10.4324/9781003327189

Typeset in Times New Roman
by Apex CoVantage, LLC

This book is dedicated to my family and friends, to the many students I have taught over the years, and to the great teachers, mentors, colleagues, and collaborators I have had.
To Robert, Isla, and Kira: You are my world. I am grateful for you every day.
To my parents and my brother: You are my foundation. Thank you for always being there and supporting me.
To Dr. Lois Boynton and Dr. Daniel Riffe: You have provided so much educational inspiration. Thank you for that and for your continued friendship and mentorship over the years.

CONTENTS

List of Contributors   x

PART 1
Introduction and Foundations   **1**

1 A Public Relations Approach to Public Health and
   Social Change   3
   Brooke W. McKeever

2 Public Relations and Understanding Culture as a Social
   Determinant of Health   14
   María E. Len-Ríos, Rachel Young, and Amanda Hinnant

3 Ethical Relationships and Responsibilities Contribute to
   Social Good   31
   Lois A. Boynton

4 "Racism is a U.S. public health crisis": How Public
   Relations and Intersectionality Interact to Form This
   Reality of Public Health Today   47
   *Jennifer Vardeman, Natalie T. J. Tindall, Jeremy
      Cajina-Clark, and Monica L. Ponder*

PART 2
Concepts and Competencies 65

5 Exploring the Intersections of Stewardship in Public
Relations and Public Health 67
Geah Pressgrove and Richard Waters

6 Advocacy, Activism, and Gun Violence Communication 83
Minhee Choi

7 Crisis Communication for Social Good 98
Lucinda Austin, LaShonda Eaddy, Xuerong Lu,
and Yan Jin

8 Health Justice for the Past, Present, and Future:
Exploring the Linkage between Social Movements and
Public Relations 116
Candice L. Edrington and Sarah A. Aghazadeh

PART 3
Places and Spaces 131

9 Nonprofit Organizations: A Force for Good 133
Brooke W. McKeever

10 High Stakes, Low Trust: Government Public Relations 148
Abbey Blake Levenshus

11 Proving It with Action: Embracing a Responsibility to
Advocate for Social Change 166
Holly Overton and Nicholas Eng

PART 4
Examples from Abroad 181

12 Managing Digital Strategic Communication during the
COVID-19 Pandemic: Insights from Italian Ministries
and Governmental Institutions 183
*Alessandro Lovari, Francesca Comunello, Alessandra
Massa, Francesca Ieracitano, and Alberto Marinelli*

13 A Decade of Communicating about Mental Health after
Crises in Christchurch, New Zealand 198
Wan Chi Leung, Georgia Williams, and Kaaren Mathias

Index *215*

CONTRIBUTORS

Sarah A. Aghazadeh, Auburn University, USA

Lucinda Austin, University of North Carolina at Chapel Hill, USA

Lois A. Boynton, University of North Carolina at Chapel Hill, USA

Jeremy Cajina-Clark, University of Houston, USA

Minhee Choi, Texas Tech University, USA

Francesca Comunello, Sapienza University of Rome, Italy

LaShonda Eaddy, Pennsylvania State University, USA

Candice L. Edrington, University of South Carolina, USA

Nicholas Eng, University of Georgia, USA

Amanda Hinnant, University of Missouri, USA

Francesca Ieracitano, Sapienza University of Rome, Italy

Yan Jin, University of Georgia, USA

María E. Len-Ríos, University of Minnesota, USA

Wan Chi Leung, University of Canterbury, New Zealand

Abbey Blake Levenshus, Butler University, USA

Alessandro Lovari, University of Cagliari, Italy

Xuerong Lu, Oregon State University, USA

Alberto Marinelli, Sapienza University of Rome, Italy

Alessandra Massa, Sapienza University of Rome, Italy

Kaaren Mathias, University of Canterbury, New Zealand

Holly Overton, Pennsylvania State University, USA

Monica L. Ponder, Howard University, USA

Geah Pressgrove, West Virginia University, USA

Natalie T. J. Tindall, University of Texas at Austin, USA

Jennifer Vardeman, University of Houston, USA

Richard Waters, University of San Francisco, USA

Georgia Williams, University of Canterbury, New Zealand

Rachel Young, University of Iowa, USA

PART 1

Introduction and Foundations

1

A PUBLIC RELATIONS APPROACH TO PUBLIC HEALTH AND SOCIAL CHANGE

Brooke W. McKeever

Introduction to This Book

A presentation before the American Public Health Association in 1949 by Dr. Vlado A. Getting, then commissioner of the Massachusetts Department of Public Health, stated that the attainment of public health objectives could be "hastened by the employment of a continuing, good public relations program" (Getting, 1949, p. 1561). He describes public relations as "a science through which an organization" may secure the "public recognition and approval which is necessary to success" (Getting, 1949, p. 1561). He goes on to discuss the objectives of public relations in detail, including internal relations, the dissemination of information, community organization, professional relationships, and governmental relations. Some of the strategies mentioned in his presentation, more than 70 years ago, are still used by public relations practitioners today.

In some ways, public relations has remained incredibly stable over the years. Of course, the advent of the internet and social media, the development of on-line communities, and other technological innovations such as artificial intelligence (AI) have led to changes in public relations and communication (both good and bad) including increased forms of social networking and support, and faster spreading misinformation and disinformation. These challenges and opportunities have been particularly salient in recent years, as an unprecedented pandemic has affected people and communities across the globe. During this time, we have seen individuals and organizations from the public, private, and nonprofit sectors engaged in strategic communication in various forms. Some of those forms of communication are new (since what Dr. Getting described in his speech), but some remain tried and true. His presentation concluded by stating that, "while never

DOI: 10.4324/9781003327189-2

before have people been as aware of health as they now are, we have still fallen short of creating proper demand for the attainment and maintenance of optimal health" (Getting, 1949, p. 1566). The same could be said today, following more than three years of an ongoing pandemic, which coincided with global events related to social justice, economic and workforce changes resulting from the pandemic, and ongoing concerns related to climate change and the environment.

With this history and these events as a backdrop, this book explores public relations for public health and social good. It applies a relationship-building and management approach to strategic communication for behavior and social change. It examines principles and concepts that are important in public relations and explains how they have been applied in research and practice by nonprofit, government, and corporate entities working to understand and improve public health and social conditions. Many organizations attempt to influence prosocial behavior, such as donating one's time, money, or talents, or participating in advocacy or activism efforts. This book explores research and practice related to communication and other factors involved in motivating such behaviors.

While many people have written about public relations and public health over the years (see, e.g., Ki et al., 2022; Park & Reber, 2010; Springston & Lariscy, 2005; Wise, 2001), the ongoing COVID-19 pandemic has made health and risk communication more visible to the public. Additionally, we have witnessed the importance of prosocial behaviors, such as wearing a mask in public, staying home and/or practicing social distancing, and getting vaccinated to protect oneself and others against COVID-19. Prosocial behaviors such as donating, volunteering, or participating in other forms of advocacy and activism have also been highly visible in recent years, as nonprofit organizations work toward social justice for various issues and corporations become more involved in corporate social advocacy and activism (Ciszek & Logan, 2018; Kim et al., 2020).

Because of events that took place in 2020–2021, issues related to trust, empathy, the need for clear communication, working in partnership with others, and relationship building with different publics have had a renewed focus for media and scholars (Abbott, 2021; Furr-Holden et al., 2021; Guidry et al., 2021). However, these issues are not new, and public relations and health communication has a long history of studying and grappling with some of these issues. A recently published article, written by the editor, demonstrates how we can apply lessons from the past to the current pandemic and to strategic communication moving forward to help improve health and social conditions (McKeever, 2021). More specifically, the article looks at media advocacy efforts from Surgeon General C. Everett Koop in the 1980s regarding HIV/AIDS and draws parallels to leadership and communication (or the lack thereof) related to COVID-19 during the 2020s. Similarly, a website for the Center for the Study of Tobacco and Society, hosted by the University of Alabama, explores the failures and successes of public health efforts to curtail tobacco use in the U.S. by examining advertisements, media coverage, and campaigns that resulted from public relations and health communication efforts (https://csts.ua.edu/). While much of the work related to public health and social change is carried out by nonprofit or government entities, corporations have also been involved in such efforts, particularly in recent years with the increase in corporate social responsibility, advocacy, and activism. Educational institutions, such as universities, are also involved in some of these efforts, and of course colleges and universities are invested in educating the next generation of public relations and public health communicators.

This book explores these topics with a focus on research and how research has been or can be applied to practice, and campaigns or other real-world examples of communication affecting public health or social change. Each chapter ends with questions to consider and references for further reading. The chapters are written by leading scholars in the fields of public relations, health, and strategic communication. They are written for undergraduate and graduate students as well as for scholars studying these topics and practitioners working in these areas. The goal of this book is to examine and describe relevant topics, campaigns, strategies, and communication that has already happened related to public health and social good so that we might continue to understand, communicate, and explore to improve conditions in these areas moving forward. In the editor's opinion, communication successes and failures, especially those related to public health, social change, and behavior change, can best be understood by looking back—so we can continue to make improvements in communication and in society as we move forward.

A Public Relations Approach to Public Health and Social Change

So, what is meant by a public relations approach to public health and social change? Public relations is based on relationship management. It involves communication, of course, but where PR has differentiated itself from other fields like marketing and advertising is in its focus on relationships. Social marketing has long been viewed as a way to approach communicating about health and social issues. In this sense, social marketing has been defined as, "the use of commercial marketing principles and techniques to promote the adoption of a behavior that will improve the health or well-being of the target audience or of society as a whole" (Weinreich, 2010, p. 4). However, this book argues that a *public relations approach* may be more effective than social marketing or other approaches to public health and social change. By focusing on relationships, key relational outcomes like trust, commitment, satisfaction, control mutuality, and more can be realized or honed through public relations strategies like stewardship (the focus of Chapter 5). When relationships are managed well, there tends to be less fall out, less need for crisis communication (the focus of Chapter 7)

FIGURE 1.1 A public relations approach to public health and social change.

or other possible negative repercussions of communication that does not keep relationships at the forefront.

Public relations strategies can influence prosocial behavior (advocacy, fund-raising, voting, vaccinating, etc.) and those behaviors can influence public health and social change. Figure 1.1 provides a simple visual depiction of this process.

While the model is simple, we know the paths to prosocial behaviors and to successful outcomes in public health or social change can be complex and fraught with impediments. Some of the chapters in this book highlight macro-level approaches, such as media advocacy, which is essentially public relations for public health. Chapter 6, for example, describes media advocacy as an approach to prevent gun violence. Media advocacy involves influencing the media and public agendas so that public health and social issues are on those agendas. Public relations can be helpful in framing issues so that people view them as public health issues at all or in ways that elevate social issues to levels of importance that are necessary for pursuing social change. Offering or pushing for solutions, which sometimes occurs through advocacy or activism, is the third step in the media advocacy process. Public relations is instrumental here as it focuses on relationships as part of working toward solutions. Other chapters in this book focus on other important elements that should be considered in applying public relations to public health or social issues, such as culture and intersectionality, ethics, and more. The chapters are outlined further below.

As further evidence of the need for and appropriate timing of this book, in the fall of 2023, the Commission on Public Relations Education (CPRE) released its 50th anniversary report, which was produced following more than a year of research, including brainstorming sessions, surveys, and focus groups with public relations educators and practitioners from groups like the CPRE, PR Council, and Page Society. The research resulted in seven key findings and calls to action. More information can be found at https://www.commissionpred.org/navigating-change-report/.

One key finding and call to action focuses on public relations' role as a social and cultural practice that generates public engagement and discourse around issues that shape society. PR practitioners and educators agree that public relations drives social change, and as such, students need to be prepared for the social role of organizations in which they may work. In this book, there is a section that focuses on nonprofit, government, and corporate entities that students may work in one day. Each chapter outlines the opportunities and challenges of working in these sectors when it comes to influencing public health or social change. The CPRE report notes that educators and students "must be courageous in addressing challenging issues including gender identity, sexuality, racism, ableism, poverty" (CPRE Executive Summary, p. 7). As we move forward as communicators, educators, and researchers in this field, we should consider how social change issues can be integrated into organizational missions and public relations programs so that they are driving forces rather than separate practices or pieces of content produced as afterthoughts. A chapter later in this book (Chapter 9) touches on this as well, in describing partnerships between nonprofit organizations and corporations or other types of entities that may work together to influence public health or social change. Indeed, it will take organizations and many individuals working together to bring about such change. This book attempts to describe ways in which we have worked and can continue working together toward such goals. The next section provides a preview of the other chapters in this book.

Chapters in This Book

This book is divided into four parts. Part 1 provides an introduction and the foundation for the book, with this first chapter explaining the need for this book, the public relations approach to public health and social change, and outlining the rest of the book for readers. The other chapters touch on foundational concepts that are important for understanding and approaching public relations for public health and social good. For example, Chapter 2: Public Relations and Understanding Culture as a Social Determinant of Health by María Len-Ríos, Rachel Young, and Amanda Hinnant explains that many factors outside individual control affect people's health status and outcomes; these are the social determinants of health. They describe how public relations professionals address and influence the social determinants of health through a variety of ways, such as by changing public opinion and social norms, framing the way audiences understand health issues, raising awareness of health issues among citizens through media, and influencing policymakers who make laws and legislation. The authors emphasize that there are many types of organizations involved in shaping a nation's health, and it is critical to understand how they use public relations to do so.

In Chapter 3: Ethical Relationships and Responsibilities Contribute to Social Good, Lois A. Boynton shares her expertise on ethics and emphasizes the importance of an ethical approach to public relations. The CPRE Executive Summary (2023, p. 6), mentioned earlier in this chapter, called ethics "an essential but neglected competency." As Boynton points out in her chapter, informing and persuading in an ethical manner requires PR practitioners to rationally apply professional values, particularly when facing dilemmas. Individuals communicating with various publics must balance competing loyalties, understand the influence of many standpoints, and advise organizational leaders about societal obligations. Her chapter includes two helpful tables: one that lists and links to multiple ethics codes of public health and public relations professional associations; and one that compares three ethical decision-making models that communication practitioners can use in work and in life.

Chapter 4, titled "Racism is a U.S. public health crisis": How Public Relations and Intersectionality Interact to Form this Reality of Public Health Today, by Jennifer Vardeman, Natalie T. J. Tindall, Jeremy Cajina-Clark, and Monica L. Ponder, takes a critical look at public relations, public health, and intersectionality and how they interconnect. They argue that the field of public relations is slowly realizing how multiple identities matter to the persistence of public health issues, and how various communication strategies and tactics contribute to these issues. This chapter provides an overview of why and how public relations and communications practitioners working in the field of public health should consider intersectionality as a foundation upon which to rethink work practices. The chapter includes several examples of health issues and campaigns to demonstrate factors contributing to persistent racial and social disparities and discusses solution-based skills and strategies that may help students and practitioners moving forward in this field. The chapter ends with recommendations for future research and practice.

Part 2 of this book focuses on concepts and competencies that are important for understanding, studying, and working in public relations as it relates to public health, social change, or social good. For example, Chapter 5: Exploring the Intersections of Stewardship in Public Relations and Public Health, by Geah Pressgrove and Richard Waters, provides an in-depth look at a very important concept in public relations: stewardship. As the authors summarize, their book chapter explores the convergence between stewardship-oriented public health and public relations literature, revealing connections between these well-established domains. They argue that stewardship offers an ethical decision-making framework for public health, while in public relations, stewardship aids in enhancing symmetrical relationship building and maintenance. This chapter also highlights eroding public trust worldwide, exacerbated by COVID-19, which the authors say underscores the importance of stewardship as the fifth step in the public relations process. The chapter concludes with a helpful table, highlighting the intersection of stewardship in public relations and public health. The authors advocate for collaborative research to bridge the gap between typical public health and public relations perspectives, which might enhance effective communication, stakeholder engagement, and both fields moving forward.

Chapter 6: Advocacy, Activism, and Gun Violence Communication, by Minhee Choi, starts by defining and differentiating advocacy and activism, two concepts that are used in public relations, particularly as it relates to public health or social issues. As Choi notes, the concepts have been used interchangeably in research and in media, communication, and popular culture, so this chapter is helpful for better understanding these important concepts. She uses gun violence communication as a case study for exploring advocacy and activism and outlines the public health approach to communicating about various issues, including gun violence.

Chapter 7: Crisis Communication for Social Good by Lucinda Austin, LaShonda Eaddy, Xuerong Lu, and Yan Jin, introduces crisis communication as an important and defining concept and competency in public relations. Indeed, some might say that crisis communication is one area that differentiates public relations from other fields, like advertising and marketing. In some people's minds, crisis communication is synonymous with public relations, though in reality it is a small part of the practice (typically, and thankfully); however, it is also a crucial part of public relations, and it is highly relevant to public health, social issues, social change, and social good. This chapter provides an overview of prominent theories, including the Situational Crisis Communication Theory and the Social-Mediated Crisis Communication Model. It discusses crisis communication as it applies to public health, social change, and social good, emphasizing disaster communication, health crises, and nonprofit crises with an overview of and case example for each. The chapter concludes with emerging trends and future directions in crisis communication in the digital world, touching on important concepts such as misinformation, media affordances, and media convergence.

Chapter 8: Health Justice for the Past, Present, and Future: Exploring the Linkage between Social Movements and Public Relations, by Candice L. Edrington and Sarah A. Aghazadeh, takes an interesting look at social movements and public health from a public relations perspective. The authors argue that public health serves as both a focus and a consequence of various social movements. This chapter centers public health, specifically physical and mental health, in the examination of behaviors associated with social change. It takes a historical approach, highlighting past and present social movements organized by groups such as the Black Panthers, to help us understand the role strategic communication plays in improving public health and social conditions. This chapter underscores the importance of social movements in U.S. history and shows how public relations has affected and been affected by public health and social movements over time.

In Part 3 of this book, authors highlight the places and spaces or sectors where public relations affects public health, social change, or helps to bring about social good. This part of the book is meant to provide a glimpse into the similarities and differences of the nonprofit, government, and corporate sectors, and discusses some research relevant in the three fields. It is also meant to provide students with an idea of what it would be like to work in these different sectors. For example, Chapter 9: Nonprofit Organizations: A Force for Good, by the editor of this book, shows how the nonprofit sector has played a part in some of the most successful public health communication and social change efforts. It focuses on the importance of donors and volunteers in the nonprofit sector, and notes that these stakeholders are a key differentiating factor in thinking about the nonprofit sector compared to corporate or government sectors. The chapter highlights research that has been conducted in nonprofit public relations and provides examples of nonprofit organizations that have led successful health communication campaigns or social change movements. It also touches on the different types of nonprofit organizations, including international nongovernmental organizations (NGOs), and describes partnerships between nonprofit and other types of organizations as an area where maximum impact can be made (in terms of practice), and where more research is needed.

The next chapter focuses on government communication. Chapter 10: High Stakes, Low Trust: Government Public Relations, by Abbey Levenshus, describes how government entities are uniquely positioned in both power and potential consequences because of their authority, mission, and resources. The author notes that in the U.S., public trust in government remains at historically low levels while misinformation continues to rise. Because of these challenges, she recommends a relational approach to strategic government communication. In addition to providing definitions, the chapter highlights relevant government public relations research on topics such as public health, risk and crisis communication, and social media management. It concludes that a relational approach can help government organizations carry out ethical, effective communication, underscoring the themes of relationship management and ethics that are found elsewhere in this book.

Rounding out this section of the book, Chapter 11: Proving it with Action: Embracing a Responsibility to Advocate for Social Change, by Holly Overton and Nicholas Eng, focuses on the role of corporations in public relations as it relates to public health and social change. It examines the role of corporations in creating social change and how public expectations of their role have shifted in recent years. The authors argue that it is no longer acceptable for companies to engage in lip service; they need to demonstrate their values and prove their intentions with action. This chapter defines corporate social responsibility (CSR) and corporate social advocacy (CSA) and describes how they contribute to social change. It concludes with recommendations for those wanting to practice or research corporate PR that aims to bring about social change.

The last part of this book, Part 4, provides two sweeping examples of public relations for public health and social good from abroad. While much of this book focuses on examples from the U.S., the final two chapters of this book are written by authors who are from and/or living in Italy and New Zealand. For example, in Chapter 12: Managing Digital Strategic Communication During the COVID-19

Pandemic: Insights from Italian Ministries and Governmental Institutions, a team of authors from Italy—Alessandro Lovari, Francesca Comunello, Alessandra Massa, Francesca Ieracitano, and Alberto Marinelli—wrote about the transformation that took place in communication practices during the COVID-19 pandemic. They describe how Italy, as one of the first Western countries to be affected by the pandemic, quickly came under pressure to manage emergency communication, which was largely done by Italian government organizations. The chapter discusses qualitative research, in the form of in-depth interviews with social media managers and heads of communications for 23 Italian government institutions. Findings from the research highlight the strategic role of the Ministry of Health in informing Italian citizens, promoting prosocial behaviors, and countering misinformation and disinformation.

Finally, Chapter 13: A Decade of Communicating about Mental Health after Crises in Christchurch, New Zealand, by Wan Chi Leung, Georgia Williams, and Kaaren Mathias discusses how mental health and wellbeing campaigns responded to crises in Christchurch, Canterbury, New Zealand. An earthquake, mass shootings, and strict lockdowns during COVID-19 affected the mental health of many people in Christchurch, a relatively small city in New Zealand. In response, government and nongovernmental organizations created public health campaigns to reach at-risk communities in the city, including indigenous people and language minorities of New Zealand and Pacific Islands. This chapter touches on culture, crisis communication, NGOs, and other aspects that flow throughout this book. The international case study provides an interesting and unique perspective and overview of campaigns that addressed an important public health issue, mental health, over time.

Conclusion

As readers will see, the chapters that follow this one in this book underscore the importance of taking a relational approach to communicating about public health and social issues. By laying a foundation for the public relations approach to public health and public good, introducing different concepts and competencies that are important in PR as it affects public health and social change, describing different places and spaces where this type of communication takes place, and providing examples from different international contexts, it is hoped that this book will be helpful to students hoping to practice or study public relations. It may also interest those already working in public relations, who are making a difference or hoping to make a change through their work in terms of public health, social good, or social change. There are threads that run throughout the book, highlighting some of the most important aspects of research and practice in these areas.

The editor has worked in this field, studied it, and taught many students, both undergraduate and graduate, over many years. I have found public relations to be an incredibly rewarding field, particularly when it focuses on public health or social issues. The beauty of PR is that it applies to any field or topic, and it is always changing. Yet the important aspects of it remain consistent: ethics, writing, research, relationships, and more. Readers can apply what they learn from this book to research, practice, teaching or to otherwise make a difference in whatever way they see fit. If that happens, the goal of this book will be realized.

References

Abbott, B. (2021, July 8). Covid-19 vaccination drive reaches frustration stage— Persuading the hesitant. *The Wall Street Journal.* https://www.wsj.com/articles/ stalled-covid-vaccination-outreach-hesitancy-11625754826

Center for the Study of Tobacco and Society. (2023). The University of Alabama. https:// csts.ua.edu/

Ciszek, E., & Logan, N. (2018). Challenging the dialogic promise: How Ben & Jerry's support for Black Lives Matter fosters dissensus on social media. *Journal of Public Relations Research, 30*(3), 115–127. https://doi.org/10.1080/1062726X.2018.1498342

Commission on Public Relations Education. (2023). Navigating change: Recommendations for advancing undergraduate public relations education (an executive summary and a call to action). http://www.commissionpred.org/wp-content/uploads/2023/10/ CPRE-Executive-Summary-FInal-Final.pdf

Furr-Holden, D., Adeoye-Olatunde, O., Buys, D. R., & McKeever, B. W. (2021, Aug. 27). How public health partnerships are encouraging COVID-19 vaccination in Mississippi, Michigan, Indiana, and South Carolina. *The Conversation.* https:// theconversation.com/how-public-health-partnerships-are-encouraging-covid-19-vaccination-in-mississippi-michigan-indiana-and-south-carolina-166005

Getting, V. A. (1949). Public relations in public health. *American Journal of Public Health and the Nation's Health, 39*(12), 1561–1566. https://doi.org/10.2105/ajph.39.12.1561

Guidry, J. P., O'Donnell, N. H., Austin, L. L., Coman, I. A., Adams, J., & Perrin, P. B. (2021). Stay socially distant and wash your hands: using the health belief model to determine intent for COVID-19 preventive behaviors at the beginning of the pandemic. *Health Education & Behavior, 48*(4), 424–433. https://doi.org/10.1177/10901981211019920

Ki, E. J., Kang, D. Y., & Huang, M. (2022). The state of health public relations: A content analysis of published articles in seven communication journals from 2001 to 2021. *Public Relations Review, 48*(5), 102255. https://doi.org/10.1016/j.pubrev.2022.102255

Kim, J. K., Overton, H., Bhalla, N., & Li, J. Y. (2020). Nike, Colin Kaepernick, and the politicization of sports: Examining perceived organizational motives and public responses. *Public Relations Review, 46*(2), 101856. https://doi.org/10.1016/j. pubrev.2019.101856

McKeever, B. W. (2021). Public relations and public health: The importance of leadership and other lessons learned from "Understanding AIDS" in the 1980s. *Public Relations Review, 47*(1), 102007. https://doi.org/10.1016/j.pubrev.2020.102007

Park, H., & Reber, B. H. (2010). Using public relations to promote health: A framing analysis of public relations strategies among health associations. *Journal of Health Communication, 15*(1), 39–54. https://doi.org/10.1080/10810730903460534

Springston, J. K., & Lariscy, R. A. W. (2005). Public relations effectiveness in public health institutions. *Journal of Health and Human Services Administration, 28*(2), 218–245. https://www.jstor.org/stable/41288065

Weinreich, N. K. (2010). *Hands-on social marketing: A step-by-step guide to designing change for good.* Sage Publications.

Wise, K. (2001). Opportunities for public relations research in public health. *Public Relations Review, 27*(4), 475–487. https://doi.org/10.1016/S0363-8111(01)00102-3

2

PUBLIC RELATIONS AND UNDERSTANDING CULTURE AS A SOCIAL DETERMINANT OF HEALTH

María E. Len-Ríos, Rachel Young, and Amanda Hinnant

Imagine two children who live a few miles apart in a major city. One grows up drinking clean water, attending high-quality schools in a safe environment, has stable housing and access to healthy foods. The other grows up drinking water with lead contamination, attending school in a high-crime neighborhood, living in a series of rundown homes, and without consistent access to fresh and plentiful food. You can see implicitly that the health of these two children is likely shaped by factors far beyond their individual control. Some situations we don't have to imagine. For instance, when Russian forces invaded Ukraine, many Ukrainian children lost access to pediatric cancer care. Some spent time in bunkers and shelters, which is not good for a compromised immune system as it can expose a child to infection. Place, one type of social determinant of health, matters when it comes to health outcomes.

The term *social determinants of health* (SDH) refer to the social, cultural, and environmental factors that influence the health status of individuals and groups. These factors are the focus of this chapter. First, we explain how cultural influences shape SDH with public relations being a cultural force that acts as a determinant of health. Second, the chapter explores how communication tactics, such as episodic and thematic framing, shape understandings of SDH. Lastly, this chapter reviews the various types of public relations that influence culture and health outcomes.

In the 1950s, studies in the United Kingdom found that people with lower socioeconomic status died earlier and had overall worse health than those with higher socioeconomic status, even when both groups had access to the same universal health coverage (Marmot et al., 1991). Other social factors associated with health outcomes include housing and daily living conditions, quality

DOI: 10.4324/9781003327189-3

education, access to health care, neighborhood, the built environment (e.g., trails and parks), employment, social support, and discrimination (Braveman & Gottlieb, 2014; see Figure 2.1). SDH have been described as "the causes of the causes" (Braveman & Gottlieb, 2014, p. 19) and the "upstream" or "distal" factors that set the context for health and wellness. The choices *individuals* make about what to eat and when to exercise are "downstream" or "proximal" factors, but which choices are available and whether those choices are easy or difficult to make are influenced by *upstream* factors like income, neighborhood safety, and amenities like affordable grocery stores or nearby parks, which typically result from governmental and commercial decisions.

Upstream factors also coexist and intersect in ways that can make it easier or more difficult to maintain good health. Taken together, these upstream factors act directly on health, construct the social and built environments in which people make their health choices, and constrain people's health options. Marginalized groups, those who have experienced societal discrimination and neighborhood

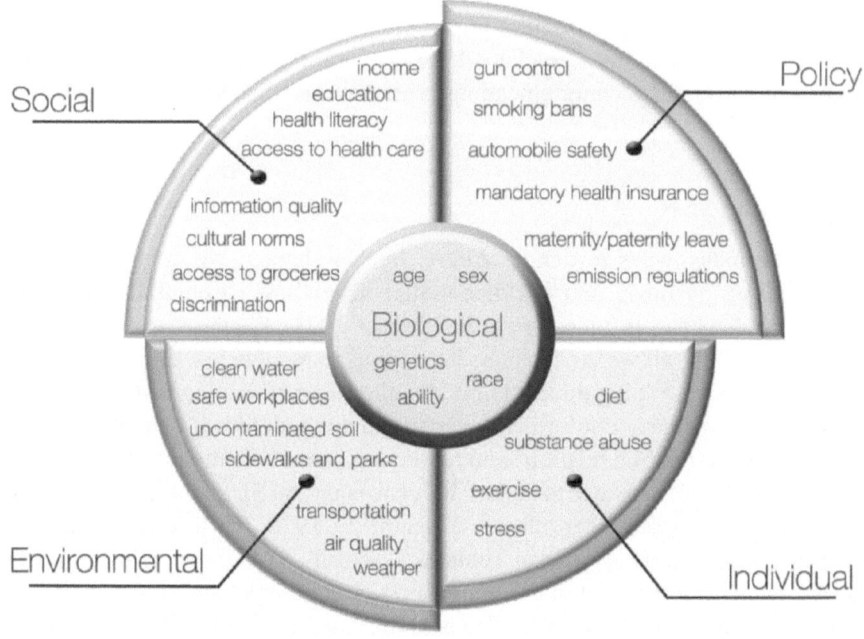

FIGURE 2.1   This diagram depicts the factors involved in social determinants of health.

Sources: Adapted from G. Dahlgren & M. Whitehead, Policies and strategies to promote social equity in health. Stockholm, Sweden: Institute for Future Studies. It appeared in A. Hinnant & M. E. Len-Ríos (2020). Rx for communicating about health inequalities. In M. E. Len-Ríos and E. L. Perry, *Cross-cultural journalism and strategic communication: Storytelling and diversity*, 2nd ed. Routledge.

segregation, may confront stress and loss of opportunity from individual or systemic racism and are often more likely to live in poverty, with unsafe or unstable housing, and with lack of access to employment, high-functioning schools, and health care (Braveman et al., 2011; Williams & Mohammed, 2013). Thus, while many communication campaigns focus on improving health through individual behaviors, it is easy to see that changing individual downstream factors can only get us so far when upstream factors constrain the options available to individuals.

And how are public relations practitioners involved in social determinants of health? Let's consider the prior example of Ukrainian children with cancer. In this case, the nonprofit St. Jude Global joined with several partners to jumpstart SAFER (Supporting Action for Emergency Response) Ukraine (St. Jude Global, n.d.). St. Jude used public relations, and the services of public relations agency Finn Partners, to increase awareness of its efforts to help children with cancer access care that was disrupted because of war. St. Jude's communication campaign helped raise awareness, funds, and partnership support to offer Ukrainian children with cancer and their families ways to continue treatments inside Ukraine or in other countries ("Four Ukrainian Children Flown," 2022; Nye, 2022). As we can see, addressing SDH often requires financial, political, and public support, and public relations has a crucial role in encouraging individuals to act. Thus, some public relations communications work can be considered a key influence on SDH.

Culture and SDH

There are many ways to define culture. In this chapter, we define culture as shared ideas, meanings, and worldviews that inform how we communicate along with our beliefs and attitudes about life (Geertz, 1973). Because culture serves as a background for all we do, it can be hard for us to recognize—until we encounter another way of doing things. Public relations and marketing communication, as part of the media and information environment, both reflect culture and influence it. Because public relations and marketing communications determine how we see health, we consider them key influences on the SDH, the factors outside our individual choices that affect our health. In 1928, PR pioneer Edward L. Bernays was paid by American Tobacco Company to increase sales of Lucky Strike cigarettes by changing societal norms about women smoking, which was disapproved of at the time. To counteract the upstream cultural influence, Bernays appealed to a value held by society—individual freedom—to develop the "Torches of Freedom" campaign (Tye, 1998). In this sense, cultural norms and practices create a system that influences individual behaviors. Bernays and tobacco company executives worked to change the culture that affected individual behavior and in effect helped change societal systems—not necessarily for the better—and it was big business.

When we think of PR efforts to improve public health, much emphasis is placed on downstream factors (people changing their behaviors), yet many times it is the upstream factors—the societal rules and regulations—that control individual behaviors. For example, the U.S. Surgeon General published his report on the health hazards of smoking on January 11, 1964 (Centers for Disease Control and Prevention-CDC, n.d.-a). As with smoking, marketing and PR efforts also influence these upstream factors. Indeed, after cigarette smoking was deemed a health hazard, the U.S. government enacted laws to help curb smoking, including banning broadcast advertising of tobacco, limiting the purchasing age, and prohibiting smoking in certain places (e.g., airplanes, government buildings). Even so, cultural factors and myths, like the myth that cigarettes signify coolness, rebellion, and independence, keep people smoking. Critical to note, cultural factors and social determinants are variable across countries and even within communities. So, when we consider campaigns and SDH, we must consider whether there are similarities or differences in culture that may affect health outcomes at both the systemic and individual level.

Today, the nonprofit Truth Initiative studies tobacco-related media messages that are seen by young people. The organization advocates for media environments that do not normalize smoking in culture. The organization publicizes its research to put pressure on media companies and legislators to constrain the use of tobacco-related products on screens. For instance, the Truth Initiative's study found that the Netflix show *Stranger Things*, popular among teens and young adults, had increased depictions of smoking four-fold since its first season (Keveney, 2020). Their work is in the battleground area of the social determinants of health as they focus on the environment in which teens are immersed because research shows lifelong smokers start by the age of 26 (CDC, n.d.-b). The media environment has an effect on perceptions of social norms and serves as a social determinant of health, and the Truth Initiative engages in media relations work to advocate for reducing the presence of tobacco product depictions in pop culture.

SDH and the culture of health can also influence how professional communicators frame audience messages. Much of health and science communication have relied on the idea that scientists have information that audiences need, and if the information is properly communicated, audiences will make good, healthful choices. In science communication, this is a dissemination or deficit model of communication (Bubela et al., 2009)—the expectation being that if people have the right information, they will make the right choices. What this perspective misses is that individuals might reject the scientific information or may face systemic constraints and not be able to act on it (e.g., lack money, access). Thus, there has been a move away from a deficit model toward a broader view of factors that influence whether individuals accept messages.

In considering the individual and systemic levels, we can look at alcohol consumption. Consuming alcohol in excess can have harmful effects on health, including death. At the individual level, alcohol awareness campaigns are used to reduce individual drinking for the public good. For instance, on college campuses researchers have conducted social norm campaigns to combat the idea that "everyone is drinking" by sharing campus statistics about drinking prevalence with the idea that college students will feel freer to decline consuming alcohol when they realize that many college students are not drinking or not drinking to excess (DeJong, 2010; Su et al., 2018). This campaign is one example of how communicators can use social factors in their messaging to go beyond the basic sharing of risk information.

Of course, there are other systemic factors that affect alcohol consumption, including availability, price, and law enforcement. In fact, some researchers have been critical of social norms campaigns because sometimes research results have indicated that the campaigns did not work as intended. Follow-up studies and analysis have shown, however, that social norms campaigns have worked when the availability of alcohol on campus was considered (DeJong, 2010). When there was a high availability of alcohol, social norms campaigns did not work as well. This finding again points out the complex interactions among social determinants and that the circumstances of one's environment may play an influential factor in determining the health outcome.

There is evidence across countries to support the finding that social determinants play a role in population health. A study on the same topic, of 15 low- to middle-income countries (e.g., Brazil, Hungary, Mexico), found that, similar to high-income country results, limiting physical availability of alcohol (e.g., licensing sales and distribution, store density in communities, and store hours) was associated with lower drinking volume. Similarly, when beer prices were high, people drank beer less often. Interestingly motor vehicle laws about drunk driving did not affect consumption, which the study's researchers said may be tied to matters of enforcement (Cook, Bond, & Greenfield, 2014). In other words, if individuals do not think they'll be stopped by the police, they may be less likely to worry about drunk driving because they do not expect to get caught.

Virtual environments may also be places that influence health behaviors. Researchers have examined whether adolescents' attitudes toward drinking and perceptions of their self-efficacy to refuse a drink can be affected by interacting with virtual characters or avatars in video games. The authors of one recent study found that, indeed, social norms, depicted in a virtual environment using fear appeals (a serious car accident), appeared to affect drinking attitudes and perceptions of the increased ability to say no to a drink (Hong et al., 2023), even though it may be a short-lived effect.

In examining strategic messaging to improve public health related to alcohol consumption, we can see that systems are associated with effects on individual alcohol consumption, and the culture in which an individual lives will provide a context for the behavior. These contextual factors go beyond choice.

How Different Communication Devices Influence How Audiences Perceive Determinants of Health

The way we receive information can affect how we think about finding solutions to health problems, and public relations professionals know that how they prepare their communications can affect whether journalists want to tell their stories. News and lifestyle media outlets have historically centered on individual determinants of health as both cause and solution for countless personal health problems and even for broader public health issues like opioid use (e.g., individual addiction v. criminal fraud in marketing and distribution of prescription opioids on behalf of a pharmaceutical company). These are downstream factors. Norms of journalism structure and ideology have led to a focus on individual behavior over SDH because the former provides direction for individual action and the latter are complicated and controversial (Hinnant et al., 2017). Moreover, SDH do not attract news attention because the issues are constant, slow-moving, and abstract, while individual determinants meet several newsworthiness standards being novel, disruptive, personalized, and unusual (Galtung & Ruge, 1965; Young et al., 2017). Another reason individual risk factors and treatments dominate journalism is because they are the subject of most research and intervention (Braveman et al., 2011). Reinforcing this pattern is the findings that show us story framing in news that focuses on an individual (e.g., a young woman's fight against breast cancer, a child's struggle with lead poisoning from contaminated water) increases perceived news issue importance among audiences (Grabe et al., 2017).

The prevalence of health inequalities in certain groups is a more specific, yet still complex topic in health journalism, and SDH largely shape these inequalities. When journalists cover health inequalities, like other topics, there is a focus on individual experiences with disease rather than the social factors at play. Coverage of health inequalities, while important for informing policy and the public (Niederdeppe et al., 2013), can have negative effects on at-risk audiences and for shaping public opinion on several factors, so coverage needs to be carefully considered. To elaborate, one study shows that focusing on health inequalities in colorectal cancer mortality rates discouraged African Americans from undergoing preventative screening (Nicholson et al., 2008). Specifically, Africans Americans who read news stories emphasizing health disparities compared to White Americans without mentioning progress experienced more negative emotions, which led to less intention to be screened for colorectal cancer. Conversely, another study showed that focusing on progress made toward increased equality could decrease support of majority groups for political action to address social determinants of health; when White Americans were reminded of civil rights progress, they were less likely to support policies addressing social inequities, including health disparities (Eibach & Purdie-Vaughns, 2011). Thus, public relations professionals know that how you tell a story can influence how audiences think about health issues.

In terms of how these broader issues play out in communication, we look to more specific communication devices, such as framing. Framing, which is the process of making certain aspects of reality more salient than others in a story (Entman, 1993), determines whether a health story emphasizes individual causes and solutions or social causes and solutions. Thematic framing, which deals with broad issues and the background context for an issue, contrasts with episodic framing, which provides concrete details of a specific individual or event as means to represent an issue (Iyengar, 1991). Like journalistic coverage generally, most health stories would be characterized as episodic (e.g., by focusing on a patient's experience) (Dunwoody, 2021). It follows that thematic framing cultivates audience attributions of responsibility for problems to societal forces, while episodic framing leads audience members to blame individuals for problems. To extend the attribution of responsibility further, thematic framing and SDH fosters a feeling of social responsibility for solutions, while episodic framing and a focus on individual determinants of health leads audiences to expect individuals to solve their own problems (Cho & Salmon, 2007).

Episodic frames use stories of everyday people, anecdotes, or "exemplars," while thematic frames provide base-rate information, such as statistics, policies, or legislation, and additional context. According to Gibson and Zillman (1994), episodic frames use "exemplifying information, or exemplars, about individuals whose circumstances illustrate the phenomenon under review," such as personal details about how someone has coped with a situation. Thematic frames provide "base-rate information"—such as statistics, numerical data, or risk calculations— which details "the number or proportion of people or things involved in a given social phenomenon" (pp. 603–604). SDH are difficult to capture within the episodic framework favored by news media and audiences.

Because discrimination, prejudice, and racism are social determinants of health (Paradies et al., 2015), communicators need to consider diversity, equity, and inclusion in the framing of their health communications. There are ways that communication practitioners can develop both a more equitable and responsible approach to sharing episodic, individual stories. When scouting sources, both expert and lay people, practitioners typically prioritize mostly visible kinds of diversity, such as race, ethnicity as well as other less visible types of diversity. Additionally looking for experts and other sources who come from, serve, and speak to different types of communities can provide added context. In sharing personal stories, it is more accurate when practitioners find people whose experiences are representative of the realities of the health situation, and not promote outlier cases or ones that are overly sensational. For example, even though American Indians and Alaska Natives face greater risk of cirrhosis and chronic liver disease than the national average, including the story of a teenager with cirrhosis would give a mistaken idea about risk as it relates to age. Journalists writing about this health inequity between AI/AN and other racial groups might find the specific case of the teenager to be compelling due to its novelty, but it does not give an accurate idea of who mainly suffers from cirrhosis (someone middle-aged).

Accurate communication about SDH is of critical importance, and avoiding unintended effects resulting from certain common storytelling tactics requires time, attention, and critical thinking.

Domains Where Public Relations Affects Public Health

Public Relations, Media Relations, and Influencing Health News Coverage

There is no shortage of health information that a person can sleuth on the Internet or in news publications. Health information can originate from many sources, including for-profit hospitals, pharmaceutical companies, medical device manufacturers, etc. Other purveyors of health information include nonprofit hospitals, community health organizations, associations like the American Diabetes Foundation, and advocacy groups like Breast Cancer Action. Still, medical societies, universities, local libraries, state and local health departments, U.S. federal health agencies, and health agencies operating worldwide all provide a wealth of information online. As noted previously, much of this information is aimed at the individual with the operating premise that if individuals engaged in healthful behaviors, health in communities would and could improve.

In addition to content they produce for organizations directly, strategic communicators have a hand in shaping what information gets placed in news. Public relations textbooks suggest upwards of 40 percent of news articles originate from a variety of public relations sources (Lattimore et al., 2009). Journalists, when asked, often say that they rely more on non-public relations sources for their story ideas, such as looking at what other news organizations are covering, using their own interests and curiosity about an idea, or following up on ideas from their news audiences. Among public relations sources, journalists have said they rely more on university and nonprofit sources for their story ideas (Len-Ríos et al., 2009). There is a concern that news from corporate sources treat news audiences like consumers, rather than individuals with health needs (Crosswell & Porter, 2018). What could be the concern with treating health information as a commercial commodity?

In considering strategic communication for the public good, we know that companies, in the age of corporate social responsibility or corporate purpose, have refocused their efforts to show their value in doing public good (Bortree, 2014), and they can do so in many ways, but they often do so only in ways that serve their corporate purpose and not beyond that. A good question to consider—what if the only public good an organization contributes to is one that furthers its own financial interests?

Lobbying to Influence Health Policy Affecting SDH

Lobbyists, a vocation within the realm of public relations, influence SDH indirectly by influencing legislators who set the laws that regulate businesses and the health care industries (e.g., pharmaceutical companies, medical device makers, health-care providers). Lobbying can be defined as "the practice in which a sponsoring organization pays someone (ideally a person with government experience and influential contacts) to persuade elected officials to vote according to the sponsor's wishes" (Parvanta et al., 2018, p. 125). As is clear from the previous alcohol examples, lobbyists use news media and health messaging as methods to influence the public to sway legislators and their legislation that governs the city, state, and country. It is no secret that companies and advocacy organizations hire PR firms to lobby government officials to support legislation that would benefit their organizational goals. Yet, most folks are unfamiliar with who is lobbying Congress on farm subsidies that may affect which foods will be in plentiful supply at the grocery store. It is easier for individuals to keep up with health news that affects them, so they probably know it is bad to sit at their desk all day, but are not familiar with legislation that affects what's at the grocery store.

The 2005 film *Thank You for Smoking* depicted lobbyists representing the tobacco, alcohol, and firearms industries, and provided a satire for how money influences U.S. politics and the ecosystem in which we live. As one lobbyist says in the film, "I speak on behalf of cigarettes" (Reitman, 2006). These industries make big money and use it to lobby legislators to grow their economic power. In the health space, tobacco lobbyists are some of the most sophisticated professionals in their techniques, and in the age of vaping, it is probably still true. Under fire in 2019 for the sharp increase in teenage vaping, Altria, which owns former tobacco giant Phillip Morris, invested in Juul and some Phillip Morris executives moved from Altria to lead Juul Labs Inc. (Maloney, 2019). While the U.S. Food and Drug Administration (FDA) was investigating Juul's marketing practices and their impact on youth vaping, the company lost its market leadership position to other e-cigarette manufacturers. These new vape brands have removed tobacco-based nicotine and have substituted it with synthetic nicotine, thus, at the time, bypassing regulation by the Food and Drug Administration as they were only legislated to regulate tobacco and, not all forms of nicotine, by Congress. In April 2022, Congress gave the FDA power to regulate all forms of nicotine (FDA, 2023). Vape products that include synthetic nicotine are increasingly being sold with the popular fruit and mint flavorings that so attract young vape users (Jewett, 2022b; Park-Lee, et al., 2021).

In terms of SDH, this example shows just how regulation of products through health policies can affect the health of a country and community. Research shows that nicotine has negative effects on teen brain development (Park-Lee, et al., 2021) and causes lung damage (Jewett, 2022a). In U.S. culture, children are considered a special protected class, and more precaution is taken with their health, so there is a response to the vaping industry. Grassroots advocacy organization Parents Against Vaping E-Cigarettes (Petersen, 2019) was founded when one parent discovered that an e-cigarette representative from Juul had appeared at one of her children's schools as part of an anti-smoking group and told the children that vaping was safe (Petersen, 2019; read more here: https://www. parentsagainstvaping.org/our-story). It is important that health communicators understand that on any issue there are multiple groups jockeying for their message to be heard the loudest, and usually the group with most resources wins— though it also helps to have the better story.

Incredibly, creating grassroots advocacy organizations to promote smoking has been a tactic of tobacco manufacturers for years, and is a practice known in the public relations industry as "astroturfing." Of course, AstroTurf is a registered trademark for the company that produces synthetic turf grass that is used in sports stadiums. In public relations it refers to something similar—providing a manufactured substitute for something real. More specifically astroturfing refers to an organization financially sponsoring the formation of a citizens' group, or front group, around an issue to create the perception that there are concerned citizens who, independent of the organization, represent a point-of-view that endorses the organization's position (Mayer, 2007). The result is that an organization creates an advocacy group meant to be presented as "grassroots" (grass is to turf as a grassroots organization is to a fake astroturf organization) that grew organically out of community concern (Leiser, 2016). In the case of e-cigarettes, Juul, as identified by journalists, supported the Switch Network, which journalists say was meant to appear as a grassroots organization serving to get Juul users to share why they had switched from cigarettes to vaping to attract potential converts (LaVito, 2019). In fact, vaping companies like Juul were asserting that their products were better for public health because they were not as harmful as combustible cigarettes. The science is still accumulating, but there are health risks to vaping, especially for young people (Bracken-Clarke, 2021; Jewett, 2022a).

What is important to recognize about lobbying is: the policy and legislative arena is where many decisions get made about social determinants of health. PR professionals represent corporations, health-care organizations, citizen groups, and particular industries. They influence policy decisions that ultimately trickle down and affect communities. The downstream effects of not regulating products like Juul are possibly: a need for more health and substance abuse counselors at middle schools and high schools; greater security for school restrooms; poorer health and elevated health costs for families who have children who sustain lung damage; and, perhaps, depending on marketing targets, disparities in health among groups within society.

Health Partnerships

Many times, corporations, nonprofits, or governments partner to solve health problems. This happens at both upstream and downstream levels. Having transportation, a car, a bus line nearby, or a person able to take you to a doctor's appointment is a social determinant of health. People without means to get to doctors' appointments are susceptible to poorer health as they lack primary health care. People who miss appointments are often charged a missed appointment fee. Rideshare companies, like Uber and Lyft, have been in talks to partner with local governments, nonprofits, and medical centers to help individuals get to their health-care appointments. Federal Medicaid recipients are supposed to be provided rides to their medical appointments, but they have been left waiting due to a shortage of availability of rides. This may require patients to stay hospitalized longer—not being able to be discharged—or in missing appointments, which are difficult to get (Johnson, 2018; Johnston, 2019). Of course, rideshare companies opened this service to build business, yet, even so, they are helping hospitals solve transportation issues for their patients (Wolfe & McDonald, 2020). It is a win–win, and strategic communication has been key to developing these partnerships. Thus, the SDH can be modified by organizations that partner to solve problems in systems that prevent individuals from getting the health care they need.

Government Campaigns to Influence Individual and Community Health

Even though there is so much information produced about how to be healthful, a nation's health is not determined alone by access to information and must consider the countervailing forces that promote unhealthful consumption (e.g., snacks and candies) and promote unhealthful behaviors (e.g., tobacco). New York City's Mayor Michael Bloomberg led an effort in the late 2000s to manage the sale of sugary drinks in the city as the Health Department said that in 2010 about 60 percent of New York City residents were obese or overweight (Targeted News Service, 2010). The Health Department led public education campaigns to educate City residents through subway posters with headlines such as, "Are you pouring on the pounds?" and visuals identifying how many sugar packets are in large soft drinks (Targeted News Service, 2010). The mayor proposed limiting the maximum size of soft drinks in city managed venues to 16 ounces (Swann, 2014). Bloomberg contended that sugary drinks were tied to obesity, and that reducing the serving size would help individuals keep their weight in check and, therefore, reduce the potential that New Yorkers would eventually develop weight-related complications like diabetes and heart disease.

This effort was ultimately unsuccessful, and it brought strong opposition from the American Beverage Association, the industry lobbying group for soft drink companies like Pepsi Co., Coca-Cola, and others. They feared a loss of revenue from reduced sales, as well as worried the campaign's purpose would spread to other locations outside of New York City. They created a coalition of groups called New Yorkers for Beverage Choices and argued that New Yorkers should be left to make their own choices about their health (Petrecca, 2012). Do these arguments sound familiar? Choice? Freedoms? These are value propositions that work incredibly well in some cultures that believe in individual determinism.

More recently in our public health history, government communicators have had to make choices communicating around the COVID-19 pandemic. The U.S. federal government largely left communications to the states and to a politicized and embattled CDC—first under the Trump administration, then under the Biden administration. When historians study how the U.S. and the world handled the pandemic, how will they evaluate consideration of SDH? Each country's culture influenced their approach to prevention, mitigation, testing, and vaccination. There are many questions about who had vaccine access and which countries were first able to get access to vaccines for their citizens, among questions about cost of care at the local level, etc. How were the most vulnerable in societies, the elderly and the immunocompromised, protected? Countries handled the pandemic differently with China taking a zero-COVID policy, with New Zealand closing the country, to the U.S.'s varied state-by-state approach. Country, region, and zip code mattered.

An examination of who died during the pandemic in the U.S. has shown that there are racial disparities, and these have been a result, in many ways, of SDH. More people of color face discrimination in health care, so when regulations are put in place, they and their communities are typically not prioritized. A result of the U.S.'s historical legacy of White supremacy and discrimination, a SDH, people of color are more likely to work in frontline jobs at increased risk of exposure to the virus. In Greenville County, South Carolina, for instance, the state's Department of Health and Environmental Control's Diversity, Equity, and Inclusion Office (DEIO) found that from the beginning of the pandemic until Dec. 15, 2020, 27 percent of hospitalizations were from Greenville's Black community, who comprised 18.4 percent of the population. Conversely, Latinos had 20 percent of the county's COVID-19 cases in August of 2020, and by Dec. 15, 2020, they comprised only 12.9 percent of cases. The drop was attributed to an educational outreach campaign in Spanish via online and radio ads in addition to emails to Hispanic businesses. The county also invested in connecting at-risk communities with testing and other resources. This partial success in Greenville demonstrates that SDH include in-culture communication as well as access to sound health information and clinic resources (Navarro, 2021).

There will be many health public relations lessons from the COVID-19 pandemic concerning providing for the public good. Even as parts of the nation "returned to normal," in 2021 and 2022, there were immunocompromised children who could not return safely to school, and the pandemic left an estimated 10.5 million children worldwide without primary caregivers, with children in Africa and Southeast Asia disproportionately affected (Hillis et al., 2022). In not preventing those deaths, surviving children will contend with downstream effects. To protect them, children will need nurturing care, protection from violence, and access to good education (Hillis et al., 2022). The inability to effectively prevent deaths requires decisions down the line on how to fix the consequences.

Summary

In the beginning of this chapter, you were asked to consider two children who lived near each other but whose living conditions and opportunities for health were very different. This example illustrates how conditions people are born into and live in can determine their exposure to pollutants, their safety, their opportunities to achieve good health through preventive measures like exercise and healthy food, and the type of messages they're exposed to. The chapter has illustrated how these SDH are represented in media, and how the choices of media and public relations professionals can also act on social determinants of health. You have read about how lobbying for laws and policy can shape safety and access to resources that may place limitations on individual options for self-care. We have also talked about how awareness and promotion of different health issues and products can all contribute to environments that promote health for some while creating health risks and disparities for others.

Despite their importance, there is relatively little money spent trying to address SDH. A 2020 assessment of U.S. health systems investments identified just 9.1 percent of expenditures went to programs promoting upstream SDH, with most investment going to housing, food security, and employment programs (Horwitz et al., 2020). The U.S. has consistently ranked last among high-income nations for providing access to health care, quality of insurance, and suffers the disparities in access across its population, with Norway, the Netherlands, and Australia ranking at the top for health care (Parker, 2021). The Commonwealth Fund's research shows that the U.S. deviates from other high-income countries by not providing universal health care or comprehensive social services for the young, which affects population outcomes as individuals age (Parker, 2021). While important, a preponderance of consumer health information cannot improve health if the systems in society do not support health.

The bottom line to remember with the social determinants of health: the context for a person's life matters because it determines what choices are available to them. It is not solely a matter of what individuals can do for themselves. Not only is it important for strategic communicators to frame messages for a target audience so they understand the social determinants that may be at play in their options, but it is also important to engineer an environment that leads to better upstream conditions for better health.

Discussion Questions

1. What would it take for the public to become *as aware and knowledgeable* about *how* the SDH affect individual health as they are about the caloric value of different foods?
2. Pick a country and identify one of its major health problems. What are the upstream factors that influence that health problem? Are the health problems equally distributed across the population?
3. It is challenging to make a story about SDH come alive and feel relevant to audience members. Can you think of other ways to make such a story compelling without using personal narratives of ordinary people (exemplars)?
4. Lobbying requires that a PR professional choose a side in a policy debate. Do all sides necessarily serve the public good? Should they when it comes to health?

Further Reading

Braveman, P., & Gottlieb, L. (2014). The social determinants of health: It's time to consider the causes of the causes. *Public Health Reports, 129*(1_suppl2), 19–31.

Niederdeppe, J., Bigman, C. A., Gonzales, A. L., & Gollust, S. E. (2013). Communication about health disparities in the mass media. *Journal of Communication, 63*(1), 8–30. https://doi.org/10.1111/jcom.12003

Williams, D. R., & Mohammed, S. A. (2013). Racism and health I: Pathways and scientific evidence. *American Behavioral Scientist, 57*(8), 1152–1173.

References

Bortree, D. S. (2014). The state of CSR communication research: A summary and future direction. *Public Relations Journal,* 8(3). Available online: http://www.prsa.org/Intelligence/PRJournal/Vol8/No3/

Bracken-Clarke, D., Kapoor, D., Baird, A. M., Buchanan, P. J., Gately, K., Cuffe, S., & Finn, S. P. (2021). Vaping and lung cancer: A review of current data and recommendations. *Lung cancer (Amsterdam, Netherlands), 153,* 11–20. https://doi.org/10.1016/j.lungcan.2020.12.030

Braveman, P., Egerter, S., & Williams, D. R. (2011). The social determinants of health: Coming of age. *Annual Review of Public Health, 32,* 381–398. DOI: 10.1146/annurev-publhealth-031210-101218

Braveman, P., & Gottlieb, L. (2014). The social determinants of health: It's time to consider the causes of the causes. *Public Health Reports, 129*(1_suppl2), 19–31. DOI: 10.1177/00333549141291S206

Bubela, T., Nisbet, M., Borchelt, R. et al. (2009). Science communication reconsidered. *Nature Biotechnology, 27*, 514–518. https://doi.org/10.1038/nbt0609-514.

Centers for Disease Control and Prevention (n.d.-a) *History of the Surgeon General's reports on smoking and health.* Retreived from June 15, 2023 from https://www.cdc.gov/tobacco/sgr/history/index.htm.

Centers for Disease Control and Prevention (n.d.-b) *Youth and tobacco use.* Retreived from June 6, 2023 from https://www.cdc.gov/tobacco/data_statistics/fact_sheets/youth_data/tobacco_use/index.htm

Cho, H., & Salmon, C. T. (2007). Unintended effects of health communication campaigns. *Journal of Communication, 57*(2), 293–317. https://doi.org/10.1111/j.1460-2466.2007.00344.x

Cook, W. K., Bond, J., & Greenfield, T. K. (2014). Are alcohol policies associated with alcohol consumption in low- and middle-income countries? *Addiction, 109*(7), 1081–1090. https://doi.org/10.1111/add.12571.

Crosswell, L., & Porter, L. (2018). *Politics, propaganda, and public health: A case study in health communication and public trust.* Lexington Books.

DeJong, W. (2010) Social norms marketing campaigns to reduce campus alcohol problems. *Health Communication, 25*(6–7), 615–616, DOI:10.1080/10410236.2010.496845.

Dunwoody, S. (2021). Science journalism: Prospects in the digital age. In *Routledge handbook of public communication of science and technology* (pp. 14–32). Routledge.

Eibach, R. P., & Purdie-Vaughns, V. (2011). How to keep on keeping on: Framing civil rights accomplishments to bolster support for egalitarian policies. *Journal of Experimental Social Psychology, 47*(1), 274–277. https://doi.org/https://doi.org/10.1016/j.jesp.2010.10.005

Entman, R. M. (1993). Framing: Toward clarification of a fractured paradigm. *Journal of Communication, 43*(4), 51–68. https://doi.org/10.1111/j.1460-2466.1993.tb01304.x

Food and Drug Administration (2023, March 17). *FDA updates regulatory documents to include "non-tobacco nicotine" products.* Retrieved June 15, 2023 from https://www.fda.gov/tobacco-products/ctp-newsroom/fda-updates-regulatory-documents-include-non-tobacco-nicotine-products.

Four Ukrainian children flown to US for cancer treatment. (2022, March 22). *Agence FrancePresse.* Available from NewsBank: Access World News – Historical and Current.

Galtung, J., & Ruge, M. H. (1965). The structure of foreign news: the presentation of the Congo, Cuba and Cyprus crises in four Norwegian newspapers. *Journal of Peace Research, 2*(1), 64–90. https://doi.org/10.1177/002234336500200104

Geertz, C. (1973). *The interpretation of cultures* (Vol. 5043). Basic Books.

Gibson, R., & Zillmann, D. (1994). Exaggerated versus representative exemplification in news reports: Perception of issues and personal consequences. *Communication Research, 21*(5), 603–624. https://doi.org/10.1177/00936509402100500

Grabe, M. E., Kleemans, M., Bas, O., Myrick, J. G., & Kim, M. (2017). Putting a human face on cold, hard facts: Effects of personalizing social issues on perceptions of issue importance. *International Journal of Communication, 11*, 23, 907–929.

Hillis, S., N'konzi, J.N., Msemburi, W., et al. (2022, Sept. 6) Orphanhood and caregiver loss among children based on new global excess COVID-19 death estimates. *JAMA Pediatrics.* Published online. DOI:10.1001/jamapediatrics.2022.3157

Hinnant, A., Subramanian, R., & Jenkins, J. (2017). The media logic of health journalism: Strategies and limitations in covering social determinants. *Australian Journalism Review, 39*(2), 23–35. https://search.informit.org/doi/10.3316/ielapa.360354422169050

Hong, T., Cabrerea, J., & Beaudoin, C. E. (2023). Disentangling real-world and virtual-world social norms: The persuasive elements and social psychological effects of a serious game, *Telematics and Informatics Reports*, 9, Article 100038, https://doi.org/10.1016/j.teler.2022.100038.

Horwitz, L., Chang, C., Arcilla, H., & Knickman, J. (2020). Quantifying health systems' investment in social determinants of health, by sector, 2017–19. *Health Affairs, 39*(2), 192–198. https://www.healthaffairs.org/doi/10.1377/hlthaff.2019.01246.

Iyengar, S. (1991). *Is anyone responsible? How television frames political issues.* University of Chicago Press.

Jewett, C. (2022a, March 8). The loophole that's fueling a return to teenage vaping. https://www.nytimes.com/2022/03/08/health/vaping-fda-nicotine.html.

Jewett, C. (2022b, Sept. 6). Juul settles multistate youth vaping inquiry for $438.5 million. https://www.nytimes.com/2022/09/06/health/juul-settlement-vaping-crisis.html.

Johnson, C. Y. (2018, March 1). Uber and Lyft think they can solve one of medicine's biggest problems: Ride-sharing companies want to help you get to your doctor's appointments. *The Washington Post*. Retrieved from Factiva.

Johnston, C. (2019, March 31). Ride plans need assist: Senator sponsors a bill providing transportation options for patients. *Tampa Bay Times*. Retrieved from Factiva.

Keveney, B. (2020, September 1). Exclusive: Report finds TV tobacco imagery persists, and says young viewers turn to vaping. *USA Today*, https://www.usatoday.com/story/entertainment/tv/2020/09/01/study-finds-tv-smoking-images-raise-chances-youths-start-vaping/3423268001/.

Lattimore, D., Baskin, O., Heiman, S. T., & Toth, E. L. (2009). *Public relations: The profession & the practice*, 4th ed. McGraw-Hill.

LaVito, A. (2019, Oct. 1). Juul hires 'political dark arts' firm led by ex-Clinton campaign director in its fight for survival. CNBC.com. https://www.cnbc.com/2019/10/01/vaping-company-juul-recruits-customers-for-shadow-grassroots-lobbying-campaign.html

Leiser M. (2016). AstroTurfing, 'CyberTurfing' and other online persuasion campaigns. *European Journal of Law and Technology, 7*(1), 1–27. https://ejlt.org/index.php/ejlt/article/view/501/636

Len-Ríos, M. E., Hinnant, A., Park, S., Cameron, G. T., Frisby, C. M., & Lee, Y. (2009). Health news agenda building: Journalists' perceptions of the role of public relations. *Journalism & Mass Communication Quarterly, 86*(2), 315–331. https://doi.org/10.1177/107769900908600204

Maloney, J. (2019, Oct 01). Juul hires another top Altria executive: Altria's head of regulatory affairs to take over similar role at e-cigarette startup. *Wall Street Journal (Online)*.

Marmot, M. G., Stansfeld, S., Patel, C., North, F., Head, J., White, I., . . . & Smith, G. D. (1991). Health inequalities among British civil servants: The Whitehall II study. *The Lancet, 337*(8754), 1387–1393. DOI: 10.1016/0140-6736(91)93068-k

Mayer, R. N. (2007).Winning the war of words: The "front group" label in contemporary consumer politics. *The Journal of American Culture, 30*(1), 96–109. https://doi.org/10.1111/j.1542-734X.2007.00467.x

Navarro, M. (2021). Virus hits minority groups hardest. *The Greenville News*. A2.

Nicholson, R. A., Kreuter, M. W., Lapka, C., Wellborn, R., Clark, E. M., Sanders-Thompson, V., Jacobson, H. M., & Casey, C. (2008). Unintended effects of emphasizing disparities in cancer communication to African-Americans. *Cancer Epidemiology Biomarkers & Prevention, 17*(11), 2946–2952. DOI: 10.1158/1055-9965.EPI-08-0101

Niederdeppe, J., Bigman, C. A., Gonzales, A. L., & Gollust, S. E. (2013). Communication about health disparities in the mass media. *Journal of Communication, 63*(1), 8–30. https://doi.org/10.1111/jcom.12003

Nye, J. (2022, November 14). SAFER Ukraine: A Global Effort to – Oncology Nurse Advisor. *Ocology Nurse Advisor*. NewsBank database.

Paradies, Y., Ben, J., Denson, N., Elias, A., Priest, N., Pieterse, A., Gupta, A., Kelaher, M., & Gee, G. (2015). Racism as a determinant of health: A systematic review and meta-analysis. *PLoS One*, *10*(9), e0138511. DOI: 10.1371/journal.pone.0138511. PMID: 26398658; PMCID: PMC4580597.

Park-Lee, E., Ren, C., Sawdey, M. D., et al. (2021). Notes from the field: E-cigarette use among middle and high school students—National Youth Tobacco Survey, United States, *MMWR Morbidity and Mortality Weekly Report*, *70*, 1387–1389. DOI: http:// dx.doi.org/10.15585/mmwr.mm7039a4.

Parker, C. (2021, August 5). U.S. medical system ranks last among 11 high-income nations in new study. *The Washington Post*. Retrieved from EBSCO database.

Parvanta, C. F., Nelson, D.E., & Harner, R. N. (2018). *Public health communication: Critical tools and strategies*. Jones & Barlett Learning.

Petersen, A. (2019, September 21.). Getting through to your teen about the dangers of vaping. *The Wall Street Journal Online*. *https://www.wsj.com/articles/getting-through-to-your-teen-about-the-dangers-of-vaping-11569070800*

Petrecca, L. (2012, July 17). Fight over sugary-drinks ban gears up. *USA Today*. Retrieved from Factiva.

Reitman, J. (Director). (2006). *Thank you for smoking* [film]. Room 9 Entertainment.

St. Jude Global. (n.d.). *SAFER Ukraine*. St. Jude Global. Retrieved June 13, 2023 from https://global.stjude.org/en-us/saferukraine.html#sectioned_content-f76d0774-5bb8-409a-8478-0dca7d514a18=2.

Su, J., Hancock, L., Wattenmaker McGann, A., Alshagra, M., Ericson, R., Niazi, Z., Dick, D. M., & Adkins, A. (2018). Evaluating the effect of a campus-wide social norms marketing intervention on alcohol-use perceptions, consumption, and blackouts. *Journal of American College Health*, *66*(3), 219–224. https://doi.org/10.1080/07448481.2017. 1382500

Swann, P. (2014). *Cases in public relations management: The rise of social media and activism*. Routledge.

Targeted News Service. (2010, August 2). HD Health Department launches new effort to wean New Yorkers from sugary beverages. Retrieved from Factiva.

Tye, L. (1998). *The father of spin: Edward L. Bernays and the birth of public relations*. Random House.

Williams, D. R., & Mohammed, S. A. (2013). Racism and health I: Pathways and scientific evidence. *American Behavioral Scientist*, *57*(8), 1152–1173. https://doi.org/10. 1177/0002764213487340

Wolfe, M. K., & McDonald, N. C. (2020). Innovative health care mobility services in the U.S. *BMC public health*, *20*(1), 906. https://doi.org/10.1186/s12889-020-08803-5

Young, R., Subramanian, R., Miles, S., Hinnant, A., & Andsager, J. L. (2017). Social representation of cyberbullying and adolescent suicide: A mixed-method analysis of news stories. *Health Communication*, *32*(9), 1082–1092. https://doi.org/10.1080/104 10236.2016.1214214

3

ETHICAL RELATIONSHIPS AND RESPONSIBILITIES CONTRIBUTE TO SOCIAL GOOD

Lois A. Boynton

Being ethical is integral to how we conduct research, create messages, and build diverse, inclusive, and healthy relationships among individuals and organizations seeking social change. Making ethical decisions involves a rational process. Any individual judgment also must reflect our responsibilities to others as we put our values into action. Importantly, making ethical decisions and resolving ethical dilemmas reflect core ideals of public relations and relationship management. We should approach our decision making symmetrically, grounded in interdependence, and a willingness to invest in and build trusting, open, committed, and engaged relationships (Ledingham & Bruning, 1998).

The Basics

We often think of ethics as knowing and acting in ways that reflect what we *should* do, rather than being tempted to act in ways we know we shouldn't. But that's the easy part . . . or relatively so. Challenges erupt when we face ethical dilemmas—when the values upon which we base our ethical actions are in conflict, and we cannot apply them concurrently (Kidder, 2005). For example, there are values-based reasons why a practitioner might not divulge details about why an executive left a company, and there are values-based reasons to make that information known. But the practitioner cannot simultaneously disclose details and not disclose details. These right-versus-right situations require us to work together and apply reasoning skills to ascertain which rationale to implement and what intentions led us there. It's also important to avoid paralysis of analysis;

DOI: 10.4324/9781003327189-4

ultimately, we must act in "a morally appropriate way forward" (American Public Health Association, 2019, p. 7) and justify why that action is the best option. Resolving dilemmas may not give you relief, however. A former student discussed how she resolved a work dilemma, adding, "I know I did the right thing, but I still wanted to take a shower after it was all over."

What Is Ethical Public Relations?

It's no secret that public relations has yet to shed the image of propagating spin and half-truths. There are many examples of practitioners who crossed the line. The now-defunct British agency Bell Pottinger was felled in 2017 by its unscrupulous campaign "to exploit racial tension in South Africa to further its client's agenda" (Arenstein, 2017). It was expelled from the Public Relations and Communications Association, despite initial claims of being "the victim of a smear campaign" (Sweney, 2017). More recently, 5WPR agency CEO Ronn Torossian ultimately confessed to owning and operating Everything-PR, a purported news site he used to hype his company and clients while debasing his competitors (Hastings, 2022). Although not a Public Relations Society of America member, Torossian was blasted by the New York chapter's board for his "cowardly and blatant violation of PRSA's Code of Ethics, a stain on our profession [that] undermine[s] our role as guardians of facts and integrity for those we serve" (New York Chapter, 2022). And even the most ethical practitioners may face challenges from a client or manager who would compromise ethical practices in favor of short-term gains.

Yet, for about 75 years, practitioners and scholars have focused on developing and applying ethical standards to values-based public relations. The vast majority of practitioners find value in building stakeholder relationships grounded in honesty, transparency, integrity, accountability, and respect. These are particularly relevant for nonprofit and government agencies supporting public health initiatives as well as for-profit organizations advocating for social good.

Why, then, is it difficult to improve the image-makers' image? Perhaps it results from public relations practitioners having a built-in ethical dilemma of balancing competing loyalties—to their organization/clients and to society (Fitzpatrick & Bronstein, 2006). Consider these examples: Furnishing teens with condoms and communicating about avoiding risky behaviors may reduce sexually transmitted diseases while also infuriating some parents who object to pre-marital sex (Guttman, 2000). The need for organ donations clashed with personal and religious beliefs in Australia (Merminod & Benaroyo, 2022), and fear appeals with graphic images to discourage unhealthy habits created harmful distress for some, according to a UK study (Brown & Whiting, 2014). Often-effective anti-smoking campaigns also inadvertently created lung cancer stigma among patients who didn't smoke (Riley et al., 2017). Some researchers determined artificial intelligence may help health communicators reach target audiences with nuanced messages, but "it also has the potential to create, sustain, or exacerbate inequities" (Fisher & Rosella, 2022). Advocating behaviors on hot-button political topics such as vaccines, gun safety, and abortion accessibility also may create dilemmas when values of personal autonomy clash with standards for societal well-being (Guttman, 2000).

Almost 20 years before the COVID-19 pandemic, Guttman (2000) foreshadowed recent dilemmas about health message reliability: "Should the interventionists disseminate what they believe is the best information they currently have, even if it may prove to be inaccurate?" (p. 180). In early 2020, the Centers for Disease Control and Prevention tweeted that masks were not necessary for people outside health-care professions; rather, handwashing and staying home if sick were effective ways to prevent the spread of coronavirus, pre-vaccine. In less than three months, messages shifted and mask mandates were in place, leaving some people confused and others frustrated ("Advice," 2020; CDC, 2020; "COVID-19 Infection," 2021; Simmons-Duffin, 2021). Dr. Anthony Fauci, former director of the National Institute of Allergy and Infectious Diseases, explained that recommendations changed—and likely would change again—based on available data about this ever-evolving contagion (Cercone, 2022).

Our Obligations to Others

Ask researchers about the Institutional Review Board process, and they will probably tell you it's a very involved (and sometimes frustrating) process for research project approval. But there's a valid reason for the checks and balances that date back to the discovery of the egregious Tuskegee Study. The 40-year experiments, which began in 1932, subjected African American men to needless suffering and death by withholding treatment for the sexually transmitted disease syphilis. Study communication misled predominantly poor African Americans by promising "free blood test; free treatment, by County Health Department and Government Doctors," as well as free meals and transportation. Fliers also expressed a sense of urgency: "YOU MAY FEEL WELL AND STILL HAVE BAD BLOOD. COME AND BRING ALL YOUR FAMILY." What was designed as a six-month, small community study progressed until 1972, when Associated Press reported a whistleblower's revelation that government experiments continued even after penicillin was invented in the mid-1940s and found to be an effective treatment for syphilis (Brown, 2017; Heller, 2017). It would be another 25 years, May 1997, before survivors, victims, and their families received an apology, issued by then-President Bill Clinton ("Clinton Apologizes," 1997).

In addition to financial settlements, Congress passed the National Research Act in 1974. The Department of Health Education and Welfare created regulations to prevent research subject exploitation. Resulting Institutional Review Boards in academic and research settings review study proposals to ensure potential participants receive information essential for making an informed decision to participate or not and to ensure researchers do not employ unsafe or unethical practices (APA, n.d.). Non-academic organizations also may apply for federalwide assurance of compliance to Office for Human Research Protections' guidelines protecting research participants' rights ("Assurance Process," n.d.).

Overall, public relations practitioners and health communicators do not intentionally design campaigns that cause such harm. But there are instances when errors presumed unintentional occur that could have been avoided had the practitioner taken time to understand their stakeholders and the influence of their own background. As the National Institutes of Health (n.d.) notes, "Mental shortcuts activate implicit biases that lead to errors in judgment. We can act impulsively and based on emotion, overweigh certain evidence, ignore baselines, and only recall certain aspects of information to inform a judgment" (p. 12). Correcting these often-institutionalized biases calls for intentionality, particularly among the powerful and privileged.

The process starts with understanding my standpoint and acknowledging how my experiences and position in society affect whom I socialize with, what information I find useful, as well as my perceptions of myself and others. Individuals in underrepresented populations have broader perspectives because they must adapt to the dominant culture while retaining their own cultural, racial, ethnic, and/or gender identities ("Standpoint," n.d.). This may manifest as code switching, reflecting how marginalized people adapt their language, look, and behaviors to align with the dominant group. While this may improve their ability to be accepted, it also may compromise personal authenticity and harm their mental health (Washington-Harmon, 2022).

Those with societal privilege may not recognize challenges facing individuals who lack power (Bajracharya, 2018; "Standpoint," n.d.). This is not to say privilege is bad. Communicating successfully, however, relies on my determination to learn from those whose realities differ and help change systems that continue to privilege some groups over others. Businesses, in particular, argues Logan (2021), must address racial inequities, "because they historically have perpetuated and profited from racial oppression" (p. 6).

Consider how race can affect acceptance of helpful treatments. Several public health advocates want to change statistics around HIV among African Americans, mainly women, particularly since medications have existed for ten years to significantly reduce the chance of contracting HIV. Of the three versions of pre-exposure prophylaxis—PrEP—available, only one has been advertised, which currently is not recommended for women. Campbell et al. (2022) explain how "stigma, discrimination and poverty" can affect public health outcomes. "We have over 400 years of anecdotal reference that show sex for Black women is often not centered around sex positivity or as a mutually beneficial, pleasure filled experience."

Other communicators also must appreciate the power of words. A July 2022 article called a COVID-19 mutation a "new 'Ninja' COVID variant," language that Poynter writer Al Thompkins quoted in his column. The next day, Thompkins (2022) published part of an email received from an Asian American Journalists Association program director, who pointed out how this stereotype can fuel xenophobia: "Just as Covid hasn't let up, neither has hate against AAPIs." The publication subsequently changed its headline, calling the variant "relentless" (Axe, 2022).

It's also important to avoid some standpoint stumbling blocks. Essentialism may lead to assumptions that everyone in a particular demographic has the same beliefs, experiences, or even biogenetics. Inaccuracies arise when we accept these stereotypes—consider the rich cultural differences among Asian Americans or the varying viewpoints of faith leaders. Health-care advocates are not immune (if you'll pardon the pun) from these generalizations. For example, Valles (2012) raised concerns about "misguided essentialism" when health researchers made no distinction between high blood pressure risks among African Americans born in the U.S. and African immigrants to America (p. 407). In a more recent commentary, Waters et al. (2021) point out how cancer-predictive models distinguish Black from white races, but do not address potential differences among bi-racial or multi-racial individuals.

Another standpoint shortcoming to avoid is dualism, which leads to "us versus them" thinking that judges one perspective to be "better" than the other. For example, rational actions often hold superiority over emotional actions. Dualism lacks context and negates how complex humans are ("Standpoint," n.d.).

Corporate Social Responsibility and Social Advocacy

For-profit companies approach societal responsibilities differently than nonprofits and government public health agencies, since businesses also have obligations to investors. Not long ago, businesses contended a company's sole purpose was to ensure its owners got a return on their investment. Fledgling efforts to promote corporate social responsibility as an ethical obligation were dismissed as running counter to America's free enterprise system. Libertarian economist Milton Friedman (1970) argued that a board of directors pays a CEO to "conduct the business in accordance with their desires, which generally will be to make as much money as possible while conforming to the basic rules of the society, both those embodied in law and those embodied in ethical custom." Friedman did not expound upon what those ethical customs entail, although he conceded, "corporate executives can legitimately focus on fulfilling other ends, as long as they are specifically directed by their employers" (Ruger, 2011, p. 148). While executives may support causes out of their own wallets, expecting corporations to do likewise was, according to Friedman, nothing more than socialism.

Despite Friedman's distain for CSR, some business owners broadened their corporate responsibilities to include customers, employees, suppliers, communities, social activist groups, and shareholders. With the CSR business model, "companies make a concerted effort to operate in ways that enhance rather than degrade society and the environment" (Fernando, 2022). Business ethicist Archie Carroll (1991) identified four CSR foundations, two professed by Friedman—economic and legal—plus ethical and philanthropic. Steurer et al. (2012) explain, "respective management practices go beyond what the law requires, but not meaning that these management practices are left entirely to the discretion of managers" (p. 207).

In 2019, executives from 181 companies in the US Business Roundtable—from Aflac to Zebra Technologies—issued a 300-word "Statement on the Purpose of a Corporation" (2019), pledging "a fundamental commitment to *all* of our stakeholders"—customers, employees, suppliers, communities, and shareholders. The updated statement concludes, "Each of our stakeholders is essential. We commit to deliver value to all of them, for the future success of our companies, our communities and our country." Skeptics didn't think the statement went far enough to indicate how and when CEOs would make this stakeholder shift. They had a point; critics soon scolded corporate boards for boosting CEO pay and bypassing opportunities to invest in other stakeholders' needs (Daniels, 2022; Liu, 2022).

CSR is not just an American business commitment. Individual companies, government agencies, NGOs, and coalitions in Europe, Asia and the Pacific islands, Africa, and the Americas employ these principles, too. Business collaborative CSR Europe (2022) guides companies through changing corporate sustainability and responsibility criteria required by 2024 in European Union countries; the Argentine Institute of Corporate Social Responsibility (2020) provides CSR tools for businesses operating there.

In some countries, CSR efforts became necessary to control international corporations taking advantage of lax regulations. Some oil production companies in Nigeria have dumped toxic wastes in water sources, primarily in farming and fishing communities. On the plus side, NGOs like the Red Cross and UNICEF provide disaster relief and disease treatments. At the height of the COVID-19 pandemic, about 200 Nigerian businesses and citizens donated 39.6 Naira—$93.5 million US dollars—to purchase crucial medical equipment needed in clinics and food for about 8 million citizens in need during lockdowns. This Coalition Alliance Against COVID-19 also developed communication campaigns to build citizen awareness about the disease (Coalition, 2020; Osemeke et al., 2016).

SMRT Corporation, which manages Singapore's public transportation systems, focuses its CSR efforts on community service and volunteerism. Its railway management team organized a blood donation program with the Singapore Red Cross, setting up blood drives at high-traffic train stops. The communication department promotes volunteer activities and tracks participation (Ping, 2005). CSR begins with SMRT's corporate culture: "When a business is well-managed, it will find that it is natural to be socially responsible" (p. SG-15).

In these examples, CSR equates to giving back to communities through philanthropic efforts that simultaneously improve the company's brand image. Their contributions are important, but stakeholders also expect businesses to be accountable and measure the impact of their care of employees, their communities, and the environment. Why this shift? Many of today's stockholders prefer investing in companies that employ environmental, social, and corporate governance (ESG) standards—tangible measurements to show "how companies treat their staff, manage supply chains, respond to climate change, increase diversity and inclusion, and build community links" ("Understanding," 2021). Certain companies take this commitment further through B Corporation certification.

Familiar brands like Ben & Jerry's, Counter Culture Coffee, Patagonia, and Toms made long-term commitments by earning B Corporation certification. Founded in 2006, B Labs has certified 5,024 companies worldwide as of mid-2022. According to its website:

> B Corp Certification is a designation that a business is meeting high standards of verified performance, accountability, and transparency on factors from employee benefits and charitable giving to supply chain practices and input materials. . . . [which] build trust with consumers, communities, and suppliers; attract and retain employees; and draw mission-aligned investors.
>
> *("About," n.d.)*

Many global health companies also commit to these stringent criteria and agree to re-certification every three years: Todo Works, a Korean maker of electric wheelchairs; Servioptica, an eye-care company in Colombia; and U.S.-based equalityMD, mental health providers for the LBGTQ+ community, among others ("Looking," n.d.).

Corporate social advocacy emerged as stakeholders upped the CSR ante, expecting companies to augment their support of "safe" causes, such as donating food to soup kitchens, by using their corporate clout to take a stance on controversial social issues such as gay and trans rights, immigration, or health impacts of climate change (Rim et al., 2020). Taking a position on a cause is not the same as lobbying, which companies undertake based on self-interests. Rather, an organization applying CSA takes a stance on a divisive social issue despite knowing that acting on its values may alienate some stakeholders. Hence, a company's leadership should anticipate potential blowback before stepping into the spotlight (Dodd & Supa, 2014).

For example, Dick's Sporting Goods discontinued sales of assault weapons and high-capacity magazines following the 2018 Parkland, Florida, mass shooting. Chairman and CEO Edward Stack, well aware that some customers would disapprove, "called on elected officials to pass what the company called 'common sense' gun reforms" (Gaither et al., 2018, p. 182).

Despite initial multi-million-dollar losses, Dick's recovered financially, and, importantly, kept its values-based mission intact (Fitzgerald, 2022).

From both an ethics and business perspective, corporate social advocacy is not for the faint of heart. Avoiding an issue can generate disapproval among some stakeholders, but so can window-dressing advocacy that might be seen as "pandering and exploitative for the sake of driving profits." For stakeholders to take companies seriously, marketing expert Alex Davidson advised companies begin at home, by employing inclusive and equitable HR practices. Moving into marketing, "if they're a company claiming to support the LGBTQ+ community, they should be doing it all year, not just during Pride Month. Consumers are very savvy and will grow distrustful of organizations pandering through 'rainbow capitalism'" (Today@Wayne, 2022).

No matter how ethical companies believe their stances are, they must understand no stakeholder group is completely homogeneous; some within a stakeholder group may support a corporation's stance on a controversial issue while others may object. "Fostering consensus may be impossible," explained Stanford Law professor Mike Callahan (2022). "Building trust through a transparent process may be the best path forward." Proactive planning includes identifying how corporate values and business priorities mesh with a social cause.

Doing Ethics

"With great power comes great responsibility" – whether attributed to Voltaire or Spiderman's Uncle Ben, this quote reinforces the importance of resolving ethical dilemmas professionally, by applying agreed-upon standards, or codes (Kidder, 2005). As the American Public Health Association (2019) states, "A code is like a promise to society, . . . concerning how and for what ends [practitioners'] professional knowledge and authority should be used." Public health professionals "are expected to put the public interest and the public trust ahead of their personal interests and to never misuse their office or authority for personal gain" (p. 2).

Public relations professional associations also have codified ethical standards to help their members determine the best course of action, particularly when facing right-vs-right dilemmas. Standards are based on expectations such as accuracy, integrity, transparency, respecting client confidentiality, fairness, and avoiding conflicts of interest (see Table 3.1). The UK's Public Relations and Communication Association code (2019) calls on health communicators to be transparent and create accurate information that won't "mislead, misinform, cause or be detrimental to health" (p. 3). However, codes do not present the "right" answer for dilemmas; according to IABC, they serve "as a guide to making consistent, responsible, ethical, and legal choices in all our communication" (IABC, 2011). Decisions "grow from a process that promotes rational discourse against emotional tensions" (Kidder & Born, 2002, p. 14).

TABLE 3.1   Ethics codes of public health and public relations professional associations

American Public Health Association Code of Ethics: https://www.apha.org/-/media/files/pdf/membergroups/ethics/code_of_ethics.ashx

IABC Code of Ethics for Professional Communicators: https://www.iabc.com/About/Purpose/Code-of-Ethics

International Public Relations Association Code of Conduct : https://www.ipra.org/member-services/code-of-conduct/

Public Relations and Communications Association Professional Charter and Codes of Conduct: https://www.prca.org.uk/about-us/pr-standards/professional-charter-and-codes-conduct

PRCA Health Public Relations and Communications Code of Conduct, pp. 3–4: https://www.prca.org.uk/sites/default/files/downloads/PRCA%20Codes%20of%20Conduct%20-%2028th%20Feb%202019.pdf

PR Council Code of Ethics and Principles: https://prcouncil.net/join/the-pr-council-code-of-ethics-and-principles/

Public Relations Society of Japan Code of Ethics: https://prsj.or.jp/association-en/prsjcode/code-of-ethics/

Public Relations Society of America Code of Ethics: https://www.prsa.org/about/prsa-code-of-ethics

Public Relations Society of Kenya Code of Ethics: https://www.prsk.co.ke/code-of-ethics/

Note: Accessed April 24, 2024

Practitioners may consult any number of decision-making processes that provide structure to resolve ethical dilemmas, such as the Potter Box, Bok model, and Navran model (see Table 3.2). Each approaches analysis differently, but a common aspect is we shouldn't make decisions in a vaccum. Rather, we benefit from working together to identify the dilemma, facts of the case, competing values, possible solutions, and "what ifs" before deciding. These models help practitioners tackle a wide range of ethical challenges, such as those described above. It's also helpful to employ ethical guidelines to communication tactics you produce. The TARES test, described next, is designed specifically for evaluating persuasive materials.

TABLE 3.2 Ethical decision-making models

Potter Box[a] *4-step process*	*Bok model*[b] *3-step process*	*Navran model*[c] *6-step process*
1. What are the facts of this situation?	1. Consult your conscience.	1. Identify the ethical problem.
2. What ethical values are at play, both personal and professional?	2. Seek expert advice to identify potential solutions.	2. Identify possible solutions.
3. How can ethical principles of philosophers inform your analysis?	3. Hold a public discussion with those affected/involved in the dilemma. Conduct in your head if needed.	3. How viable are these alternative solutions?
4. To whom are you loyal? Prioritize them.	Make a decision.	4. Select a solution.
Revisit steps as needed.		5. Impliment that solution.
Make a decision.		6. Evaluate the decision and outcomes.

[a] Franquet-Santos-Silva, M., & Ventura-Morujão, C.-A. (2017). The Potter box model of moral reasoning. *El Profesional de la Información, 26*(2), 328–335. https://doi.org/10.3145/epi.2017.mar.20

[b] Wilkins, L., Painter, C., & Patterson, P. (2022). *Media ethics: Issues and cases* (10th ed.). Rowman & Littlefield.

[c] Luttrell, R., & Ward, J. (2018). *A practical guide to ethics in public relations.* Rowman & Littlefield.

Before practitioners take advocacy messages public, they should have a process in place to assess whether the item is ethical, so they might avoid unintentional slights and work through dilemmas that often stem from competing loyalties to the organization and society. The TARES test explores five factors: truthfulness, the persuader's intent, degree of respect and equity toward stakeholders, as well as the message's contribution to social good (Baker & Martinson, 2001). Here are considerations for each step:

Truthfulness assesses whether verbal and visual claims are truthful and accurate. While primarily focusing on whether the message is factual, this step also includes whether the audience finds the source trustworthy and reliable (Baker & Martinson, 2001). For example, some critics called the NFL hypocritical for its significant support of anti-violence charities by airing their PSAs during games, but it applied lax punishment when players committed violent acts (McManus, 2015; NFL, n.d.; Vrentas, 2022).

Authenticity reflects the persuader's intention and whether or not they act on their values by doing the right thing for the right reasons (Baker & Martinson, 2001). For example, organizations should employ fear appeals judiciously. Overly graphic PSAs showing deadly car crashes resulting from texting while driving or physical deformities brought about by smoking could be disturbing and demotivate audiences. Stereotypes also may harm the organization's credibility.

Respect involves how the organization treats those it wishes to persuade. Baker and Martinson (2001) advise asking, "Have I respected the receivers of this persuasive message by appealing to their higher inclinations and their basic goodness, by not pandering, exploiting, or appealing to their lower or baser inclinations?" (p. 165). Respectfulness also involves a willingness to take full, open responsibility for message content.

Equity asks us to consider whether power differentials can affect stakeholders' ability to understand the message (Baker & Martinson, 2001). Public health workers interact with some stakeholders who grasp scientific and medical jargon with ease. There are many, however, who find it difficult to follow jargon-heavy messages. Persuaders also must consider language barriers. For example, a winter storm hit Seattle, Washington, in 2006, and left more than 1 million residents without power for about a week. Although desperate times call for desperate measures, many people who used charcoal grills and generators indoors became severely ill from carbon monoxide poisoning; the vast majority of them did not speak English. Following this disaster, several government agencies, NGOs, and local businesses collaborated to create safety messages in multiple languages and formats. The "Take Winter by Storm" campaign included radio PSAs, posters, safety preparedness checklists, fact sheets, and additional resources distributed through businesses, clinics, churches, nonprofit agencies, and other groups, particularly in immigrant communities. The major undertaking began by distributing materials in seven languages; within five years, the materials were available in 24 languages (University of Minnesota, n.d.).

Social responsibility, the final TARES step, addresses two key questions: (1) Does this message provide "a positive contribution to the common good" (Baker & Martinson, 2001, p. 168) or (at least) one that does not cause harm? and (2) Does this message increase or decrease stakeholders' trust in persuasive messages in general? Ultimately, persuaders must hold themselves accountable to those they hope to influence. As Franklin (2022) recommends, "enduring commitments convey enduring values. Don't chase the issue of the day; respond thoughtfully on issues that matter to your values."

You'll notice the five categories are not mutually exclusive. However, overlaps may help persuaders explore potential impacts of their messages—positive and negative, intentional and unintentional—before releasing them publicly.

Conclusion

Advocating for social good is a crucial role for public relations practitioners, one that requires employing persuasion ethically, especially when facing dilemmas. We're obligated to assess potential consequences, consult codes, balance loyalties, and consult peers to find viable solutions that meet ethical obligations. Yet, communication for social change can be fraught with ethical challenges—addressing implicit biases, including voices of marginalized stakeholders, avoiding misinformation and disinformation, among others. We also can't rest on our laurels when it comes to changing dynamics, whether societal or technological. Politicized social and health concerns have created enormous contention in communities, businesses, and even among families. Further, the potential breakthroughs that AI offers communicators also introduce potential pitfalls, as these programs already have the unfortunate ability to "learn and amplify biases present in data" (Fisher & Rosella, 2022). Bottom line: creating effective and ethically sound communication to build relationships takes effort and commitment to contribute to social good.

Discussion Questions

1. Assess a public service announcement using the TARES test. Then assess a political campaign ad. What ethical differences do you notice?
2. Award-winning artist/activist Alexandra Bell evaluated *New York Times* news stories to show how implicit racial biases affected coverage (International Center of Photography, 2018). Considering standpoint theory, apply her approach to health articles and resources. What do you recommend these messengers do?
3. Select a controversial social issue and assess how effectively corporate leaders have advocated about that issue.
4. Table 3.1 includes PR and public health association ethics codes. How well do they tackle issues facing today's professionals? What would you add or change?
5. How might the Bok model and Potter Box aid in resolving health communication dilemmas (Cogar, 2012, pp. 6–9; Table 3.2)?

Further Reading

Cogar, M. (2012). *Ethical decision-making for scholastic media publications.* https://teachingjournalismethics.files.wordpress.com/2012/09/cogar-ethicaldecision-makingmodels1.pdf
International Center of Photography (2018). *2018 Infinity Award: Applied—Alexandra Bell* [Video]. YouTube. https://www.youtube.com/watch?v=-MHXY6vIoe4

References

About B Corp certification. (n.d.). B Corporation. Retrieved August 11, 2022, from https://www.bcorporation.net/en-us/certification

Advice on the use of masks in the context of COVID-19. (2020, April 6). World Health Organization. https://apps.who.int/iris/bitstream/handle/10665/331693/WHO-2019-nCov-IPC_Masks-2020.3-eng.pdf

American Public Health Association. (2019). Public health code of ethics. https://www.apha.org/-/media/files/pdf/membergroups/ethics/code_of_ethics.ashx

APA (n.d.). Frequently asked questions about institutional review boards. American Psychological Association. Retrieved 7/20/2022, from https://www.apa.org/advocacy/research/defending-research/review-boards

Arenstein, S. (2017, September 13). To celebrate ethics month, we bring you 'reputation launderer' Bell Pottinger from across the pond. *PR News*. https://www.prnewsonline.com/prnewsblog/to-celebrate-ethics-month-we-bring-you-reputation-launderer-bell-pottinger-from-across-the-pond/

Argentine Institute of Corporate Social Responsibility. (2020). https://intranet.eulacfoundation.org/en/mapeo/argentinean-institute-corporate-social-responsibility-iarse

Assurance process frequently asked questions (FAQs). (n.d.). Office for Human Research Protections. https://www.hhs.gov/ohrp/register-irbs-and-obtain-fwas/fwas/assurance-process-faq/index.html

Axe, D. (2022, July 15). This relentless COVID variant is the most dangerous one yet. *The Daily Beast*. https://www.thedailybeast.com/why-the-new-ba5-covid-variant-is-the-most-dangerous-one-yet

Bajracharya, S. (2018, January 6). Standpoint theory. Businesstopia. https://www.businesstopia.net/mass-communication/standpoint-theory.

Baker, S., & Martinson, D. L. (2001). The TARES test: Five principles for ethical persuasion. *Journal of Mass Media Ethics*, *16*(2), 148–175. doi:10.1080/08900523.2001.9679610

Brown, D. L. (2017). 'You've got bad blood': The horror of the Tuskegee syphilis experiment. *The Washington Post*. https://www.washingtonpost.com/news/retropolis/wp/2017/05/16/youve-got-bad-blood-the-horror-of-the-tuskegee-syphilis-experiment/

Brown, S. L., & Whiting, D. (2014). The ethics of distress: Toward a framework for determining the ethical acceptability of distressing health promotion advertising. *International Journal of Psychology*, *49*(2), 89–97. doi: 10.1002/ijop.12002

Callahan, M. (2022, May 9). Companies are facing more social pitfalls than ever. What's a forward-thinking board to do? *The Barron's Daily*. https://www.barrons.com/articles/companies-are-facing-more-social-pitfalls-than-ever-politics-supreme-court-51651867415

Campbell, D. M., Copeland, R., Cowlings, P. D., Marshall, N., & McKinley-Beach, L. (2022, July 14). What's up with HIV prevention and Black women? *Word in Black*. https://wordinblack.com/2022/07/whats-up-with-hiv-prevention-and-black-women/

Carroll, A. B. (1991). The pyramid of corporate social responsibility: Toward the moral management of organizational stakeholders. *Business Horizons*, *34*(4), 39–48. https://doi.org/10.1016/0007-6813(91)90005-G

CDC [@CDCgov]. (2020, Feb. 27). CDC does not currently recommend the use of face-masks to help prevent novel #coronavirus. Take everyday preventive actions, like staying [Tweet; link to website]. Twitter. https://twitter.com/cdcgov/status/12331347 10638825473?lang=en

Cercone, J. (2022, February 9). DeSantis ad on Fauci 'flip-flops' leaves out reasons for guidance changes. *Tampa Bay Times*. https://www.tampabay.com/news/health/2022/02/09/desantis-ad-on-fauci-flip-flops-leaves-out-reasons-for-guidance-changes/

Clinton apologizes to Tuskegee experiment victims. (1997, May 16). CNN. https://edi tion.cnn.com/ALLPOLITICS/1997/05/16/tuskegee.apology/

Coalition Alliance Against COVID-19. (2020, November). Press conference on activities by CACOVID. https://www.cbn.gov.ng/Out/2020/CCD/CACOVID%20press%20 conference%20FINAL.pdf

Cogar, M. (2012). *Ethical decision-making for scholastic media publications*. https:// teachingjournalismethics.files.wordpress.com/2012/09/cogar-ethicaldecision-mak ingmodels1.pdf

COVID-19 infection prevention and control. Living guideline: Mask use in community settings. (2021, December 22). World Health Organization. https://apps.who. int/iris/bitstream/handle/10665/350927/WHO-2019-nCoV-IPC_masks-2021.1-eng.pdf

CSR Europe. (2022, July 6). New social and environmental reporting rules for large companies from 2024. https://www.csreurope.org/newsbundle-articles/new-social-and-environmental-reporting-rules-for-large-companies-from-2024

Daniels, C. (2022, April 14). Is corporate America no longer interested in purposeful business? *PR Week*. https://www.prweek.com/article/1753148/corporate-america-no-longer-interested-purposeful-business

Dodd M. D., & Supa, D. W. (2014). Conceptualizing and measuring "corporate social advocacy" communication: Examining the impact on corporate financial performance. *Public Relations Journal*, *8*(3), 2–23. https://www.bellisario.psu.edu/assets/ uploads/2014DODDSUPA.pdf

Fernando, J. (2022, May 27). Corporate social responsibility. Investopedia. https://www. investopedia.com/terms/c/corp-social-responsibility.asp

Fisher, S., & Rosella, L. C. (2022). Priorities for successful use of artificial intelligence by public health organizations: A literature review. *BMC Public Health*, *22*, 2146. https:// doi.org/10.1186/s12889-022-14422-z

Fitzgerald, J. (2022, April 18). Dick's Sporting Goods followed its conscience on guns—and it paid off. Harvard Business School. https://hbswk.hbs.edu/item/ dicks-sporting-goods-followed-its-conscience-on-guns-and-it-paid-off

Fitzpatrick, K., & Bronstein, C. (2006). *Ethics in public relations: Responsible advocacy*. Sage.

Franklin, D. (2022, July 19). Data illuminates difference between corporate values and political stands. *PR News*. https://www.prnewsonline.com/values-politics-bpi-data/?oly_enc_id=8464G9080634B5M

Friedman, M. (1970, Sept. 13). A Friedman doctrine—the social responsibility of business is to increase its profits. *New York Times*. Section SM, 17. https://www.nytimes. com/1970/09/13/archives/a-friedman-doctrine-the-social-responsibility-of-business-is-to.html

Gaither, B. M., Austin, L., & Collins, M. (2018). Examining the case of DICK's Sporting Goods: Realignment of stakeholders through corporate social advocacy. *Journal of Public Interest Communications*, *2*(2), 176–201. doi:10.32473/jpic.v2.i2.p176

Guttman, N. (2000). *Public health communication interventions: Values and ethical dilemmas*. Sage.

Hastings, R. (2022, March 7). Hey business leaders, let's tackle bad PR behavior together. *PR News*. https://www.prnewsonline.com/torossian-ethics-money-business

Heller, J. (2017, May 10). AP was there: Black men untreated in Tuskegee syphilis study. AP. https://apnews.com/article/business-science-health-race-and-ethnicity-syphilis-e9dd07eaa4e74052878a68132cd3803a

IABC code of ethics for professional communicators. (2011). International Association of Business Communicators. https://www.iabc.com/About/Purpose/Code-of-Ethics

International Center of Photography (2018). *2018 Infinity Award: Applied—Alexandra Bell* [Video]. YouTube. https://www.youtube.com/watch?v=-MHXY6vIoe4

Kidder, R. M. (2005). *Moral courage.* W. Morrow.

Kidder, R. M., & Born, P. L. (2002). Moral courage in a world of dilemmas. School Superintendents Association. https://www.proquest.com/docview/219278877

Ledingham, J. A., & Bruning, S. D. (1998). Relationship management in public relations: Dimensions of an organization-public relationship. *Public Relations Review, 24*(1), 55–65. https://doi.org/10.1016/S0363-8111(98)80020-9

Liu, J. (2022, April 18). CEOs made a median $20 million last year—254 times more than the average worker. CNBC. https://www.cnbc.com/2022/04/18/ceos-made-a-median-20-million-last-year254-times-more-than-the-average-worker.html

Logan, N. (2021). A theory of corporate responsibility to race (CRR): Communication and racial justice in public relations. *Journal of Public Relations Research, 33*(1), 6–22. https://doi.org/10.1080/1062726X.2021.1881898

Looking for a B Corp? (n.d.). B Corporation. Retrieved August 11, 2022, from https://www.bcorporation.net/en-us/find-a-b-corp

McManus, J. (2015). As the NFL rolls out anti-violence messages, Greg Hardy acts out. ABC News. https://abcnews.go.com/Sports/nfl-rolls-anti-violence-messages-greg-hardy-acts/story?id=34746356

Merminod, G., & Benaroyo, L. (2022). Ethical issues in public health communication: Practical suggestions from a qualitative study on campaigns about organ donation in Switzerland. *Patient Education and Counseling, 105,* 881–886. https://doi.org/10.1016/j.pec.2021.07.012 0738-3991/

National Institutes of Health (n.d.). NIH implicit bias refresher course. Retrieved August 11, 2022, from https://diversity.nih.gov/sites/coswd/files/images/NIH_Implicit_Bias_Refresher_Course.pdf

New York Chapter of the Public Relations Society of America. (2022, February 17). PRSA-NY's board of directors issues statement regarding disinformation on Everything-PR [Press release]. https://www.prsany.org/news/596046/PRSA-NYs-Board-of-Directors-Issues-Statement-Regarding-Disinformation-on-Everything-PR.htm

NFL. (n.d.). Addressing and preventing domestic violence and sexual assault. https://www.nfl.com/causes/dvsa/

Osemeke, L., Adegbite, S., & Adegbite, E. (2016). Corporate social responsibility initiatives in Nigeria. In S. O. Idowu (Ed.), *Key initiatives in corporate social responsibility: Global dimension of CSR in corporate entities* (pp. 357–375). Springer. https://doi.org/10.1007/978-3-319-21641-6_17

Ping, H. Y. (2005). Corporate social responsibility in Singapore: Institutions, frameworks and practices. Asia-Pacific Economic Cooperation. https://www.apec.org/docs/default-source/Publications/2005/12/Corporate-Social-Responsiblity-in-the-APEC-Region- Current-Status-and-Implications-December-2005/TOC/Singapore.pdf

Riley, K. E., Ulrich, M. R., Hamann, H. A., & Ostroff, J. S. (2017). Decreasing smoking but increasing stigma? Anti-tobacco campaigns, public health, and cancer care. *AMA Journal of Ethics, 19*(5), 475–485. doi:10.1001/journalofethics.2017.19.5.msoc1-1705

Rim, H., Lee, Y. A., & Yoo, S. (2020). Polarized public opinion responding to corporate social advocacy: Social network analysis of boycotters and advocators. *Public Relations Review, 46*(2), 101869. https://doi.org/10.1016/j.pubrev.2019.101869

Ruger, W. (2011). *Milton Friedman.* New York: Continuum.

Simmons-Duffin, S. (2021, May 15). Confused by CDC's latest mask guidance? Here's what we've learned. NPR. https://www.npr.org/sections/health-shots/2021/05/14/996879305/confused-by-cdcs-latest-mask-guidance-heres-what-weve-learned

Standpoint theory. (n.d.). Communication studies. Retrieved August 11, 2022, from http://www.communicationstudies.com/communication-theories/standpoint-theory

Statement on the purpose of a corporation (2019, August 19). Business Roundtable. https://s3.amazonaws.com/brt.org/May-2022BRTStatementonthePurposeofaCorporationwithSignatures.pdf

Steurer, R., Martinuzzi, A., & Margula, S. (2012). Public policies on CSR in Europe: Themes, instruments, and regional differences. *Corporate Social Responsibility and Environmental Management, 19*, 206–227. doi: 10.1002/csr.264

Sweney, M. (2017, September 4). Bell Pottinger expelled from PR trade body after South Africa racism row. *The Guardian.* https://www.theguardian.com/business/2017/sep/04/bell-pottinger-expelled-from-pr-trade-body-after-south-africa-racism-row

Today@Wayne. (2022, June 9). *Taking a stand: Deciphering corporate social, political stances.* Wayne State University. https://today.wayne.edu/news/2022/06/09/taking-a-stand-deciphering-corporate-social-political-stances-48436

Thompkins, A. (2022, July 15). A word about words. Poynter: Covering COVID-19. https://mailchi.mp/poynter/xy73rkah81?e=50d36f3703

Understanding and adopting ESG – An overview. (2021, March 25). Lexology. https://www.lexology.com/library/detail.aspx?g=80bbe258-a1df-4d4c-88f0-6b7a2d2cbd6a

University of Minnesota Center for Infectious Disease Research and Policy. (n.d.). Resources about winter weather and carbon monoxide address preparedness needs of new immigrants. Retrieved August 11, 2022, from https://www.cidrap.umn.edu/practice/resources-about-winter-weather-and-carbon-monoxide-address-preparedness-needs-new

Valles, S. A. (2012). Heterogeneity of risk within racial groups, a challenge for public health programs. *Preventive Medicine, 55*, 405–408. http://dx.doi.org/10.1016/j.ypmed.2012.08.022

Vrentas, J. (2022, July 13). NFL players pay a small price when accused of violence against women. *New York Times.* https://www.nytimes.com/2022/07/13/sports/football/nfl-players-pay-a-small-price-when-accused-of-violence-against-women.html

Washington-Harmon, T. (2022, May 23). Code-switching: What does it mean and why do people do it? Health. https://www.health.com/mind-body/health-diversity-inclusion/code-switching

Waters, E. A., Colditz, G. A., & Davis, K. L. (2021). Essentialism and exclusion: Racism in cancer risk prediction models. *Journal of the National Cancer Institute, 113*(12), 1620–1624. doi: 10.1093/jnci/djab074

4

"RACISM IS A U.S. PUBLIC HEALTH CRISIS"

How Public Relations and Intersectionality Interact to Form This Reality of Public Health Today

Jennifer Vardeman, Natalie T. J. Tindall, Jeremy Cajina-Clark, and Monica L. Ponder

Introduction

This chapter appears in a text that examines the theoretical and applied contexts of public relations, social conditions, and public health. Because of the complexity of this issue, we will work backwards, to some extent. We will first discuss the societal problem of the state of public health today, describe how identity factors into the problems, and then make connections to this "industrial" issue through the lens we all understand, public relations. We hope to demonstrate the power of public relations by examining its role in an extremely serious problem our country faces today that affects hundreds of millions of people and costs the country billions of dollars. The problem is a racist public health system.

Current Context: Racial Disparities

In 2020, the Centers for Disease Control and Prevention named racism a "serious public health threat" (CDC, 2021; Vestal, 2020). The previous term "health disparities" is now more discreetly labeled "racial disparities." However, this somewhat limited moniker is larger in scope: although race is the leading factor by which communities experience disparate health outcomes, race is largely correlated with class, and even more, with gender and disability. So, the industry term that is increasingly being adopted to acknowledge the effects of racism in public health (Feagin & Bennefield, 2014)—intersectionality—further describes the depth of health disparities in a community.

We are at a critical moment in history regarding negative health outcomes among certain U.S. populations. The COVID-19 epidemic demonstrated that in

DOI: 10.4324/9781003327189-5

stark ways. It is now well-documented that COVID-19 was worse for working-class, predominantly Black and brown communities, as well as for women in these communities. What has been less discussed is what role public relations—a strategically managed communication function—played in the critical racial disparities crisis we see today. It should be noted that when we state or declare "public relations," we include health public relations under that umbrella. Bard-han (2002) defined public relations as "any planned communicative action that aims to develop mutually beneficial relationships between multiple stakehold-ers" (p. 224), which riffs on the oft-used definition for public relations. Although most applied intersectionality research in public relations has been conducted in public health or health-care contexts, only 27 articles in a 20-year span across the top seven communication journals have grappled to some extent with political, cultural, and social issues related to health (Ki et al., 2022). Most of the inter-sectional work has not been labeled as or considered health public relations, yet their work resides in that domain. This chapter provides the theoretical framing for a future study in which we ask leaders in the field to answer:

> How did/does public relations (including health public relations) contribute to the persistence of racial disparities in the United States? In what ways has the field and practice of public relations (including health public relations) exacerbated racial disparities?

We believe the answer lies in a historic and persistent decontextualization of pub-lic relations strategies and tactics outside the lens of intersectionality. While inter-sectionality has become more recognized in the past 12 years in public relations research as an important consideration in research and campaigns (see Vardeman, Tindall, Saad, & Smith, 2023), its application to health specific issues and organi-zations has not been widely acknowledged. Said another way, public health poli-cymakers and analysts understand the effects of discrimination on the field more now, but those groups have not begun to explore how strategic communication (as differentiated from interpersonal forms of health communication) contributes to the endurance of racial disparities. This chapter will identify some unique factors that sit at the nexus of intersectionality, public relations, and health contexts, and why this connection provides important methodological, theoretical, and practical guidelines for public relations scholarship and practice, overall.

Contextual Definitions

We cannot address these questions without defining intersectionality, public health, and the specific area of public relations we use to study the former two, critical health communication:

Intersectionality. To frame our work, we first must discuss what is intersectional-ity. Coined by Kimberlé Crenshaw, intersectionality is "a prism from which to view a range of social problems to better ensure inclusiveness of remedies, and to identify opportunities for greater collaboration between and across social movements" (Crenshaw & Harris, 2013, p. 3). This approach is a tool that allows researchers to make prominent the invisible exclusions that define a public's privileges and oppressions. Intersectional theory asserts that people are often disadvantaged by various sources of oppression: their class, gender identity, race, sexual orientation, religion, and other identity markers. Within our work, we view intersectionality as a critical approach to understanding how the various identities held by a public influences and mediates the receptiveness, tolerance, resistance, and acceptance of certain campaign messaging.

Public health. Public health focuses on the concerns that affect the "health of the population of a particular community or country" (Koplan et al., 2009, p. 1994). We conceptualize public health as part of a general system of measuring and addressing large-scale health problems in a community, overlapping with concepts like *health care* and *population health,* among other terms, when discerning the need for and context within which communication campaigns are used to change large-scale health outcomes. Because of the complexity and vast scope of culture, industry, and economic systems across multiple countries but specifically within the United States context, public health has been rhetorically referred to as a "wicked," ongoing problem that requires deliberative democracy, and a component of that deliberative democracy is communicating within the paradoxes (Johnston & Gulliver, 2021).

Critical health communication. Critical health communication is a challenge to the quantitative social psychological models and methods that have dominated health communication. The field serves as a clarion call for scholars to address questions and structures that perpetuate social inequities. Lupton (1994) argued the field of health communication needed to engage in greater interdisciplinarity and integrate more critical cultural and political theory and approaches within its work. Of critical importance, Lupton (1994) stated that a turn toward advocacy and reshaping the political agenda was a necessity: "A sophisticated understanding of the power of discourse in shaping social responses to illness and disease is vital to inform the activities of health communicators acting as advocates to improve the conditions in which the practices of everyday life are carried out" (p. 63).

Intersectionality in Health and Public Relations Context

During the last 15 years, intersectionality has evolved from an incipient flash point to a sustaining area of inquiry and analytical frame within the public relations body of knowledge. In this section we will provide insight into the launch and integration of intersectionality into public relations research and the prominent foci for intersectional research.

Extant Research

The early wave of research on diversity was muted in its declarations about power as well as the entanglements created by multiplicative identities. Prior research viewed identity in silos. Women were studied, racial minority groups were studied, but those with multiple identities that experienced marginalization (e.g., women of color) presented an opportunity for researchers and practitioners to apply simplistic "one-size-fits-all" studies and solutions. The unintended consequence of studying practitioners and publics more homogeneously was that their different, nuanced experiences were minimized in the canon of public relations scholarship (Place & Vardeman-Winter, 2018), and real-world publics were under- or mis-represented in campaign programming (Tindall & Vardeman-Winter, 2011).

Earlier scholars studying race and gender in public relations were reluctant to explore the differences residing within groups, leading to flattened descriptions and perspectives. Aldoory and Toth (2021) remarked that "to generalize female public relations practitioners based on White women alone oversimplifies the experiences of public relations people living as women" (p. 164). Efforts to include other standpoints have been frequent and sustained. Sha (2006), in a clear exploration of the salience of cultural identity in messaging and the value of the situational theory of publics' referent criterion, provided a path for future work within the public relations context that used culture-centered approaches and queried how perception and meaning are shaped by the confluence of identities. Pompper (2005) nudged the concept of intersectionality into the literature through the application of critical race theory (a first for public relations scholarship) and by explicitly stating that scholarship should be "conscious of difference and race, ethnicity, and culture" (p. 140). Golombisky (2015) offered a sharp rebuke to the feminist theory projects within the scholarship, arguing for the "embrace [of] intersectionality as theory and method of accounting for positionality" (p. 390) and a turn from gender equality toward social justice within public relations "as a practice, discipline, and social phenomenon" (p. 390). Vardeman and Tindall (2010), prompted by their graduate studies at the University of Maryland at College Park and their dissertation projects which engaged with feminist thought, critical studies, and intersectional thinking, were the first to comprehensively fuse intersectionality with public relations and articulate how intersectionality could be used as an analytic framework (Vardeman et al., 2023).

Typology of Intersectional Work

With time came greater sophistication and a deeper plumbing and application of the theoretical. The interest in intersectionality spurred new researchers and research ideas that could be divided into two camps: those looking at intersectionality framed by the organization, function, and practice of public relations, and those focusing on the groups of individuals who are targeted for specific communications and understanding how the identities possessed by members of those groups inform their understanding, appreciation, and involvement with messaging. Scholars demonstrated the necessity of the theory to the body of knowledge and the pertinence of the concept to public relations practice, and many of these projects wrestled with the praxis of public relations messaging and segmentation surrounding public health concerns.

Practitioner-Focused Works

This corpus examines the roles and experiences of communicators, their autonomy, power, and responsibilities within their organizations. Aldoory and Toth (2021) explored the meaning and value of intersectionality to the profession. Place (2022) investigates the way PR practitioners incorporate intersectionality into listening strategies to understand publics with intersecting, complex identities. Edwards (2022) investigates how practitioners of color manage their intersectional properties and the impacts their intersecting identities have on their professional lives. She finds that practitioners of color are constantly compromising between speaking out against discrimination they experience, and maintaining their silence (Edwards, 2022). The challenge they face is not about whether to openly take a stand against discrimination, but about how to resist in ways that preserves their "sameness" and does not threaten their careers. The study reveals how intersectionality can be used to view public relations as a "racial project" that promotes identities that serve projects and clients while leading practitioners of color to behave in ways that mask their "risky" identities (Edwards, 2022). By shining a light on the frustrating reality of PR practitioners of color, Edward's study combats the notion that PR is a post-racial field and reveals the way this line of thinking leads to the reinforcement of racial power structures in PR rather than improves the lives of practitioners with different identities.

Publics-Focused Works

This stream of research focuses on the groups of individuals who are targeted for specific communication campaigns and understanding how the identities possessed by members of those groups inform their understanding, appreciation, and involvement with messaging. Studies in this vein explore which identities become salient in different contexts, and how these layered identities shift a public's decision-making processes. Several projects examined how practitioners shaped health communication campaigns in benefit (or in detriment) of the intersectional concerns faced by the targeted publics or audiences. Turpin (2013) explored how targeted HIV/AIDS messaging campaigns missed how the multitude of constraints faced by Black women limited their message process and ramped up their fear of stigmatization. In their autoethnographic work on women and weight-loss messaging, Johnson and Eaves (2013) filled a gap by using an auto-ethnographic approach and intersectional analytic lens to dissect how women comprehend and process certain health messages. The study examined weight loss across two women's experiences who have different identities, and implications for segmentation of publics in campaign messages suggested that health is a particularly relevant context to explore intersectionality in communication messaging. These two female scholars' different perceptions of weight, body image, and health messaging showcased how the segmentation of publics in campaign messaging requires more matter and substance than demographic traits; their exploration resulted in the following telling conclusion: their project "reveal[ed] the need for more methodologies such as autoethnography that will uncover the multiple identities and experiences of an organization's public" (Johnson & Eaves, 2013, p. 113).

In summary, over the span of 15 years, intersectionality was an idea met with perplexity that transcended into the mainstream of public relations research. There is the concern that intersectionality has become a stand-in for diversity or a wrongly used descriptive term for multifaceted identity (Aldoory & Toth, 2021). Vardeman et al. (2023) detailed the growing pains for intersectional work within public relations over the past ~12 years, particularly considering recent anti-racist and anti-sexist social movements/events in the United States, namely Black Lives Matter and the Women's March on Washington. We will detail next specific characteristics that make intersectionality in public health and public relations an important and unique site of analysis.

Why Intersectional Public Relations Is Imperative to Public Health

Anytime there's a disproportionate amount of risk/disease in a community, this indicates a problem of disparate information flow at some level. Here, we discuss four sites where public relations has contributed to an absence of intersectional considerations in public health communication campaigns. These exist at the conceptual design, methodological, strategic segmentation, and tactical implementation levels.

Conceptual Design Requires Cultural Contextualization and Collaboration

Racial disparities persist in public health because many health practitioners of all disciplines live in a different power dynamic than the people whose everyday lived experiences are the ones reflected in racial disparities statistics.

Policymakers and those working for large-scope and hierarchically structured organizations come from culturally white and higher educated and higher income backgrounds; and those who experienced the highest rates of morbidity and mortality of disease and negative health conditions are those of low-income communities of color. This is not just a racial injustice issue; it is also one that is intricately intertwined with class and gender, as well as other identities of age, nationality, disability, and sexual orientation, among others. This *policymaker– public gap* (Vardeman-Winter, Jiang, & Tindall, 2013) results in significant issues at the conceptual design stage of public health interventions if intersectional collaboration is not considered.

When conducting research, intersectionality theory should be taken into consideration from conceptualization as it can provoke important considerations for interactions throughout the entire study (Abrams et al., 2020; Tan et al., 2023). It can be applied with recruiting participants, while collecting data, and disbursing the findings. The reason intersectionality should be applied is whether subconsciously or not, the similarities and differences between participants and researchers might influence some of the research. Intersectionality is meant to be practiced.

Collaboration is also essential to activating intersectional research. This is largely due to the socioeconomic gap that exists between public relations strategists within organizations and their campaign target groups for interventions. Abrams et al. (2020) recommends a triangulation approach be taken when collecting data. Taking this approach of combining methods, theories and data sources will be able to achieve more inclusivity related to the topic being studied or presented. Before recruiting participants, working with those communities to build out interview guides and research questions will reduce power imbalances within the process.

Oppositional Sensitivities in Segmentation Design

The highly publicized deaths and police violence against Black and brown people around the summer of 2020 forced many middle- and upper-class white people to acknowledge and accept the catastrophic problems for people of color in America. Specifically, Black Americans faced dual epidemics in 2020 with some of the worst COVID outcomes and an apex of public brutality. Health communicators and policymakers noticed the detrimental and uneven effects the intervention campaigns were having on communities of color and of low income: Hull et al. (2020) from *Health Communication* wrote that, "Masks are the new condoms," and argued that racist structures in (non-intersectional) campaigns enable Black Americans to have the highest mortality from COVID (as they have in the HIV epidemic).

A wave of diversity, equity, and inclusion initiatives and dialogues sprang up among organizations, industry associations, ad hoc committees, and community groups. The purpose, in some ways, was for white practitioners and professionals to further reify abject discrimination as unacceptable in workplaces, unearth subtle and unacknowledged racism, and include historically unseen groups in programming. For public health practitioners, it seems a new awareness for unidentified discrimination would be the primary goal during the next major intervention. However, a lack of intersectional understanding in segmenting publics thwarted some otherwise well-intentioned major public health interventions.

Monkeypox Targets: The Real versus the Intervention

In May 2022, the first case of the monkeypox virus in the U.S. was reported in Massachusetts (Kornfield & Knowles, 2022). Since then, cases have risen to more than 25,000 in October 2022, with 99 percent of all monkeypox cases in men and 94 percent of all cases in men who have sex with men (MSM) (Centers for Disease Control and Prevention [CDC], 2022g; Soucheray, 2022). At the start of the outbreak, white men were the most affected demographic, but as the virus spread and vaccine distribution began, queer men of color quickly became the most affected group by the monkeypox virus (CDC, 2022d).

When looked at through the lens of the situational theory of publics, this is a narrowly identified public to target. Problem recognition is high because MSM are aware that the monkeypox virus is spreading through their community. Many of them are also knowledgeable about how it spreads and what they can do to minimize their risk (Morning Consult, 2022). As a whole, constraint recognition is low because the only constraints to stop the spread of monkeypox in this public lie in the reduction of certain lifestyle habits. This includes reducing the number of sexual partners they might have, ceasing having anonymous sex, and reducing the use of apps to find sexual partners, habits that gay men have already begun to adopt (CDC, 2022c). Internal and external involvement recognition are also high. MSM know that they are the most at-risk group, and they recognize monkeypox as a threat to their community (Morning Consult, 2022). This combination of variables would make the MSM community an aware public for a health organization to target. However, the problem with this approach is that it does not take into account the intersecting identities of people within this community.

When broken down further, the MSM community is not made up exclusively of white men. There is a large percentage of people of color who either self-identify or are ascribed as MSM, and the variables for them look different. Problem recognition for this public would remain largely the same. Monkeypox affects Black and brown queer men the same way that it affects white MSM. The difference occurs with constraint recognition. Overall, constraint recognition was low among MSM, but extra constraints exist for queer people of color that do not exist for the MSM community as a whole because of their race(s) (discussed next).

Perceived constraints for people of color in this context relate to another salient segmentation variable: referent criterion. Members of this public might pull knowledge about responding to a viral outbreak and associated vaccines from the time of the COVID-19 vaccine rollout. People of color experienced significant constraints to accessing the vaccine then even though they were getting infected at disproportionate rates (Recht & Weber, 2021). Many members might also remember how people of color, Black people especially, were largely overlooked by the government, organizations, and outreach campaigns during the AIDS epidemic (Royles, 2017). This knowledge leads to heightened constraint recognition in this public. They face barriers that other members of the wider public do not have to overcome. Thus, involvement recognition would be even higher for this public: not only are they part of the most affected group overall, they are the most affected subgroup within the larger public. While this public might simply be aware when it comes to changing behavior, this mix of variables could easily make them a frustrated, active public that health organizations would look over simply because they did not consider their intersecting identities.

The public health messaging around monkeypox has further exacerbated the monkeypox outbreak. Coming off the heels of the rise of Asian discrimination that COVID helped foster, many health officials are scared of stigmatizing the MSM community through their messaging (Cahill, 2022). While this sensitivity is well-intentioned, it has led to many health organizations creating vague messages about monkeypox that downplay the fact that it is spreading in the MSM community and, rather, initial alerts suggest monkeypox to be indiscriminately spreading among the general population (Downs, 2022). Even the CDC is having trouble finding a balance in creating messages that target this public without stigmatizing them, which can be easily observed in their ready-to-print materials for partners to disseminate to their publics (CDC, 2022a). These materials are factually accurate, they have inclusive language and images, and they even have an entire selection of pride-themed materials. One thing that is noticeably absent in all of these materials is any mention of MSM (CDC, 2022f). This overcompensation in the name of de-stigmatization is prevalent in the messaging of many health organizations leading to confusion among those most at risk and those at very low risk (Kupferschmidt, 2022). There is no clear solution for this problem, but one thing is for certain—health organizations need to message clearly and honestly about monkeypox in order to combat the spread of the virus, misinformation, and stigma.

Even more, the issue of intersectionality is one where some health communicators fall short yet again. Health organizations have such a heightened awareness of the MSM community because of history's failings that they do not realize they are overlooking another identity of many in the MSM community. The monkeypox virus originated in Africa, and while some health organizations tiptoe around MSM, they have been less cautious about the way they frame their messages about its origins. The CDC and the World Health Organization make it clear on their websites where the first cases of monkeypox outside of Africa came from and how it arrived in the U.S.: through contact with prairie dogs that were housed with Gambian rats (CDC, 2022b; World Health Organization [WHO], 2022a). The images that these two organizations use are also cause for concern. At the top of its page on monkeypox, the WHO has a banner image of a Black person's hand infected with the monkeypox virus, and most of the graphics that the CDC uses also depict Black individuals with the disease (CDC, 2022e; WHO, n.d.). This has led to concerns about the framing of monkeypox as an "African disease" (Nsofor, 2022). Like the issue of the MSM community, there is no clear solution, but health organizations must be aware of the multiple intersecting identities of their publics and how their messaging affects them.

Methods That Focus on the Community Rather Than Individual

As noted in Vardeman et al. (2023), one reason for the lag in uptake of intersectional analyses in professional and intellectual fields like public relations is the difficulty in methodologically analyzing the effects of co-occurring multiple identities upon workplace bias and/or publics' decision-making. Despite the difficulties, scholars (e.g., Bowleg, 2008, 2012) have worked to demystify and clarify ways we can do intersectional research. We want to offer a challenge to readers to pick methods that are not often used in public relations or public health spaces (ethnography, autoethnography).

Having multiple perspectives is crucial to comprehending the bigger picture, whether that be in research or in public relations campaigns. When recruiting participants, Abrams et al. (2020) recommends expanding efforts into smaller communities such as community centers, empowerment groups, advocacy organizations, and other public organizations. Additionally, other strategies recommended are quota and purposive sampling, venue-based or time-location sampling. These original recruitment strategies will increase the opportunities for connections with people who may have disadvantages and allow for a broader perspective to be reached.

Triangulated analyses will produce the best understanding of how multiplicative identities affect health status if both quantitative and qualitative methods are used. Most intersectional work in public health/health-care public relations has been conducted using qualitative methods. However, there are an increasing number of studies about public health that explore intersectionality using quantitative methods (Agénor, 2020; Bauer et al., 2021; Jiang et al. 2011; Logie et al., 2022). Public relations scholars should examine analytical methods used in intersectional studies outside our field and map our particular concepts to those analytical trends and methods.

To this point, Tan et al. (2023) recommended priority actions for achieving health equity (in tobacco control interventions) using intersectionality approaches. These actions include using more qualitative and mixed methods that leave room for interpretation and rich description of experience; enacting policies that improve living conditions and support sustained behavior change among communities; requiring integrated intersectionality training across disciplines (physical and social sciences alike) that will "ensure that intersectionality-grounded research questions are asked and answered" (p. 2); partnering with communities at every phase of research, incenting scholars from a variety of backgrounds to pursue intersectional projects; and promoting person-first language rather than identity-first labels that are negatively valued. Finally, intersectionally informed reform suggests that population health is a more apt approach to improving public health rather focusing on the microlevel (e.g., individual solutions for systemic causes and issues) (Agénor, 2020).

Messaging Requires Culturally Contextualized Cues

One of the most tangible and salient examples of problematized intersectionality in public health PR research has been the persistence of misappropriate cultural cues in our campaigns. These miscues have been documented in public relations research over the past 12 years (Curtin & Gaither, 2007; Vardeman et al., 2023). In their thorough critique of presuppositions of the intellectual and practical domains of public relations, Vardeman, Tindall, and Jiang (2013) described the "researcher and practitioner challenge" as "those who attempt to span the boundaries between organizations and publics cannot *not* be an individual situated in a particular intersection and an employee of an organization in a particular industry, portraying a distinct organizational identity" (p. 290). In every interaction and within every campaign decision being made, a practitioner or a researcher is acting from an informed perspective or position that pulls from the multiple streams of influence and referent criteria the person has. This is how miscues happen. For example, Long (2006) viewed the National Heart, Lung, and Blood Institute's Heart Truth campaign as a success from its branding and social marketing perspective. However, in Tindall and Vardeman's (2011) work on the Heart Truth campaign as a platform to understand minoritized female publics' connection and resistance to heart disease messaging, that campaign suffered due to the initial and subsequent graphics, photography, and messaging created in the comfort of PR firms and government officers that did not appeal to or consider the intended publics with the highest likelihood of heart disease. Heath (2016) found that the messaging of HIV and AIDS campaigns provided a cloistering effect for middle-class Black women in Atlanta. These women did not see themselves within the intended target audience or their concerns reflected in the campaigns. As Heath noted, "race, gender, and hierarchies of class shape their thoughts and beliefs about agency or choice about relationships as well as privilege and status relating to HIV perceptions and risk" (p. 112).

Systemic Reform of Political Economy of Public Health Communication

Abject and subtle forms of racism and discrimination alike are enabled by capitalist economies. This economic system allows for revenue to largely outweigh public well-being, and the legislative process for the latter is often corrupted by profitable corporations. Public health measures and interventions, then, are left with far smaller coffers upon which to enact and enforce risk-adverse/pro-health interventions. This bleak state of the economic status of U.S. public health can be seen in recent studies and commentaries by public health researchers examining the tobacco industry's stark statistics of smoking trends among Black communities coupled with the now discoverable marketing and advertising strategies of Black and brown communities by tobacco manufacturers (cf. Garrett et al., 2014: Zavala-Arciniega et al., 2023). Scholars in the tobacco control space are advocating for a paradigm shift toward intersectional-informed approaches for reform (Tan et al., 2023), and they suggest starting with examining power structures between communities and corporations:

> we must identify the pervasive and powerful structural factors that shape the lived experiences of individuals and communities affected by oppression. We must then begin to understand how these factors result in individual, societal, and intergenerational harms from commercial tobacco use.

> *(p. 74)*

The heightened targeting/marketing of flavored cigars and menthol cigarettes to Black youth and men is a prime example of institutional racism and residential segregation and requires intersectionality to uncover the overwhelming use of menthol cigarettes in the Black community compared to other racial groups (Kong et al., 2019). Menthol cigarettes also have a higher usage among women than men, LGTBQ people, and kids (Christensen, 2022, April 22). A systematic review found that higher concentrations of tobacco retailers have been located in lower-income areas and areas with greater proportions of Black residents; the review also found more instances of menthol cigarettes marketing in stores in urban area neighborhoods and neighborhoods with more Black residents (Kong et al., 2019, p. 619).

Health communication scholarship and practice have focused excessively on reducing risk by encouraging changes in individual behaviors. This "personal responsibility" approach assumes that by focusing on the individuals, they'll be able to alleviate the structural impact of being Black in the United States (Hull et al., 2020, p. 1740). When the pandemic hit, the reality was there wasn't equal protection from the COVID-19 virus within the different racial groups due to social-structural and contextual factors. Face masks and social distancing weren't as effective in bringing down the positive cases of COVID-19 because the same health behaviors present various levels of protection due to exposure and social imbalances that ultimately affect the risk and recovery. When the COVID-19 vaccines rolled out to communities, it presented another opportunity for racial and other biases into clinical decisions about who is a "good candidate" to receive it (Hull et al., 2020, p. 1741).

Moving Forward: Recommendations for Future Research and Practice

Based upon the work we have done before and the scholarship laid out in this chapter, we offer the following recommendations for practitioners and scholars:

- Within public relations, public health should be reframed within a lens of power and identity. Public health scholars have moved toward holistic reform to consider power and identity in each of their research processes. Now is the time for public relations people to take up the same mantle when doing health communication and public health work. Power and identity surface in every interaction a person has with the world, including our campaign activations, calls to actions, and key messages.
- Regaining trust and credibility is a common need between public health and public relations. According to the 2022 Edelman Trust Barometer, the default mode within society is one of distrust of societal institutions. Richard Edelman (2022) wrote that "we need to move from outrage to optimism, fears to confidence, insinuation to fact" (¶ 15). Trust and credibilty are the bedrocks for reputation and relationship, the two things of value for public relations. In public health, Larson and Heymann (2010) expressed the need and importance of public trust in the enterprise of public health. The hallmarks of trust that both public relations and public health should center in their activities are transparency, honesty, community, and care.
- Public relations should adopt a *prosocial imperative* that is infused with care and empathy and promises science-informed and community-based communication policies. Prosocial behavior is an assumed intent in some aspects of public relations research and practice. However, prosocial covers a wide swath of intentions, behaviors, and concepts. Within the multiple definitions of prosocial behavior, Pfattheicher et al. (2020) found that most define the intentional acts that are valuable to the larger society and that promote beneficence and the well-being of others. For this model to work in public

relations, we believe that we need to consider empathy, care, evidence, and community as core constructs. Of this laundry list of concepts, both empathy and care are the two components that need clearer definition within the public relations context. Yeomans (2016) noted that empathy is an underserved, under-researched ideal within public relations and called for the reframing of empathy as a "transformative potential for the individual as empathiser with disadvantaged, marginalised or oppressed groups in achieving social justice goals" (p. 87).

Discussion Questions

1. Given the constantly changing manifestation of race, diversity, equity, gender, and other identities in our society, how do you see intersectionality being employed in public health PR campaigns in the next several years?
2. How should PR practitioners in nonprofits explain the concept of intersectionality to managers or community partners who may not understand how to incorporate messages targeting multiple communities or varying intersectional identities?
3. Consider other concepts/theories/models of identity that have been employed in public relations scholarship (e.g., corporate social responsibility of race, whiteness theory, queer theory, requisite variety, among others). What does intersectionality offer uniquely to challenges PR practitioners face in public health? How can intersectionality complement other approaches?

Further Reading

Bowleg, L. (2008). When Black+ lesbian+ woman≠ Black lesbian woman: The methodological challenges of qualitative and quantitative intersectionality research. *Sex Roles*, *59*, 312–325.

Cho, S., Crenshaw, K. W., & McCall, L. (2013). Toward a field of intersectionality studies: Theory, applications, and praxis. *Signs: Journal of Women in Culture and Society*, *38*, 785–810.

Feagin, J., & Bennefield, Z. (2014). Systemic racism and US health care. *Social Science & Medicine*, *103*, 7–14.

Vardeman, J., Tindall, N.T.J., Saad, N., & Smith, L. (2022). "Revisiting intersectionality: The stray, strain, and performativity of social identity dimensions in public relations over the past decade." In D. Pompper, K. R. Place, & C. K. Weaver (Eds.), *Routledge companion to public relations* (pp. 74–88). Routledge: New York.

References

Abrams, J., Tabaacc, A., Jungd, S., & Else-Queste, N. (2020). Considerations for employing intersectionality in qualitative health research. *Social Science Medicine*, *258*: 113138. DOI:10.1016/j.socscimed.2020.113138

Agénor, M. (2020). Future directions for incorporating intersectionality into quantitative population health research. *AJPH, 110*(6), 803–806. DOI: 10.2105/AJPH.2020.305610.

Aldoory, L., & Toth, E. L. (2021). *The future of feminism in public relations and strategic communication: A socio-ecological model of influences*. Lanham, MD: Rowman & Littlefield.

Bardhan, N. R. (2002). Accounts from the field: A public relations perspective on global Relations AIDS/HIV. *Journal of Health Communication, 7*:3, 221–244, DOI: 10.1080/10810730290088102

Bauer, G. R., Churchill, S. M., Mahendran, M., Walwyn, C., Lizotte, D., & Villa-Rueda, A. A. (2021). Intersectionality in quantitative research: A systematic review of its emergence and applications of theory and methods. *SSM – Population Health, 14*: 100798. https://doi.org/10.1016/j.ssmph.2021.100798.

Bowleg, L. (2008). When Black+ lesbian+ woman≠ Black lesbian woman: The methodological challenges of qualitative and quantitative intersectionality research. *Sex Roles, 59*, 312–325.

Bowleg, L. (2012). The problem with the phrase women and minorities: Intersectionality— an important theoretical framework for public health. *American Journal of Public Health, 102*(7), 1267–1273. https://doi.org/10.2105/AJPH.2012.300750

Cahill, S. (2022). Monkeypox and gay and bisexual men: Fact sheet. https://health.hawaii. gov/docd/files/2022/06/Monkeypox-and-gay-and-bisexual-men-fact-sheet-06-02-2022. pdf

CDC. (2021, October 25). Racism and health. Centers for Disease Control and Prevention. https://www.cdc.gov/minorityhealth/racism-disparities/director-commentary.html

CDC. (2022a). Reducing stigma in monkeypox communication and community engagement. Retrieved September 29, 2022, from https://www.cdc.gov/poxvirus/monkeypox/ resources/reducing-stigma.html

CDC. (2022b, July 22). About monkeypox. Retrieved from https://www.cdc.gov/poxvirus/ monkeypox/about/index.html

CDC. (2022c, August 22). Impact of monkeypox outbreak on select behaviors. Retrieved from https://www.cdc.gov/poxvirus/monkeypox/response/2022/amis-select-behaviors.html

CDC. (2022d, August 22). Monkeypox cases by age and gender, race/ethnicity, and symptoms. Retrieved from https://www.cdc.gov/poxvirus/monkeypox/response/2022/ demographics.html

CDC. (2022e, August 23). Clinical recognition | Monkeypox | Poxvirus | CDC. Retrieved from https://www.cdc.gov/poxvirus/monkeypox/clinicians/clinical-recognition.html

CDC. (2022f, September 19). Print resources. Retrieved from https://www.cdc.gov/poxvirus/ monkeypox/resources/print.html

CDC. (2022g, September 22). 2022 U.S. map & case count. Retrieved from https://www. cdc.gov/poxvirus/monkeypox/response/2022/us-map.html

Christensen, J. (2022, April 22). Ban on menthol cigarettes and flavored cigars could save hundreds of thousands of lives, experts say. CNN. https://www.cnn.com/2022/04/27/ health/proposed-menthol-ban/index.html

Crenshaw, K., & Harris, L. (2013). A primer on intersectionality. Los Angeles: African American Policy Forum. Accessed via https://youthrex.com/wp-content/uploads/2019/ 02/59819079-Intersectionality-Primer.pdf

Curtin, P. A., & Gaither, T. K. (2007). *International public relations: Negotiating culture, identity, and power*. Thousand Oaks, CA: Sage Publications.

Downs, J. (2022, May 28). Gay men need a specific warning about monkeypox. *The Atlantic*. https://www.theatlantic.com/ideas/archive/2022/05/monkeypox-outbreak-spread-gay-bisexual-men/643122/

Edelman, Richard. (2022, January 18) *Breaking the Vicious Cycle of Distrust.* Retrieved March 25, 2024, from https://www.edelman.com/trust/2022-trust-barometer/breaking-vicious-cycle-distrust

Edwards, L. (2022). 'I'm a PR person. Let's just deal with it.' Managing intersectionality in professional life. *Public Relations Inquiry, 12*(1), 27–51. https://doi.org/10.11 77/2046147X221089323

Feagin, J., & Bennefield, Z. (2014). Systemic racism and US health care. *Social Science & Medicine, 103,* 7–14. DOI: 10.1016/j.socscimed.2013.09.006.

Garrett, B. E., Dube, S. R., Babb, S., & McAfee, T. (2014). Addressing the social determinants of health to reduce tobacco-related disparities. *Nicotine & Tobacco Research, 17*(8), 892–897. DOI: 10.1093/ntr/ntu266.

Golombisky, K. (2015). Renewing the commitments of feminist public relations theory from velvet ghetto to social justice. *Journal of Public Relations Research, 27*(5), 389–415. https://doi.org/10.1080/1062726X.2015.1086653

Heath, C. D. (2016). Voices from the unheard: Perceptions of HIV among middle class Black women in Atlanta. *Transforming Anthropology, 24*(2), 97–115. https://doi.org/10.1111/traa.12072

Johnson, C. R. S., & Eaves, K. L. (2013). An ounce of time, a pound of responsibilities and a ton of weight to lose: An autoethnographic journey of barriers, message adherence and the weight-loss process. *Public Relations Inquiry, 2*(1), 95–116. https://doi.org/10.1177/2046147X12460949

Johnston, J., & Gulliver, R. (2021). Public interest communication. The University of Queensland. https://doi.org/10.14264/316efde

Ki, E.-J., Kang, D., & Huang, M. (2022). The state of health public relations: A content analysis of published articles in seven communication journals from 2001 to 2021. *Public Relations Review, 48*(5), 102255. https://doi.org/10.1016/j.pubrev.2022.102255

Kong, A. Y., Golden, S. D., & Berger, M. T. (2019). An intersectional approach to the menthol cigarette problem: What's race(ism) got to do with it? *Critical Public Health, 29*(5), 616–623. https://doi.org/10.1080/09581596.2018.1478066

Koplan, J. P., Bond, T. C., Merson, M. H., Reddy, K. S., Rodriguez, M. H., Sewankambo, N. K., & Wasserheit, J. N. (2009). Towards a common definition of global health. *The Lancet, 373*(9679), 1993–1995. https://doi.org/10.1016/S0140-6736(09)60332-9

Kornfield, M., & Knowles, H. (2022, May 18). Monkeypox case confirmed in Massachusetts. *The Washington Post.* https://www.washingtonpost.com/health/2022/05/18/monkeypox-case-massachusetts/

Kupferschmidt, K. (2022, August 4). We can fight monkeypox without hysteria or homophobia. *The New York Times.* https://www.nytimes.com/2022/08/04/opinion/monkeypox-communication.html

Larson, H. J., & Heymann, D. L. (2010). Public health response to influenza A(H1N1) as an opportunity to build public trust. *JAMA, 303*(3), 271–272. doi: 10.1001/jama.2009.2023.

Logie, C. H., Earnshaw, V., Nyblade, L., Turan, J., Stangl, A., Poteat, T., Nelson, L., & Baral, S. (2022). A scoping review of the integration of empowerment-based perspectives in quantitative intersectional stigma research. *Global Public Health, 17*(8), 1451–1466. https://doi.org/10.1080/17441692.2021.1934061

Long, K. H. (2006). *Public relations and branding in health communication programs: A case study of a successful campaign* (Publication No. 1433961). [Thesis, University of Maryland, College Park]. ProQuest Dissertations & Thesis Global.

Lupton, D. (1994). Toward the development of critical health communication praxis. *Health Communication, 6*(1), 55–67. https://doi.org/10.1207/s15327027hc0601_4

Morning Consult. (2022). National Tracking Poll #2207197. https://assets.morningconsult.com/wp-uploads/2022/08/12165423/2207197_crosstabs_MC_HEALTH_MONKEY-POX_Adults_STACKED_v2_SH.pdf

Nsofor, I. (2022, June 2). OPINION: Why this Nigerian doctor is angry at media coverage of monkeypox: Goats and Soda. NPR. https://www.npr.org/sections/goatsandsoda/2022/06/02/1102199023/opinion-media-coverage-of-monkeypox-paints-it-as-an-african-virus-that-makes-me-

Pfattheicher, S., Nockur, L., Böhm, R., Sassenrath, C., & Petersen, M. B. (2020). The emotional path to action: Empathy promotes physical distancing and wearing of face masks during the COVID-19 pandemic. *Psychological Science*, *31*(11), 1363–1373. https://doi.org/10.1177/0956797620964422

Place, K. R. (2022, March 27). Toward a framework for listening with consideration for intersectionality: Insights from public relations professionals in borderland spaces. *Journal of Public Relations Research*, *34*(3). DOI: 10.1080/1062726X.2022.2057502

Place, K., & Vardeman-Winter, J. (2018). Where are the women? An examination of the status of research on women and leadership in public relations. *Public Relations Review*, *44*, 165–173. https://doi.org/10.1016/j.pubrev.2017.10.005

Pompper, D. (2005). "Difference" in public relations research: A case for introducing critical race theory. *Journal of Public Relations Research*, *17*(2), 139–169. https://doi.org/10.1207/s1532754xjprr1702_5

Recht, H., & Weber, L. (2021, January 17). Black Americans are getting vaccinated at lower rates than white Americans. *Kaiser Health News*. https://khn.org/news/article/black-americans-are-getting-vaccinated-at-lower-rates-than-white-americans/

Royles, D. (2017, July 6). Race, homosexuality, and the AIDS epidemic. African American Intellectual History Society. https://www.aaihs.org/race-homosexuality-and-the-aids-epidemic/

Sha, B.-L. (2006). Cultural identity in the segmentation of publics: An emerging theory of intercultural public relations. *Journal of Public Relations Research*, *18*(1), 45–65. https://doi.org/10.1207/s1532754xjprr1801_3

Soucheray, S. (2022, August 8). Monkeypox cases reach 7500 in US; 99% of cases in males. CIDRAP. https://www.cidrap.umn.edu/news-perspective/2022/08/monkeypox-cases-reach-7500-us-99-cases-males

Tan, A. S. L., Hinds, J. T., Smith, P. H., Antin, T., Lee, J. P., Ostroff, J. S., Patten, C., Rose, S. W., Sheffer, C. E., & Fagan, P. (2023). Incorporating intersectionality as a framework for equity-minded tobacco control research: A call for collective action toward a paradigm shift. *Nicotine & Tobacco Research*, *25*(1), 73–76. https://doi.org/10.1093/ntr/ntac110

Tindall, N. T. J., & Vardeman-Winter, J. (2011). Complications in segmenting campaign publics: Women of color explain their problems, involvement, and constraints in reading heart disease communication. *Howard Journal of Communication*, *22*, 280–301. http://dx.doi.org/10.1080/10646175.2011.590407

Turpin, T. (2013). Unintended consequences of a segmentation strategy: Exploring constraint recognition among Black women targeted in HIV/AIDS campaigns. *Public Relations Journal*, *7*(2), 96–127.

Vardeman-Winter, J. E. (2017). The framing of women and health disparities: A critical look at race, gender, and class from the perspectives of grassroots health communicators. *Health Communication*, *32*, 629–638. DOI: 10.1080/10410236.2016.1160318

Vardeman-Winter, J. E., Jiang, H., & Tindall, N. T. J. (2013). Information-seeking outcomes of representational, structural, and political intersectionality among health media consumers. *Journal of Applied Communication Research*, *41*(4), 389–411. DOI: 10.1080/00909882.2013.828360

Vardeman-Winter, J. E., Jiang, H., & Tindall, N. T. J. (2014). 'Mammography at age 40 to 49 saves lives, just not enough of them': Gendered political intersections in communicating breast cancer screening policy to publics. In C. Daymon & K. Demetrious (Eds.), *Gender and public relations: Critical perspectives on voice, image and identity* (pp. 221–246). London: Routledge.

Vardeman-Winter, J. E., & Tindall, N. T. J. (2010). Toward an intersectionality theory of public relations. In R. L. Heath (Ed.), *Handbook of public relations II* (pp. 223–236). Thousand Oaks, CA: Sage Publications.

Vardeman-Winter, J. E., Tindall, N., & Jiang, H. (2013). Intersectionality and publics: How exploring publics' multiple identities questions basic public relations concepts. *Public Relations Inquiry, 2*(3), 279–304. doi:10.1177/2046147×13491564

Vardeman, J., Tindall, N. T. J., Smith, L., & Saad, N. (2023). Revisiting intersectionality: The stray, strain, and performativity of social identity dimensions in public relations over the past decade. In D. Pompper, K. R. Place, & C. K. Weaver (Eds.), *Routledge companion to public relations* (pp. 74–88). New York: Routledge.

Vestal, C. (2020, June 15). *Racism is a public health crisis, say cities and counties.* The Pew Charitable Trusts. www.pewtrusts.org/en/research-and-analysis/blogs/stateline/2020/06/15/racism-is-a-public-health-crisis-say-cities-and-counties

World Health Organization. (2022a, May 19). Monkeypox. Retrieved from https://www.who.int/news-room/fact-sheets/detail/monkeypox

World Health Organization (WHO). (n.d.). Health topics – Monkeypox. Retrieved from https://www.who.int/health-topics/monkeypox#tab=tab_1

Yeomans, L. (2016). Imagining the lives of others: Empathy in public relations. *Public Relations Inquiry, 5*(1), 71–92. https://doi.org/10.1177/2046147X16632033

Zavala-Arciniega, L., Meza, R., Hirschtick, J. L., & Fleischer, N. L. (2023). Disparities in cigarette, e-cigarette, cigar, and smokeless tobacco use at the intersection of multiple social identities in the US adult population. Results from the Tobacco Use Supplement to the Current Population Survey 2018–2019 Survey. *Nicotine & Tobacco Research: Official Journal of the Society for Research on Nicotine and Tobacco, 25*(5), 908–917. https://doi.org/10.1093/ntr/ntac261

PART 2

Concepts and Competencies

5

EXPLORING THE INTERSECTIONS OF STEWARDSHIP IN PUBLIC RELATIONS AND PUBLIC HEALTH

Geah Pressgrove and Richard Waters

This chapter draws intersections between the robust bodies of stewardship-focused public health and public relations literature. While stewardship has been prevalent in these sectors for several decades, the potential to draw connections between these bodies of extant literature is an untapped opportunity. In public health, stewardship has been said to add value by providing an ethically based framework for decision-making (Hong, 2014) and navigating complex communication and regulatory landscapes (de Campos, 2020). Similarly in public relations literature, stewardship is a core component of symmetrical relationship maintenance (Kelly, 2001), and has demonstrated its utility as a way to improve stakeholder attitudes and behaviors (e.g., Pressgrove, 2013). Although conceptually similar, departures in dimensionality provide novel insights that can demonstrate added value for all parties. This is particularly salient at a time of eroding public trust across all sectors around the globe (Edelman, 2019), a reality compounded by the COVID-19 pandemic and the flood of communication that resulted during early lockdowns and throughout the vaccine rollout (Prah Ruger, 2020).

From the public health perspective, the World Health Organization (2000) asserts that the responsibility of a country's health system lies with the government and that such stewardship is enacted through formulating health policy, exerting influence, and collecting and using intelligence. However, many scholars posit that the WHO failed to provide an adequate roadmap for enacting such governance (Alvarez-Rosete et al., 2013), with some scholars going so far as to adopt the term governance in place of stewardship (Balabanova et al., 2008; Smith et al., 2012). Nonetheless, the term has continued to attract interest from researchers seeking to clarify the domains of the construct (e.g., Travis et al.,

DOI: 10.4324/9781003327189-7

2002; Veillard et al., 2011), exploring its applicability in developing countries (e.g., Nafees & Nayani, 2011) and applying it to specific aspects of a health system (e.g., Brown et al., 2010).

Concurrently, public relations scholarship has demonstrated the centrality of stewardship to relationship management (Hon & Grunig, 1999; Ledingham, 2001). While initially proposed as a critical component of relationship cultivation and maintenance in the nonprofit sector (e.g., Kelly, 1998), other areas of public relations literature have also adopted the concept including corporate communication (Waters, 2011b), sports communication (Waters et al., 2011), employee communication (Waters et al., 2013), crisis communication (Byrd, 2012) and political communication (Pressgrove & Kim, 2018). Notably, this body of scholarship has advanced conceptual clarity by further explicating the meanings of the dimensions of the construct (Pressgrove et al., 2015) and validating a measurement model (Pressgrove, 2017); demonstrating how stewardship can be used to deepen relationships in both domestic (e.g., Harrison et al., 2017) and international contexts (e.g., Li et al., 2020; Olinski & Szamrowski, 2020); and connected stewardship to desirable outcomes such as trust, commitment, satisfaction, the balance of power, and loyalty (e.g., Harrison, 2018; Pressgrove & McKeever, 2016; Waters et al., 2013).

In the following sections, the authors draw on the extant literature to first review the public health exposition of the normative principles and associated responsibilities involved with stewardship. Next, the authors review public relations scholarship from varied contexts to explain how this approach underpins effective relationship management, which is imperative to achieve the WHO directives. Then the authors explain the intersections and diversions, opportunities for enhanced engagement and improved conceptual understanding for research and practice. To this end, the central role of stewardship in both fields will be highlighted, as well as the meaning and principles of authentic stewardship and the responsibilities that arise when taking such an approach to relationship management.

Stewardship in Public Health

The concept of stewardship was first advanced as a critical factor for assuring the public interest is protected in the World Health Organization's 2000 World Health Report (WHO, 2000). According to the report, the objectives of a health system are to improve population health, respond to expectations and provide protection against the cost of ill health. The WHO advanced four system functions to achieve these aims: service provision, resource generation, financing, and *stewardship*. In the report, stewardship was defined as "the careful and responsible management of the well-being of the population" which was said to be "the very essence of good government" (p. viii). While it is anticipated that the idea of stewardship would have culturally specific interpretations, stewardship was described as "ethical" (p. 123), "inclusive" (p. 137), and proactive governance (WHO, 2000). Stewardship in health-care public policy has expanded beyond these ideals established by the WHO to include responsible management, a normative dimension that dissolves inequalities of the health system, and balanced intervention that stresses social accountability and eliminates conflicts of interest (Kapoor et al., 2014). This expanded view of stewardship reinforces wider dimensions of public relations, including social responsibility, equal access to all in the health system, and proper business management.

Building on this work, an independent task force convened by WHO in 2004 identified stewardship as a key area for research necessary for overcoming barriers to achieving the United Nations Millennium Development Goals, a set of eight shared goals that each UN country aims to achieve by 2030 (Task Force on Health Systems Research, 2004). These goals are explained as fundamental values countries adopt to meet the needs of the world's poorest. These goals promote health equity, gender equality, education, and sustainability; and aim to measure progress in reducing poverty, hunger, disease, and exclusion. Many of the suggested strategies to pursue these goals were rooted in stewardship and responsibility. Given its equitable approach in health-care, stewardship-focused strategic guidance and oversight are said to be key contributors to achieving the health targets of the 2030 Sustainable Development Goals, which include factors such as mitigating inequality, mobilizing capacity to improve health systems and managing low-income countries reliance on external resources (Brinkerhoff et al., 2019).

To this end, stewardship has remained a focus of inquiry among public health scholars for over two decades (e.g., Brown et al., 2010; Nafees & Nayani, 2011, Oetzel et al., 2015). In this work, stewardship has been defined in myriad ways with most definitions involving a duty by governments to act socially responsibly in the context of health system management and regulation. For example, many of the contemporary definitions draw from the work of Kass (1990) who engages principles from agency theory focused on a willingness to act as an ethical agent to earn public trust and being a good agent for the other party. Other scholars have taken a broader view indicating that

> stewardship begins with the willingness to be accountable for some larger body than ourselves—a team, an organization, a community. It springs from a set of beliefs about reforming organizations that affirm our choice for service over the pursuit of self-interest.
>
> *(Block, 1993, p. 16)*

Drawing on these definitions, Saltman (2000) advances that stewardship consists of a collective set of values and as such is a "function of governments responsible for the welfare of populations and concerned about the trust and legitimacy with which its activities are viewed by the general public" (p. 735). And, while controversial to some public health scholars (e.g., Coggon, 2011), the Nuffield Council on Bioethics (2007) advances their stewardship model that outlines ethical principles that should be considered by health policymakers. In seeking to achieve public health goals, governments should minimize intrusion or coercion in people's private lives and choices while

> provid[ing] conditions that allow people to be healthy and, in particular, to take measures to reduce health inequalities. The stewardship-guided state recognises that a primary asset of a nation is its health: higher levels of health are associated with greater overall well-being and productivity.
>
> *(p. xvii)*

Amidst these controversies and attempts to conceptualize stewardship in public health, in the years that followed the WHO's initial advancement of the concept as a critical factor in fulfilling a government's responsibilities to the health of its people, a critique was mounted that an operational definition was not explicated (Alvarez et al., 2013). This led to some scholars replacing the term with governance or leadership (e.g., Balabanova et al., 2008; Smith et al., 2012) or using the terms stewardship and governance interchangeably (Barbazza & Tello, 2014). However, as Kapoor et al. (2014) have articulated, while the thrust of the concepts is similar, they are conceptually different with governance addressing the management of health systems, while stewardship relates to the values and principles underpinning those arrangements. As Boffin (2002) opines, stewardship is a broader concept than regulation and as such is the "function that embeds the health system in wider society" (p. 6). To this end, in WHO's 2007 report titled "Strengthening Health Systems to Improve Health Outcomes" stewardship was advanced as one of the six essential building blocks in its framework labeling it, "arguably the most complex but most critical building block of any health system" (p. 6). This report outlines several examples of stewardship in public health including effective managerial oversight to ensure strategic frameworks exist, coalition building, reporting and accountability, and regulation with reviews. These descriptions of stewardship in public health share many of the same fundamental components of public relations' views of stewardship, notably relationship building with outside parties and regularly updating stakeholders.

To further the utility of stewardship as a valuable construct in the public health domain across cultures, numerous scholars took up the charge to more clearly articulate the components of stewardship. For example, Travis et al. (2002) elaborated on the stewardship concept by recommending six subfunctions including generating intelligence, formulating policy direction, ensuring tools for implementation, building coalitions, ensuring accountability, and developing a fit between policy objectives and organizational structures. An alternate list of six stewardship subfunctions was advanced by Veillard et al. (2011) and included defining the vision for strategies and policies to improve health outcomes, exerting influence, assuring good governance, ensuring alignment of system design and goals, making use of legal and regulatory instruments to steer health performance and compiling and disseminating health information and research. In more recent scholarship, Cross et al. (2018) builds on this work and advance that the six functions of stewardship are formulating policy direction, establishing policy to guide performance, ensuring alignment between structures and goals, building sustainable relationships, assuring accountability, and generating intelligence. For a review of these and related attempts to operationalize stewardship in public health see Nasiri et al. (2019).

Stewardship in Public Relations

In both theory and practice, public relations scholars have identified stewardship as a key component in understanding how organizations develop and cultivate relationships with their stakeholders (Hon & Grunig, 1999; Ledingham, 2001), particularly in the nonprofit sector (e.g., Waters, 2009; Pressgrove & McKeever, 2016). Formalizing the conceptualization of stewardship, Kelly (1998) proposed that stewardship is the fifth step in traditional public relations models composed of research, objectives, programming, and evaluation (ROPE or ROPES when stewardship is included). In her conceptualization, this vital relationship management strategy is defined by dimensions of reciprocity, reporting, responsibility, and relationship nurturing (Kelly, 1998, 2001).

Since Kelly's initial conceptualization, nonprofit scholars have advanced our understanding of how these important variables function concerning publics including donors (e.g., Waters, 2011a) and volunteers (e.g., Harrison et al., 2017; Pressgrove & McKeever, 2016). Further, public relations scholars have employed the concept to better understand relationship management in areas as diverse as corporate communication (Waters, 2011b), sports communication (Waters et al., 2011), employee communication (Waters et al., 2013), and political communication (Pressgrove & Kim, 2018). Studies have regularly found that the dimensions of stewardship have been strong predictors of trust and satisfaction with organizations. These relational outcomes have been linked to favorable attitudes toward future involvement in organizational efforts and actual behavior in current initiatives.

Kelly (1998, 2001) conceptualized *reciprocity* as acts of appreciation and friendship between an organization and its publics. This initial conceptualization centered around the notion that stakeholders who choose to become involved with an organization should be thanked and recognized for that involvement appropriately by the organization. While much of the literature has focused on demonstrations of gratitude, some scholars have more broadly interpreted this dimension as the give-and-take an organization must consider to achieve a mutually beneficial relationship. For example, this dimension of stewardship manifests in ongoing engagement efforts such as community relations activities (Waters, 2011a), inclusion in private events or offerings (Worley & Little, 2002), or attempts to demonstrate fan appreciation (Waters et al., 2011). Pressgrove (2017) sought to clarify the meaning and practical application of reciprocity by breaking down the dimension into two separate constructs—acts of regard and appropriate levels of recognition. Though incorporated into Kelly's conceptualization, the two actions are substantively different and confounded the measurement of reciprocity in studies because of these differences. To illustrate, Pressgrove and McKeever (2016) found that nonprofit donors and volunteers perceive public recognition and acts of regard differently, with regard demonstrating much greater predictive validity for important relational measures such as trust, commitment, and satisfaction.

Kelly (1998, 2001) defined *responsibility* as the interdependence that facilitates all parts working together for the whole. To this end, she offers that keeping promises, being a good citizen, and acting in socially responsible ways were all necessary to ensure goodwill and relationship maintenance (Kelly, 2001). The literature shows how this dimension of stewardship has been used to understand and meet audience expectations (Worley & Little, 2002), as well as achieve "high standards of organizational management and decision making among its leadership team" (Waters et al., 2011, p. 166). From a communication management standpoint, the dimension manifests in efforts to convey information and stories that build confidence among stakeholders (Pressgrove et al., 2015) and not betray the audience's trust (Waters, 2009). Though not explicitly linked by scholars to stewardship, responsibility permeates multiple streams of public relations scholarship. It is at the core of corporate/organizational social responsibility and sustainability efforts (Lu et al., 2021); but it also has roots in conflict resolution and crisis management as stakeholders expect organizations to act responsibly to resolve crises quickly, whether they are preventable or accidental (Ma & Zhan, 2016). Responsibility can be used to achieve consistency and harmony in public relations efforts to cultivate and maintain relationships.

Reporting goes hand-in-hand with responsibility. In her initial conceptualization of reporting, Kelly (2001) focused on accountability and the "degree to which organizations continually reinforce public confidence in the integrity and effectiveness of their performance" (p. 285). She often taught that it wasn't enough for an organization to be responsible and keep promises made to stakeholders, but organizations also had an obligation to report back to those stakeholders what was done and the outcome of their work. Eschewing one-sided persuasive promotional efforts, scholars reinforced the importance of a two-way communication approach built on the reporting strategy (Worley & Little, 2002). This can manifest as information that demonstrates the organization is meeting ethical and legal requirements of accountability (Pressgrove, 2017), informing stakeholders of progress (Waters, 2011b), sharing accurate information (Waters et al., 2011), and keeping stakeholders informed (Patel & McKeever, 2014). Throughout the literature, the spirit of openness, disclosure, access, and transparency are central to reporting. Its widespread reach throughout concepts central to ethical communication management demonstrates its importance as a function of effective public relations. In the end, reporting can be used by leadership and management to improve perceptions of credibility and trust.

Drawing on fundraising literature (Culbertson et al., 1993), Kelly (2001) focused her conceptualization of *relationship nurturing* on involvement and the importance of keeping supportive publics at the forefront of the organization's awareness. Public relations practitioners portray the relationship nurturing dimension when they enact the boundary-spanning role and actively reach out to all of the organization's stakeholders. They interact, hear stakeholder concerns, and bring those back to internal management for discussion and consideration of revising business practices. By serving as its organizational conscience, public relations practitioners allow various stakeholders to speak to and engage with organizations and expand current involvement into long-term relationships (Pressgrove et al., 2015). In effective public relations, relationship nurturing connects the disconnected dots through boundary spanning, environmental scanning, organizational conscience, and stakeholder voice. While relationship nurturing has often been viewed in public relations models as a method to keep stakeholders involved with an organization between campaigns, it is a core tenant of effective public relations.

Intersections of Stewardship in Public Health and Public Relations

When the World Health Organization defined stewardship in its 2000 World Health Report, it echoed Kelly's (1998) concept conceptualization. While Kelly focused her initial discussion on donors in the fundraising context, the WHO focused on the global population and the responsible management of its well-being. Despite the different domains, both Kelly and the WHO were concerned with organizations acting ethically and responsibly with external audiences to their respective organizations, nonprofits and health-care providers/government agencies. Their discussions about stewardship emphasized service and organizational commitment to external audiences rather than their own self-interest. In the public health domain, government agencies and health-care providers are encouraged to focus on providing equitable access to health care and reducing the level of health inequalities for overall greater well-being in society. Similarly, organizations are encouraged to balance their financial and resource needs with those of their stakeholders so that their interdependent relationship stays mutually beneficial rather than one of one-sided manipulation.

Stewardship allows government agencies, corporations, and nonprofit organizations in the public health sector and many other domains to grow their reputation based on the considerate treatment of their stakeholders. While decisions may be difficult, organizations reveal their true nature when they balance their own needs with those of the audiences. While public relations scholarship recognizes the need for a balanced, mutually beneficial relationship, public health advocates push for more government and organization sacrifice to pursue global, inclusive health outcomes (Koh, et al., 2020). Public and private actions taken by organizations can build trust in stakeholders' minds when they see concern expressed for their audiences over profits and other organizational incentives. When an organization is more trustworthy, it faces less critique and skepticism by stakeholders because of its legitimacy and interest in its audiences.

Stewardship provides a path toward trustworthiness and legitimacy, but there are flaws in the conceptualizations of stewardship by public health and public relations scholars. From the public relations perspective, public health's interpretation of stewardship is sterile and so broadly defined that it doesn't outline actions any agency could enact to truly achieve increased well-being and health outcomes. Public health scholars acknowledge that the definition espoused by the World Health Organization was idealistic and didn't define a path toward incorporating stewardship into practice, and scholars have attempted to outline what it means to be a good steward for public health. Their stewardship functions focus on management decisions and behaviors, but they rarely consider engaging the public whose health they should be improving. Their focus, instead, considers such activities as generating intelligence about public health, policy development and its alignment with organizational structures, using legal and regulatory environments to steer health programs, and developing coalitions to assure accountability (Cross et al., 2018; Travis et al., 2002; Veillard et al., 2011). These higher-level management tasks focus on a more global direction for public health while ignoring the public they presumably work for.

Public relations scholars, on the other hand, have been almost exclusively focused on specific behaviors that can be used to cultivate relationships with their stakeholders without thinking about a bigger, universal picture as public health scholars have been. Kelly's (1998, 2001) initial conceptualization of stewardship led to the development of specific explication of behaviors an organization can use to engage with its audiences. Narrowly focusing on actions that represent regard, recognition, responsibility, reporting, and relationship nurturing pigeonholed stewardship into a relationship cultivation strategy and caused scholars to overlook its overarching connections to a wide range of organizational communication practices.

As shown in Table 5.1, public relations and public health scholars can gain insights into stewardship's applicability to their disciplines by reviewing how the other discipline conceptualized the concept. Despite the two fields' different focal points, the table shows how the domains' understanding of stewardship overlaps. The first column demonstrates how public relations scholarship has outlined the five specific dimensions of stewardship, and the second column traces the public health functions of stewardship to the corresponding behavior outlined in public relations literature. The third column of the table demonstrates the potential areas of cross-pollination where public health scholars can learn how to take the public relations dimensions and expand them to be more inclusive of the full scope of public health functions. Its current exclusive focus on the bigger picture with internal, upper-management actions focused on policy and organizational structure neglects the actual interaction with the public. Similarly, public relations scholars can learn how the specific stewardship dimensions can be extrapolated to represent bigger pictures and concepts within the industry and organizational communication. For example, regard is not simply an act of expressing gratitude for their involvement with the organization; it is also a consensus-building strategy for conflict resolution or building coalitions. The fourth column provides communication examples that demonstrate how public relations and public health scholars can use the overlapping areas of stewardship to more robustly examine stewardship in their respective domains.

While Table 5.1 is not a comprehensive list of all of the attempts to define the dimensions of stewardship in public health, it does embody the essence of attempts to define the dimensions of the construct in contemporary literature operationally. The cross-pollination column is an attempt to broaden the definitions of stewardship in public relations dimensions to allow for greater use in cross-sector and international contexts while concurrently illustrating how to incorporate the aspects of relationship cultivation into the functions of stewardship in public health.

Conclusion

For public health and public relations scholars, stewardship has been a defining concept in understanding how to reach their goals. Whether that goal is improved global well-being or a long-lasting relationship, the five dimensions of stewardship—regard, recognition, responsibility, reporting, and relationship nurturing—outline specific behaviors and tasks that practitioners in these two fields can use to reach these goals simultaneously in a bigger picture, universal level and at lower organizational-stakeholder levels.

TABLE 5.1 The intersection of stewardship in public relations and public health domains.

Stewardship in Public Relations	Stewardship in Public Health	Areas of Cross-Pollination	Communication Practices Representing Stewardship in Public Health and Public Relations
Regard: personal acts of appreciation and friendship (Pressgrove, 2017)	Participation and consensus orientation (Siddiqi et al., 2009); capacity building, resource allocation/development (Nasiri et al., 2019)	Prioritizes the voices of stakeholders in decision making in a manner that promotes friendship and attempts to build consensus	Personalized messages demonstrating gratitude; collaborative listening sessions/workshops; advisory committees; private online forums/groups for information sharing and feedback loops
Recognition: public demonstrations of gratitude (Pressgrove, 2017)	Evaluation and promotion of equitable access to necessary care (PAHO, 2002)	Elevating and promoting the voices and contributions of organizations and individuals central to mission-fulfillment	Public recognition events, highlighting the contributions of stakeholders in public documents; profiling key stakeholder contributions on social media; inviting guest blogging/interviews; creating thought leadership platforms to showcase stakeholder expertise and accomplishments.
Responsibility: Keeping promises, being a good citizen, acting in a socially responsible manner (Kelly 1998, 2001)	Generating intelligence, formulating policy direction, ensuring tools for implementation (Travis et al., 2002); compiling and disseminating health information and research, ensuring alignment of system design and goals (Veillard et al., 2011); generating intelligence (Cross et al., 2018)	Acting in a socially responsible manner that is informed by and generates intelligence and is in alignment with mutually beneficial goals.	Engage in and communicate acts of social responsibility; involve important stakeholders in reviewing systems and policies to ensure actions are ethically grounded and drive social value; foster partnerships and collaborations that generate collective intelligence and address shared goals/challenges

Reporting: Accountability, meeting legal and ethical requirements, reinforcing public confidence in integrity and effectiveness (Kelly 2001; Pressgrove, 2017)	Accountabilities and partnerships (Barbazza & Tello, 2014); transparency (Siddiqi et al., 2009); ensuring accountability, developing a fit between policy objectives and organizational structures (Travis et al., 2002; Cross et al., 2018); defining the vision for strategies and policies to improve health outcomes, exerting influence, assuring good governance, making use of legal and regulatory instruments to steer health performance (Veillard et al., 2011);	Reinforcing public confidence by defining and communicating the vision in a transparent, ethical and accountable fashion that takes into account legal and regulatory landscapes.	Proactively provide voluntary and legal disclosures (e.g., annual reports, quarterly earnings reports, CSR/ESG reports) across various accessible communication channels (e.g., social media, website, email, paid advertisements); present evidence-based and data-driven information in a clear, concise, and easily understandable manner to update diverse stakeholders on important issues.
Relationship Nurturing: keeping supportive publics at the forefront, engaging in reciprocal/ mutually beneficial acts; open dialogue	Equity & inclusiveness (Siddiqi et al., 2009); intrasectoral advocacy (Boffin); Participation and consensus (Barbazza & Tello, 2014); building coalitions (Travis et al. 2002); building sustainable relationships (Cross et al., 2018)	Creating opportunities for relationships that are equitable, inclusive and sustainable that provide reciprocal benefits and stimulate open dialogue	Engage in boundary spanning efforts to involve external audiences, create dialogue and celebrate diverse opinions; act as an organizational conscience when making decisions so that stakeholders' concerns are voiced and considered; promote dialogue that allows for respectful disagreement and mutual understanding

Regard focuses on thanking an entity for its involvement in an issue or with an organization. That involvement may be focused on coalition or consensus building and resource development at higher management levels or on demonstrating gratitude to an individual for their choice to become involved with any organization, including public health agencies. Stewardship advocates that gratitude must be followed up with appropriate public or private recognition for everyone, reflecting dimensions of equity and inclusion. Whether focused on public health outcomes or providing a product or service for profit or the public good, an organization cannot achieve its end goal alone. It must recognize the external audiences that were involved in reaching whatever the desired outcome may be.

Spanning managerial and stakeholder-focused decision-making and behaviors, responsibility leads organizations to reflect on how to design best structures and systems that allow for implementing policies that lead to socially conscious planning and sustainable actions so that all stakeholders benefit. Organizations in public health and other sectors must be held accountable to their promises and ultimately communicate those promises to their stakeholders. At the upper-management level, leaders must focus on demonstrating how policies will lead to their desired outcomes and how the systems in place can achieve this. Individuals interacting with organizations and agencies should also receive updates through social media, reports posted to the organizational website, or interpersonally through phone calls or text messages from the organizational staff they work with. Regular updates demonstrate an organization's commitment to transparency and force them to be accountable for working toward long-term goals.

Relationship nurturing, the final stewardship dimension outlined by public relations scholars, requires agencies to keep their stakeholders at the forefront of the organization's mind. Public health advocates stress that these stakeholders include everyone; no one should be kept from accessing health care by implementing health policy or organizational budgeting. When an organization sincerely thinks about its decisions impacting stakeholders and reacts accordingly rather than acting blindly out of the organization's best interest, it is working more equitably to ensure careful consideration of all stakeholders.

While the authors of this chapter see clear overlap in how the conceptualizations of stewardship by public health and public relations scholars have been studied, there has been little work measuring the intersection. Hopefully, this chapter will stimulate interest in the overlap and help generate a research agenda that connects the two disciplines. Communication is at the core of public relations and is of utmost importance in public health, where significant work has gone into studying health communication at varying levels (e.g., patient care, social marketing). Stewardship is the concept that bridges public health's focus on higher-level management functions, such as structural and policy design and implementation of equitable health-care access, with communicative practices that can be used at the patient level to build trust in public health agencies.

Discussion Questions

The following questions were designed to help facilitate discussion about stewardship in the two domains as well as stimulate an active research agenda for public relations-influenced understanding of public health:

1. What specific actions (behaviors and communication) that are regularly used in the practice of health care at the individual patient level can be represented by the five dimensions of stewardship as outlined by public relations scholars?
2. What connections can be drawn between public health scholars' functions of stewardship and areas of communication that public relations practitioners regularly work with?
3. How would you propose unifying public relations and public health's understanding of stewardship in a shared concept measurement?
4. In a stewardship framework, how do public health and public relations practitioners balance organizational considerations with stakeholder needs or wants, including access to affordable health care? Is it possible to act ethically given the limitations of financial resources and capabilities?

Further Reading

Boffin, N. (2002). Stewardship of health systems: A review of the literature. Antwerp: Institute of Tropical Medicine.

Kelly, K. S. (2001). Stewardship: The fifth step in the public relations process. In R. L. Heath (Ed.), *Handbook of public relations* (pp. 279–289). Thousand Oaks, CA: SAGE.

Nasiri, T., Takian, A., & Yazdani, S. (2019). Stewardship in health, designing a multi-layer meta model: A review article. *Iranian Journal of Public Health, 48*(4), 579–592.

Saltman, R. B., & Ferroussier-Davis, O. (2000). The concept of stewardship in health policy. *Bulletin of the World Health Organization, 78*(6), 732–739.

Springston, J. K., & Lariscy, R. A. W. (2005). Public relations effectiveness in public health institutions. *Journal of Health and Human Services Administration, 28*(2), 218–245. https://www.jstor.org/stable/41288065

References

Alvarez-Rosete, A., Hawkins, B., & Parkhurst, J. (2013). Health system stewardship and evidence informed health policy. Retrieved from: https://researchonline.lshtm.ac.uk/id/eprint/3201917/1/health_system_stewardship_and_evidence_informed_health_policy.pdf

Balabanova, D., Oliveira-Cruz, V., & Hanson, K. (2008). *Health sector governance and implications for the private sector.* Rockefeller Foundation.

Barbazza, E., & Tello, J. E. (2014). A review of health governance: Definitions, dimensions and tools to govern. *Health Policy, 116*(1), 1–11. https://doi.org/10.1016/j.healthpol.2014.01.007

Block, P. (1993). *Stewardship: Choosing service over self-interest.* Berrett-Koehler Publishers.

Boffin, N. (2002). Stewardship of health systems: A review of the literature. Antwerp: Institute of Tropical Medicine.

Brinkerhoff, D. W., Cross, H. E., Sharma, S., & Williamson, T. (2019). Stewardship and health systems strengthening: An overview. *Public Administration and Development*, *39*(1), 4–10. https://doi.org/10.1002/pad.1846

Brown, L. D., Isett, K. R., & Hogan, M. (2010). Stewardship in mental health policy: Inspiration, influence, institution? *Journal of Health Politics, Policy and Law*, *35*(3), 389–405. https://doi.org/10.1215/03616878-2010-004

Byrd, S. (2012). Hi fans! Tell us your story! Incorporating a stewardship-based social media strategy to maintain brand reputation during a crisis. *Corporate Communications: An International Journal*, *17*(3), 241–254. DOI: 10.1108/13563281211253502.

Coggon, J. (2011). What help is steward? Stewardship, political theory and public health law and ethics. *Northern Ireland Legal Quarterly*, *62*(5), 599–616.

Cross, H. E., De La Cruz, M., & Dent, J. (2018). Government stewardship and primary health care in Guatemala since 1996. *Public Administration and Development*, *39*(1), 11–22. https://doi.org/10.1002/pad.1827

de Campos, T. C. (2020). Guiding principles of global health governance in times of pandemics: Solidarity, subsidiarity, and stewardship in COVID-19. *The American Journal of Bioethics*, *20*(7), 212–214. https://doi.org/10.1080/15265161.2020.1779862

Culbertson, H. M., Jeffers, D. W., Stone, D. B., & Terrell, M. (1993). *Social, political, and economic contexts in public relations: Theory and cases*. Hillsdale, NJ: Lawrence Erlbaum.

Davis, J. H., Schoorman, F. D., & Donaldson, L. (1997). Toward a stewardship theory of management. *Academy of Management Review*, *22*(1), 20–47. https://doi.org/10.5465/amr.1997.9707180258

Edelman. (2019). 2019 Edelman Trust Barometer. Edelman. Retrieved from: https://www.edelman.com/sites/g/files/aatuss191/files/2019-02/2019_Edelman_Trust_Barometer_Global_Report.pdf.

Harrison, V. S., Xiao, A., Ott, H. K., & Bortree, D. (2017). Calling all volunteers: The role of stewardship and involvement in volunteer–organization relationships. *Public Relations Review*, *43*(4), 872–881. https://doi.org/10.1016/j.pubrev.2017.06.006

Harrison, V. S. (2018). Understanding the donor experience: Applying stewardship theory to higher education donors. *Public Relations Review*, *44*(4), 533–548. https://doi.org/10.1016/j.pubrev.2018.07.001

Hon, L. C., & Grunig, J. E. (1999). Guidelines for measuring relationships in public relations. Gainesville, FL: Institute for Public Relations.

Hong, R. (2014). Quarantine and global public health law: Canadian stewardship and responsibility. *Health Law Review*, *22*, 15–25.

Hunter, D. J. (1999). *Managing for health: Implementing the new health agenda*. Institute for Public Policy Research.

Hunte, D. J., Shishkin, S., & Taroni, F. (2005). Steering the purchaser: Stewardship and government. In J. Figueras, R. Robinson, & E. Jakubowski (Eds.), *Purchasing to improve health systems performance* (pp. 164–186). Maidenhead: Open University Press.

Kapoor, N., Kumar, D., & Thakur, N. (2014). Core attributes of stewardship: Foundation of sound health system. *International Journal of Health Policy and Management*, *3*(1), 5–6. DOI: 10.15171/ijhpm.2014.52

Kass H, D. (1990). Stewardship as a fundamental element in images of public administration. *Dialogue*, *10*(2), 2–48. https://www.jstor.org/stable/25610524

Kelly, K. S. (1998). *Effective fund-raising management*. Mahwah, NJ: Lawrence Erlbaum.

Kelly, K. S. (2001). Stewardship: The fifth step in the public relations process. In R. L. Heath (Ed.), *Handbook of public relations* (pp. 279–289). Thousand Oaks, CA: SAGE.

Koh, H. K., Bantham, A., Geller, A. C., Rukavina, M. A., Emmons, K. M., Yatsko, P., & Restuccia, R. (2020). Anchor institutions: Best practices to address social needs and social determinants of health. *American Journal of Public Health, 110*(3), 309–316. https://doi.org/10.2105/AJPH.2019.305472

Ledingham, J. A. (2001). Government–community relationships: Extending the relational theory of public relations. *Public Relations Review, 27*, 285–295. https://doi.org/10.1016/S0363-8111(01)00087-X

Li, P., Men, L. R., & Yue, C. A. (2020). An exploratory study of stewardship for Chinese nonprofit organizations. *International Journal of Nonprofit & Voluntary Sector Marketing, 25*(2), 1–12. https://doi.org/10.1002/nvsm.1655

Lu, J., Liang, M., Zhang, C., Rong, D., Guan, H., Mazeikaite, K., & Streimikis, J. (2021). Assessment of corporate social responsibility by addressing sustainable development goals. *Corporate Social Responsibility and Environmental Management, 28*(2), 686–703. https://doi.org/10.1002/csr.2081

Ma, L., & Zhan, M. (2016). Effects of attributed responsibility and response strategies on organizational reputation: A meta-analysis of situational crisis communication theory research. *Journal of Public Relations Research, 28*(2), 102–119. https://doi.org/10.1080/1062726X.2016.1166367

Nafees, A. A., & Nayani, P. (2011). Stewardship in Health Policy and its relevance to Pakistan. *Journal of the Pakistan Medical Association, 61*(8), 795–800. https://ecommons.aku.edu/pakistan_fhs_mc_chs_chs/10

Nasiri, T., Takian, A., & Yazdani, S. (2019). Stewardship in health, designing a multilayer meta model: A review article. *Iranian Journal of Public Health, 48*(4), 579–592.

Nuffield Council on Bioethics (2007). Public health: Ethical issues. Nuffield Council on Bioethics: London.

Oetzel, J. G., Villegas, M., Zenone, H., White Hat, E. R., Wallerstein, N., & Duran, B. (2015). Enhancing stewardship of community-engaged research through governance. *American Journal of Public Health, 105*(6), 1161–1167.

Olinski, M., & Szamrowski, P. (2020). Stewardship concept utilization on the websites of Polish public benefit organizations. *Romanian Journal of Communication and Public Relations, 22*(2), 91–106.

Pan American Health Organization (2002). Health in the Americas. Retrieved from: https://iris.paho.org/bitstream/handle/10665.2/2746/9275115877_Vol_II_EN.pdf?sequence=5&isAllowed=y

Prah Ruger, J. (2020). Positive public health ethics: Towards flourishing and resilient communities and individuals. *The American Journal of Bioethics, 20*(7): 44–54. https://doi.org/10.1080/15265161.2020.1764145

Patel, S. J., & McKeever, B.W. (2014). Health nonprofits online: The use of frames and stewardship strategies to increase stakeholder involvement. *International Journal of Nonprofit and Voluntary Sector Marketing, 19*(4), 224–238.

Pressgrove, G. (2013). *Making stewardship meaningful for nonprofits: Stakeholder motivations, attitudes, loyalty and behaviors* (doctoral dissertation, University of South Carolina).

Pressgrove, G. (2017). Development of a scale to measure perceptions of stewardship strategies for nonprofit organizations. *Journalism & Mass Communication Quarterly, 94*(1), 102–123. DOI:10.1177/1077699016640221

Pressgrove, G., & Kim, C. (2018). Stewardship, credibility and political communications: A content analysis of the 2016 election. *Public Relations Review, 44*(2), 247–255. https://doi.org/10.1016/j.pubrev.2018.01.003

Pressgrove, G. N., & McKeever, B. W. (2016). Nonprofit relationship management: Extending the organization–public relationship to loyalty and behaviors.

Journal of Public Relations Research, *28*(3–4), 193–211. https://doi.org/10.1080/10 62726X.2016.1233106

Pressgrove, G., McKeever, B. W., & Collins, E. L. (2015). Investigating stewardship strategies on nonprofit websites. *Public Relations Journal*, *9*(3), 1–18. Available online: http://www.prsa.org/Intelligence/PRJournal/Vol9/No3/

Siddiqi, S., Masud, T. I., Nishtar, S., Peters, D. H., Sabri, B., Bile, K. M., & Jama, M. A. (2009). Framework for assessing governance of the health system in developing countries: Gateway to good governance. *Health Policy*, *90*(1), 13–5.

Saltman, R. B., & Ferroussier-Davis, O. (2000). The concept of stewardship in health policy. *Bulletin of the World Health Organization*, *78*(6), 732–739.

Smith, P. C., Anell, A., Busse, R., Crivelli, L., Healy, J., Lindahl, A. K., Westert, G. & Kene, T. (2012). Leadership and governance in seven developed health systems. *Health Policy*, *106*(1), 37–49. https://doi.org/10.1016/j.healthpol.2011.12.009

Task Force on Health Systems Research. (2004). Informed choices for attaining the Millennium Development Goals: Towards an international cooperative agenda for health-systems research. *The Lancet*, *364*(9438), 997–1003. https://doi.org/10.1016/ S0140-6736(04)17026-8

Travis, P., Egger, D., Davies, P., & Mechbal, A. (2002). Towards better stewardship: Concepts and critical issues. In C. Murray & D. Evans (Eds.), *Health systems performance assessment: Debates, methods, and empiricism* (pp. 289–300). Geneva: World Health Organization.

Veillard, J. H. M., Brown, A. D., Barış, E., Permanand, G., & Klazinga, N. S. (2011). Health system stewardship of National Health Ministries in the WHO European region: Concepts, functions and assessment framework. *Health Policy*, *103*(2–3), 191–199. https://doi.org/10.1016/j.healthpol.2011.09.002

Waters, R. D. (2009). Measuring stewardship in public relations: A test exploring impact on the fundraising relationship. *Public Relations Review*, *35*(2), 113–119.

Waters, R. D. (2011a). Increasing fundraising efficiency through evaluation: Applying communication theory to the nonprofit organization-donor relationship. *Nonprofit and Voluntary Sector Quarterly*, *40*, 458–475. https://doi.org/10.1177/0899764009354

Waters, R. D. (2011b). Redefining stewardship: Examining how Fortune 100 organizations use stewardship with virtual stakeholders. *Public Relations Review*, *37*, 129–136. https://doi.org/10.1016/j.pubrev.2011.02.002

Waters, R. D., Bortree, D. S., & Tindall, N. T. (2013). Can public relations improve the workplace? Measuring the impact of stewardship on the employer–employee relationship. *Employee Relations*, *35*(6), 613–629. https://doi.org/10.1108/ER-12-2012-0095

Waters, R. D., Burke, K., Jackson, Z. H., & Buning, J. D. (2011). Using stewardship to cultivate fandom online: Comparing how National Football League Teams use their websites and Facebook to engage their fans. *International Journal of Sports Communication*, *4*, 163–177. https://doi.org/10.1123/ijsc.4.2.163

World Health Organization (2000). The world health report 2000. Health systems: Improving performance. Retrieved from: https://apps.who.int/gb/archive/pdf_files/ WHA53/ea4.pdf

World Health Organization. (2007). Everybody's business—strengthening health systems to improve health outcomes: WHO's framework for action. World Health Organization. https://apps.who.int/iris/handle/10665/43918

Worley, D. A., & Little, J. K. (2002). The critical role of stewardship in fund raising: The coaches vs. cancer campaign. *Public Relations Review*, *28*, 99–112. https://doi. org/10.1016/S0363-8111(02)00113-3

6

ADVOCACY, ACTIVISM, AND GUN VIOLENCE COMMUNICATION

Minhee Choi

The words advocacy and activism seem to be everywhere these days. The news media, corporations, the government, and nonprofit organizations all talk about the impact of advocacy and activism. Moreover, these organizations seek to participate in many forms of advocacy and activism. With the rise of civic engagement on various socio-political issues, individuals and various organizations are vocal about issues such as racism, public health emergencies, abortion rights, climate changes, animal rights, and gun violence. Furthermore, when news media talk about social movements initiated by the public, they often use words such as advocacy, activism, or activists.

Think of the Black Lives Matter (BLM) movement. How would you describe and define this movement? Is it advocacy or activism? If you can define the BLM movement as either of the two, what made you describe the BLM movement as advocacy or activism or both? Then, how is advocacy different from activism? What are some similarities and differences between advocacy and activism? How can you differentiate these two concepts?

Although advocacy and activism are two different concepts, these two terms have been interchangeably used by the general public and even by media, communication practitioners, and scholars. Conceptualizing advocacy and activism is problematic as we have little idea of what they really mean or how they can be differentiated conceptually and practically. As people and organizations act upon various socio-political issues for social change, conceptualizing and defining these two concepts and actions are important initial steps for practitioners to communicate the issues with constituents effectively. This chapter examines the concepts of advocacy and activism to find similarities and differences between the two concepts, including strategies involving advocacy and activism

DOI: 10.4324/9781003327189-8

communication. The chapter begins by defining advocacy and activism with examples and then moves to discussing strategies involved in advocacy and activism communication. Finally, the chapter looks at gun violence communication to
exemplify advocacy communication.

Advocacy and Activism

With the rise of the civic movement in recent years, advocacy and activism
have been important terms in public communication. Naturally, public relations
should be linked to advocacy and activism because related activities get constituencies involved, mobilized, and influenced through communication. In doing
so, practitioners plan and implement strategic communication to draw planned
and expected outcomes. In public relations, advocacy and activism have been
discussed by focusing on communication campaigns and strategies from advocacy or activist organizations. However, within the past two decades, the terms
have been increasingly examined in corporate communication with concepts like
corporate social advocacy and corporate social activism, i.e., when companies
take a public stance on social-political issues (Dodd & Supa, 2014). Advocacy
and activism have been key themes in public communication and public relations
research. Thus, this section will conceptualize advocacy and activism by focusing on distinctions based on the academic literature first, and then discuss some
conceptual similarities between the two concepts.

Literature has defined advocacy and activism in various ways. *Cambridge
Dictionary* defines advocacy as "public support for an idea, plan, or way of
doing something" (*Cambridge Dictionary*, n.d.). More specifically, some academic literature defines advocacy as "activities aimed at influencing the social
and civic agenda and at gaining access to the arena where decisions that affect the social and civic life are made" (Schmid et al., 2008, p. 582). Another
definition is "any attempt to influence the decisions of an institutional elite
on behalf of a collective interest" (Jenkins, 1987, p. 297). These definitions
indicate any activities influencing a political decision-making process that represents a group of people or organization. Hence, advocacy has often been used
with words specifying certain groups, such as patient advocacy (Negarandeh
et al., 2006), employee advocacy (Thelen, 2020), or client advocacy (Sachs &
Linn, 1998). Thus, advocacy work includes ensuring that institutions or policies become increasingly responsive to individual or group needs by increasing
the power of people and groups (Wallack et al., 1993). In doing so, advocacy
involves "the set of skills used to create a shift in public opinion and mobilize
the necessary resources and forces to support an issue, policy, or constituency"
(Wallack et al., 1993, p. 27).

Whereas advocates work within the system to promote change, activists generally push to dismantle what is wrong with the system itself. Thus, activism

is defined as the "process by which groups of people exert pressure on organizations or other institutions to change policies, practices or conditions the activists find problematic" (Smith, 2005, p. 5). Another definition highlights the distinctive nature of activism, which goes beyond conventional political activities to employ "the use of direct and often vigorous action in order to challenge oppressive power relations or ideologies" (Ophélie, 2016, pp. 757–758). Some researchers suggest that activists should be willing to do any tasks to bring about change and argue that they could use any strategies to gain what they aim for (Alinsky, 1971).

The definitions of advocacy and activism from existing academic literature emphasize a series of actions to influence the decision-making process for change. In doing so, communication practitioners design and employ communication strategies to build public support and influence decision-makers. Advocacy and activism involve strategic processes to influence the public agenda. However, these definitions also show distinctive differences in terms of the two aspects. The first difference is the extent of advocating actions. Advocacy focuses more on persuading and mobilizing others to support ideas and causes, whereas activism is based more on direct actions and challenging current conditions or ideas. Activities involved in activism sometimes include more risky or even illegal actions. Hample and Dallinger (1998) noted that activists could be antisocial or even violent. The second difference is the goal of action. The motivation behind activism is more based on ultimate values and social norm changes rather than policy and system changes. Tarrow (2011) noted that "activists demand fundamental social change, the recognition of new identities, entry into the polity, the destruction of their enemies, or the overthrow of a social order – but seldom just reform" (p. 215). Therefore, movements involving activism require larger-scale changes, whereas advocacy focuses on shifting or improving current conditions or policies within the social system.

We can see multiple examples of advocacy and activism in news media. For example, we often see protests from environmental activists or animal rights activists on the news. Activist groups organize protests or demonstrations to draw attention from the media, public, and people with decision-making power in unconventional ways (DiGrazia, 2013). Moreover, the news spotlights these collective activities, as they align with news values including conflict, impact, and oddity. The groups sometimes take illegal or provocative actions, such as animal rights activists going naked on the street holding a picket about "going naked rather than wearing fur" (Yaeger, 2016). As another example, activists from the environmental protection group, Greenpeace, barricaded energy group BP's London headquarters' entrances with huge containers to condemn the company's business model focusing on the exploration of fossil fuel. Greenpeace asked for the company to align with the Paris climate agreement and develop a more sustainable, environmentally friendly business model (Murphy-Bates, 2019).

Of course, activist groups also advocate issues with attempts to change policies and improve the societal system, as we defined when we discussed advocacy. Depending on their strategic decision and campaign goals, activist groups participate in both advocacy and activism. On the other hand, advocacy groups generally do not get involved in outrageous actions or protests as they focus more on reforming and improving the system. Advocacy groups tend to work within the social system, whereas activist groups constantly work to make ultimate changes to the societal system, social values, norms, and ideas. As an example, many animal rights activists not only aim to improve conditions for animals used for human interests but also argue for equal treatment of animals with humans by challenging the idea of speciesism (Hopster, 2019), indicating human superiority results in the exploitation of animals. Ultimately, animal rights activists are against the idea of speciesism, and they argue that every creature should be respected and treated equally. This example shows that activism not only improves and reforms conditions and systems but also seeks ultimate and fundamental changes in individual and societal norms and values. Thus, we can say "advocacy" when members of animal rights groups promote campaigns to pass a bill that improves the living conditions of beagles used for experiments (Masters, 2022). We can label it "activism" when the groups argue that animals should not be used for any type of food, fashion, entertainment, or experiment, which requires long-term and large-scale changes, not only by enacting new laws, but also by transforming social values.

Now, let us return to the earlier questions regarding the BLM movement. One possible answer is that, as the movement calls for fundamental changes in social values and norms, including societal systems and policies, activism seems to be a more suitable term to define BLM. Of course, BLM has advocacy components by asking for policy reform (Taylor, 2021) . However, as racism has long been a critical but never-solved issue, the movement focuses more on altering societal norms, which requires large-scale and long-term changes beyond what is required by law.

Communication Strategies Related to Advocacy and Activism

Advocacy Communication

Communication practitioners in various fields, including political communication, health communication, and some forms of media, define and deliver an issue for the organizations they work for to shape and influence audiences' perspectives with messages that will resonate with those audiences (Hallahan, 1999). When individuals or organizations communicate in an attempt to influence or change policies, we can consider it advocacy communication. In this section, we will discuss communication strategies involving advocacy communication.

Seeking news media coverage is one basic public relations practice to reach the larger public. As strategies to shape effective messages, practitioners (1) attempt to influence the media agenda and (2) frame the issue by including, excluding, and emphasizing certain aspects of the issue. One key communication concept describing influencing the media agenda for the purpose of policy change is *media advocacy*. Media advocacy refers to "the strategic use of news media by those seeking to advance a social or public policy initiative" (Holder & Treno, 1997, p. 190). In general, media advocacy indicates how an issue is described in the media and how this media coverage may influence public opinion (Winett & Wallack, 1996). Media advocacy has been described as "influencing public debate and putting pressure on policymakers by increasing volume of the public health voice and, in turn, by increasing the visibility of values, people, and public health issues befind the voice" (Wallack et al., 1993, p. 2). One strategy of media advocacy efforts is to reframe a problem as a public health issue by addressing policy and/or economic solutions rather than individual behavior change.

Media advocacy consists of three steps: (1) agenda-setting, (2) framing, and (3) suggesting a solution or policy (Berkeley Media Studies Group, 1997; Gibson, 2010). The media increase attention to certain issues and help set the agenda. To set the agenda, practitioners promote the salience of an issue by increasing the amount of media coverage and frame the issue by emphasizing certain aspects (Wallack, 1990). Practitioners seek to emphasize issues as public health concerns by focusing on causes and solutions of an issue. When the media discuss problems and solutions, they may influence the public's perception of the issue.

To influence the media agenda effectively, communication practitioners shape messages by emphasizing a certain aspect of an issue. This process necessarily involves framing. *Framing* refers to the assumption that how an issue is described can influence the process of how audiences comprehend such issues (Entman, 1993). As one of the renowned mass communication theories, framing helps explain some successful message strategies in public relations campaigns.

Framing describes how journalists and other communicators present information in a manner that resonates with existing information regarding issues to form readers' or audiences' impressions. Communication scholars have studied framing for decades because framing is a useful theory for examining strategic messages and audience response to messages (Hallahan, 1999). This approach focuses on how the construction of messages and meanings may influence key audiences.

As a type of framing, *issue framing* is another key concept that helps explain various advocacy and activism communication. Issue framing indicates how certain issues are perceived by the public and political elites (Gamson, 1992). This concept has been largely discussed in political communication. Given the complex nature of political issues, alternative interpretations of such issues are provided by various actors, such as political candidates, elected officials, administrative agency officials, and advocacy groups. Political elites pursue is-sue-framing strategies to draw a favorable public opinion on policy positions or to win elections (Jacoby, 2000).

Issue framing is a key strategy to influence public opinion (Nelson & Oxley, 1999). When journalists and communication practitioners frame an issue, they present problems, causal attributions, evaluations, and policy directions, in an attempt to influence the public's attitude (de Vreese, 2010; Entman, 1993). How journalists and communication practitioners define a problem and describe the solutions may influence the public, which may lead to persuasion effects (Mat-thes & Schemer, 2012; Merry, 2018). Advocacy and activist groups use issue framing to highlight certain issue attributes, with the intention of influencing policy formation and public opinion on issues (Entman, 1993).

In terms of issue framing, one way to influence the public's perception is whether the story is framed as an individual or societal issue. Iyengar (1991) noted that stories are shared through either *episodic* or *thematic frames*. Episodic frame refers to stories of single events or individuals, whereas thematic frame indicates presenting an issue at the societal level with more data and population-level statistics. The episodic frame is more likely to focus on individual-level attribution and solutions related to the issue. More societal-level causes and solu-tions are examined in thematic frames. Coleman et al. (2011) examined whether a thematic frame for health news, such as obesity, diabetes, immigrant health, and smoking problems, influences individuals' attitudes about public policy re-lated to such issues. They conducted an experiment by manipulating and chang-ing each story from an individual level (episodic) to societal level (thematic) problem, in terms of defining the cause and solution of each issue. The study found that a thematic frame influenced individuals' positive attitudes toward public policy changes related to the health issues more so than an episodic frame. Defining an issue, describing the causes, and suggesting solutions are essential parts of advocacy communication. Thus, communication practitioners cannot ef-fectively deliver the advocacy messages without a fuller understanding of the effects of issue framing.

In addition to influencing policy preferences, issue framing also influences individuals' willingness to participate in civic activities related to the issue (Dardis, 2007). When issue framing is related to individuals' core values and actual behaviors, it may increase public attention and engagement with the is-sue (McGinty et al., 2016). In shaping messages, communication practitioners attempt to design messages easily accessible by individuals to become familiar with an issue.

In particular, when an issue needs engagement from the public, *mobilizing in-formation*, also known as calls to action, provides the public with specific actions to take to help create solutions (McKeever, 2013). Moreover, suggesting solu-tions for issues, including specific tactics to get the public involved in the issues, is important as it enables individuals to act. Mobilizing information includes names and contact information of people or groups, the time and venue of activities, and specific actions to facilitate involvement, such as signing a petition or sharing information (Choi & McKeever, 2022; Lemert, 1984).

Many successful examples of media advocacy and issue framing can be found in public health campaigns. As public health campaigns often attempt to affect individuals' health behaviors in mass populations, media have been used as a tool to reach large audiences. Many mass media campaigns, such as efforts surrounding smoking, alcohol use, and road safety, aim to influence individuals' decision-making processes and help individuals to adopt healthy social norms (Wakefield et al., 2010). Public health campaigns also aim to create conditions in which people can be healthy through public policy changes to help individuals change their behaviors. One of the most successful examples of adopting the public health approach can be seen in the reduction of motor vehicle deaths. The factors that cause injuries and death such as tired and drunk drivers, unyielding signs, lights, windshield glass, and non-use of seat belts were identified as risk factors. Campaigns focused on multifaceted solutions such as driver education, safer roads, safety glass, seat belts, air bags, and enforcement of traffic laws, which were consequently implemented (Hemenway & Miller, 2013).

Activist Communication

As noted earlier, communication from activists includes forms of advocacy as they exert influence on public opinion and policy. However, unlike advocacy, communication involving activism often adopts direct and radical actions, such as blockades, extreme forms of protests, or hacktivism (online forms of civil disobedience, such as hacking). One concept reflecting such activist communication is the catalytic model of issue management. Issue management is "the process by which various advocates identify, prioritize, define, analyze, promote, and seek to influence the resolution of questions of public policy" (Smith & Ferguson, 2013, p. 378). In a series of strategic issue management processes, including identifying, creating, and amplifying an issue, the catalytic model focuses on getting more people aware of and supporting an issue (Coombs & Holladay, 2010; Crable & Vibbert, 1985). The catalytic model helps explain some activists' campaign strategies discussed earlier (e.g., Greenpeace protests, going naked campaign from PETA). Activist communication should establish legitimacy, awareness, and influence for effective issue management (Coombs & Holladay, 2010). First, the issue should be considered legitimate for the public to accept it as a concern as well as the group as a representative of the issue. Second, the issue should be known to a larger number of people. Finally, activists focus on getting support from the aware public to shift their support to influence. When activists get people aware of the issue and group promoting the issue, they often use unconventional tactics to influence issue salience. To amplify issue salience, activists seek news media coverage through direct and radical tactics. Presently, activist communication on social media focuses on promoting and mobilizing issues and groups to build legitimacy and gain public attention and support. Derville (2005) found that activists' provocative tactics redefine and strengthen members' identities, give members a sense of meaning, discourage opponents, trigger reactions that generate support, and redefine organizations' political spectrums. However, activists' direct actions sometimes result in negative effects, which may lead some to equate activism with vandalism, terrorism, or extremism (Feinberg et al., 2020).

Gun Violence Communication as Advocacy Communication

One example of media advocacy and issue framing in action can be seen by examining gun violence communication. Gun violence has been a serious threat to the United States in the past several decades. A bipartisan gun control bill was passed in 2022 under a national sense of urgency to limit gun violence after the tragic mass shooting at Robb Elementary School in Uvalde, Texas. However, gun violence rates have been increasing in the US during the last few decades (Gramlich, 2022).

Gun violence issues pose unique challenges compared with many other political concerns, as politicians are likely to lead public opinion rather than follow and respond to public opinion on the issue (Lindaman & Haider-Markel, 2000). Moreover, gun violence issues exhibit considerable effects on elections, which have been magnified most recently by a series of mass shootings. Thus, issue framing of gun violence matters remarkably for politicians, advocacy groups, and the general public in the U.S.

Over the past several years, considerable efforts have been exerted by physicians, public health scholars, gun safety advocacy groups, and members of the media. They aim to raise awareness of the public health implications of gun violence following the previous success of public health approaches to address tobacco use, motor vehicle safety, drunk driving, and unintentional poisoning (Mozaffarian et al., 2013).

Although many Americans have viewed gun control as challenges to constitutional protections of gun rights and ownership, the public health approach to gun violence is based on a pragmatic approach rather than a political or dogmatic approach. A public health approach encourages policymakers to create a safe environment where individuals can learn to use guns safely (Mozaffarian et al., 2013).

Nearly 30 years ago, in 1995, the American College of Physicians raised concerns about the prevalence of gun violence in the US and called for new approaches to address gun violence as a public health problem. Despite the consistent objections by gun rights advocates in Congress to fund research on gun violence during the last two decades, gun safety advocates have increasingly called for Centers for Disease Control and Prevention (CDC) research on gun violence (DeFoster & Swalve, 2018). Medical and public health journals aim to address the most-important public health problems threatening people in society. An editorial in *The Journal of the American Medical Association* defined gun violence as a serious public health problem that harms people (Mozaffarian et al., 2013) and other journals have also published articles on gun violence. For example, Bauchner et al. (2017) noted that accurate and timely research on gun violence educates people about the risk factors and interventions that prevent injuries and deaths from guns.

The advocates also reached out to members of the media. As a result of media advocacy efforts, multiple articles emphasizing the public health approach to reducing gun violence have been published in *The Washington Post* in 2014, *Fortune* in 2017, and *The New York Times* in 2017 (Franklin, 2014; Leaf, 2017; 2018, Kristof, 2017).

The CDC lists the four main steps of a public health approach: (1) defining and monitoring the problem, (2) identifying risks and protective factors, (3) developing and testing prevention strategies, and (4) assuring widespread adoption of effective programs ("Public Health Approach," 2022, para. 5). The CDC's public health approach in the gun violence context can be defined in terms of five elements (Hemenway & Miller, 2013; Mozaffarian et al., 2013). First, this approach seeks to change the environment where the problem exists rather than only targeting changes in individuals' behaviors. Second, this approach seeks to develop methods to prevent problems by examining environmental factors. Third, this approach involves multiple strategic and tactical interventions, including taxation, funding, research, public awareness campaigns, sociocultural modifications, and comprehensive policies. Fourth, the public health approach is population-based, by providing the maximum benefit for the largest number of people ("Public Health Approach," 2022, para. 1). Finally, the public health approach seeks to develop a system wherein mistakes are easily corrected and do not lead to serious injury or death.

Based on Iyengar's (1991) discussions on issue framing, the public health framing of gun violence is in line with thematic framing. In terms of defining causes and solutions of gun violence, however, episodic frames often present mentally ill individual shooters as the main cause and suggest improved mental health-care systems as a reactive solution (McGinty et al., 2016). Thematic frames attribute responsibility to easy access to guns and gun control policy loopholes, and suggest stricter gun regulations as a proactive solution.

The way in which public health problems have been framed in news media can influence individuals' perceptions of the responsibility for the issues and solutions. Moreover, this perception can substantially affect public policy. In terms of defining causes and solutions of gun violence, news stories discussed mentally ill shooters as a significant cause of gun violence, and gun access restrictions for mentally ill individuals are frequently mentioned solutions (McGinty et al., 2016). A more recent study also found that media coverage has attributed responsibility to the mental health-care system and mentally ill individuals rather than to lenient gun control regulations (DeFoster & Swalve, 2018). The study also found a small increase in the number of articles that presented a public health frame during the study period. This result indicates the disconnected perspectives among physicians, public health advocates, gun safety advocacy organizations, and journalists in relation to defining the causes of gun violence. Regarding media framing of gun violence in terms of defining problems and suggesting solutions, a survey study found that the public health approach to gun violence is not pervasive yet among the general public (McKeever et al., 2022).

In the U.S., after years of media advocacy and advocacy communication efforts dealing with gun violence, politicians, states, and local governments have been increasingly adopting the public health approach to gun violence. President Joe Biden called for a public health approach to curb gun violence in his speech after a series of mass shooting incidents (Brown & Sakran, 2021). California and New York have declared that gun violence is a public health crisis and announced multi-faceted approaches to reduce gun violence. Various local counties collaborate with community opinion leaders, law enforcement, and gun safety advocates to promote the public health approach to lessen gun violence. As an example, King County in Seattle, WA, announced an investment increase in public health strategies to reduce gun violence. The county has focused on various multi-faceted strategies, such as research to secure hard data, hot spot remediation, and hospital-based intervention, connecting with high-risk youth for prevention, providing intensive support through community events and care teams for restoration in a timely and effective manner (Argerious, 2022).

The goal of advocacy communication on reducing gun violence is to influence gun safety policies by increasing the visibility of the issue and prevention strategies and reframing the issue as a pubic health agenda. Thus, communication practitioners' strategic communication efforts to reach out to the public, elected officials, and media will help advocacy communication on gun violence move forward.

Summary

In this chapter, we discussed the definitions of advocacy and activism by focusing on the similarities and differences between the two concepts. We also discussed some relevant concepts and communication strategies that may be helpful in designing and delivering public relations campaigns related to advocacy and activism. Then, we discussed the important roles of communication practitioners in terms of describing the causes and solutions of various public health issues and influencing audiences' attitudes on the issues. Finally, we discussed advocacy communication related to gun violence as an example of media advocacy efforts.

As communication practitioners work with various social issues, understanding conceptual differences of advocacy and activism and strategic foci based on the clarification of the concepts will help implemement effective communication strategies when practitioners encourage the publics' attitude and behavior changes related to the social issues.

Discussion Questions

1. Based on the definitions and characteristics of advocacy and activism discussed in the chapter, how would you define and describe communication efforts to reduce gun violence?
2. Think of activists' direct/illegal actions as communication strategies. Are these strategies effective/ineffective? If so, to what extent are these strategies effective/ineffective?
3. The CDC defines racism as a serious threat to public health. Explain the key features of public health framing and how racism can be framed as a public health issue.
4. When communication practitioners emphasize certain aspects of an issue (issue framing) to highlight focal points of their campaign messages, what ethical concerns should communication practitioners consider?
5. How would you differentiate activism from terrorism and vandalism? Or do they share some similarities? If so, what are some similarities and differences among activism, terrorism, and vandalism? To what extent is activism communication considered freedom of speech?

Further Reading

Effectiveness of activists' public relations:
Jahng, M. R., Hong, S., & Park, E. H. (2014). How radical is radical? Understanding the role of activists' communication strategies on the formation of public attitude and evaluation. *Public Relations Review*, *40*(1), 119–121. https://doi.org/10.1016/j.pubrev.2013.11.004
Public health framing of racism:
Racism and health. (2021). Centers for Disease Control and Prevention. https://www.cdc.gov/healthequity/racism-disparities/index.html
Public health issue framing with episodic and thematic approaches:
Kim, S. H., & Anne Willis, L. (2007). Talking about obesity: News framing of who is responsible for causing and fixing the problem. *Journal of Health Communication*, *12*(4), 359–376. https://doi.org/10.1080/10810730701326051

Zhang, Y., Jin, Y., & Tang, Y. (2015). Framing depression: Cultural and organizational influences on coverage of a public health threat and attribution of responsibilities in Chinese news media, 2000–2012. *Journalism & Mass Communication Quarterly, 92*(1), 99–120. https://doi.org/10.1177/1077699014558553

References

Alinsky, S. (1971). *Rules for radicals: A practical primer for realistic radicals*. New York: Random House. https://doi.org/10.1093/sw/17.2.113

Argerious, N. B. (2022, July 14). King country expands public health approach in response to rising gun violence. *The Urbanist*. https://www.theurbanist.org/2022/07/14/king-county-expands-public-health-approach-in-response-to-rising-gun-violence/

Bauchner, H., Rivara, F. P., Bonow, R. O., Bressler, N. M., Disis, M. L. N., Heckers, S., . . . & Robinson, J. K. (2017). Death by gun violence—a public health crisis. *JAMA Psychiatry, 74*(12), 1195–1196. https://doi.org/10.1001/jamapsychiatry.2017.3616

Berkeley Media Studies Group. (1997). Issue 1: What is media advocacy? Retrieved July 20, 2022, from http://www.bmsg.org/pdfs/Issue1.pdf.

Brown, K., & Sakran, J. V. (2021, May 3). Joe Biden demonstrates public health approach will solve America's ills. The Hill. https://thehill.com/opinion/white-house/551518-joe-biden-demonstrates-public-health-approach-will-solve-americas-ills/

Cambridge Dictionary. (n.d.). Advocacy. In *Cambridge Dictionary*. Retrieved July 22, 2022, from https://dictionary.cambridge.org/us/dictionary/english/advocacy

Choi, M., & McKeever, B. (2022). Social media advocacy and gun violence: Applying the engagement model to nonprofit organizations' communication efforts. *Public Relations Review, 48*(2), 102173. https://doi.org/10.1016/j.pubrev.2022.102173

Coleman, R., Thorson, E., & Wilkins, L. (2011). Testing the effect of framing and sourcing in health news stories. *Journal of Health Communication, 16*(9), 941–954. https://doi.org/10.1080/10810730.2011.561918

Coombs, W. T., & Holladay, S. J. (2010). *PR strategy and application: Managing influence*. Chichester, UK: John Wiley & Sons.

Crable, R. E., & Vibbert, S. L. (1985). Managing issues and influencing public policy. *Public Relations Review, 11*(2), 3–16. https://doi.org/10.1016/s0363-8111(82)80114-8

Dardis, F. E. (2007). The role of issue-framing functions in affecting beliefs and opinions about a sociopolitical issue. *Communication Quarterly, 55*(2), 247–265. https://doi.org/10.1080/01463370701290525

DeFoster, R., & Swalve, N. (2018). Guns, culture or mental health? Framing mass shootings as a public health crisis. *Health Communication, 33*(10), 1211–1222. https://doi.org/10.1080/10410236.2017.1350907

Derville, T. (2005). Radical activist tactics: Overturning public relations conceptualizations. *Public Relations Review, 31*(4), 527–533. https://doi.org/10.1016/j.pubrev.2005.08.012

de Vreese, C. H. (2010). The effects of journalistic news frames. In P. D'Angelo & J. Kuypers (Eds.), *Doing framing analysis* (pp. 187–214). Routledge. https://doi.org/10.4324/9780203864463

DiGrazia, J. (2013). Individual protest participation in the United States: Conventional and unconventional activism. *Social Science Quarterly, 95*(1), 111–131. https://doi.org/10.1111/ssqu.12048

Dodd, M. D., & Supa, D. W. (2014). Conceptualizing and measuring "corporate social advocacy" communication: Examining the impact on corporate financial performance. *Public Relations Journal, 8*(3), 2–23. https://www.bellisario.psu.edu/assets/uploads/2014DODDSUPA.pdf

Entman, R. M. (1993). Framing: Toward clarification of a fractured paradigm. *Journal of Communication*, *43*(4), 51–58. https://doi.org/10.1111/j.1460-2466.1993. tb01304.x

Feinberg, M., Willer, R., & Kovacheff, C. (2020). The activist's dilemma: Extreme protest actions reduce popular support for social movements. *Journal of Personality and Social Psychology*, *119(5)*, 1086–1111. https://doi.org/10.1037/pspi0000230

Franklin, D. (2014, May 2). Framing the danger of guns as a public health risk will change the debate over gun control. *The Washington Post*. https://www.washingtonpost.com/opinions/framing-the-danger-of-guns-as-a-public-health-risk-will-change-the-debate-over-gun-control/2014/05/02/e4a73490-cf27-11e3-a6b1-45c4dffb85a6_story.html?noredirect=on&utm_term=.7d282b3947ac

Gamson, W. (1992). *Talking politics*. New York: Cambridge University Press. https://doi.org/10.1093/sf/72.3.923

Gibson, T. A. (2010). The limits of media advocacy. *Communication, Culture & Critique*, *3*(1), 44–65. https://doi.org/10.1111/j.1753-9137.2009.01057.x

Gramlich, J. (2022, February 3). What the data says about gun deaths in the U.S. Pew Research Center. https://www.pewresearch.org/fact-tank/2022/02/03/what-the-data-says-about-gun-deaths-in-the-u-s/

Hallahan, K. (1999). Seven models of framing: Implications for public relations. *Journal of Public Relations Research*, *11*(3), 205–242. https://doi.org/10.1207/s1532754xjprr1103_02

Hample, D., & Dallinger, J. M. (1998). On the etiology of the rebuff phenomenon: Why are persuasive messages less polite after rebuffs? *Communication Studies*, *49*(4), 305–321. https://doi.org/10.1080/10510979809368541

Hemenway, D., & Miller, M. (2013). Public health approach to the prevention of gun violence. *New England Journal of Medicine*, *368*(21), 2033–2035. https://doi.org/10.1056/nejmsb1302631

Holder, H. D., & Treno, A. J. (1997). Media advocacy in community prevention: News as a means to advance policy change. *Addiction*, *92* (Suppl. 2): S189–S199. https://doi.org/10.1111/j.1360-0443.1997.tb02991.x

Hopster, J. (2019). The speciesism debate: Intuition, method, and empirical advances. *Animals*, *9*(12), 1054. https://doi.org/10.3390/ani9121054

Iyengar, S. (1991). *Is anyone responsible? How television frames political issues*. Chicago: University of Chicago Press. https://doi.org/10.7208/chicago/9780226388533.001.0001

Jacoby, W. G. (2000). Issue framing and public opinion on government spending. *American Journal of Political Science*, *44*(4), 750–767. https://doi.org/10.2307/2669279

Jenkins, J. C. (1987). Nonprofit organizations and policy advocacy. In W. W. Powell (Ed.), *The Nonprofit Sector* (pp. 296–318). New Haven, CT: Yale University Press. https://doi.org/10.1126/science.236.4804.984

Kristof, N. (2017, Nov. 6) How to reduce shootings. *The New York Times*. https://www.nytimes.com/interactive/2017/11/06/opinion/how-to-reduce-shootings.html

Leaf, C. (2017, Oct. 3). The Las Vegas shooting: A public health crisis. *Fortune*. http://fortune.com/2017/10/03/vegas-shooting-public-health-crisis/

Leaf, C. (2018, Feb. 26). Framing gun violence as a public health issue. *Fortune*. http://fortune.com/2018/02/26/gun-violence-public-health-crisis/

Lemert, J.B. (1984). News context and the elimination of mobilizing information: An experiment. *Journalism Quarterly*, *61*: 243–259. https://doi.org/10.1177/107769908406100201

Lindaman, K., & Haider-Markel, D. (2000). All issues are not created equal: Reexamining issue evolution in morality policy. Presented at the annual meetings of the Midwest Political Science Association, Chicago

Masters, K. (2022, March 8). Virginia lawmakers pass new regulations for controversial beagle breeding facility. *Virginia Mercury*. https://www.virginiamercury.com/2022/03/08/virginia-lawmakers-pass-new-regulations-for-controversial-beagle-breeding-facility/

Matthes, J., & Schemer, C. (2012). Diachronic framing effects in competitive opinion environments. *Political Communication*, *29*(3), 319–339. https://doi.org/10.1080/10584609.2012.694985

McGinty, E. E., Kennedy-Hendricks, A., Choksy, S., & Barry, C. L. (2016). Trends in news media coverage of mental illness in the United States: 1995–2014. *Health Affairs*, *35*(6), 1121–1129. https://doi.org/10.1377/hlthaff.2016.0011

McKeever, B. W. (2013). News framing of autism: Understanding media advocacy and the combating autism act. *Science Communication*, *35*(2), 213–240. https://doi.org/10.1177/1075547012450951

McKeever, B. W., Choi, M., Walker, D., & McKeever, R. (2022). Gun violence as a public health issue: Media advocacy, framing and implications for communication. *Newspaper Research Journal*, *43*(2), 138–154.

Merry, M. K. (2018). Narrative strategies in the gun policy debate: Exploring proximity and social construction. *Policy Studies Journal*, *46*(4), 747–770. https://doi.org/10.1111/psj.12255

Mozaffarian, D., Hemenway, D., & Ludwig, D. S. (2013). Curbing gun violence: Lessons from public health successes. *JAMA*, *309*(6), 551–552. https://doi.org/10.1001/jama.2013.38

Murphy-Bates, S. (2019, May 20). Greenpeace activists 'shut down' BP's London headquarters with barricades blaming the firm for 'fuelling the climate emergency'. *Daily Mail*. https://www.dailymail.co.uk/news/article-7048603/Greenpeace-activists-shut-BPs-London-headquarters-stone-barricades.html

Negarandeh, R., Oskouie, F., Ahmadi, F., Nikravesh, M., & Hallberg, I. R. (2006). Patient advocacy: Barriers and facilitators. *BMC Nursing*, *5*(1), 1–8. https://doi.org/10.1186/1472-6955-5-3

Nelson, T. E., & Oxley, Z. M. (1999). Issue framing effects on belief importance and opinion. *The Journal of Politics*, *61*(4), 1040–1067. https://doi.org/10.2307/2647553

Ophélie, V. (2016). (Extra)ordinary activism: Veganism and the shaping of hemeratopias. *International Journal of Sociology and Social Policy*, *36*(11/12), 756–773. https://doi.org/10.1108/IJSSP-12-2015-0137

Public health approach to violence prevention. (2022) Centers for Disease Control and Prevention. Retrieved from https://www.cdc.gov/violenceprevention/publichealthissue/publichealthapproach.html

Sachs, D., & Linn, R. (1998). Client advocacy in action: Professional and environmental factors affecting Israeli occupational therapists' behaviour. *Occupational Health and Industrial Medicine*, *2*(38), 71. https://doi.org/10.1177/000841749706400316

Schmid, H., Bar, M., & Nirel, R. (2008). Advocacy activities in nonprofit human service organizations: Implications for policy. *Nonprofit and Voluntary Sector Quarterly*, *37*(4), 581–602. https://doi.org/10.1177/0899764007312666

Smith, M. F. (2005). Activism. In R. L. Heath (Ed.), *Encyclopedia of Public Relations* (pp. 5–9). Thousand Oaks, CA: Sage. https://doi.org/10.4135/9781412952545.n345

Smith, M. F., & Ferguson, D. P. (2013). "Fracking democracy": Issue management and locus of policy decision-making in the Marcellus Shale gas drilling debate. *Public Relations Review*, *39*(4), 377–386. https://doi.org/10.1016/j.pubrev.2013.08.003

Tarrow, S. G. (2011). *Power in movement: Social movements, collective action and politics*. Cambridge, MA: Cambridge University Press. https://doi.org/10.2307/2083040

Taylor, K. Y. (2021, Aug 6). Did last summer's black lives matter protests change anything? *The New Yorker*. https://www.newyorker.com/news/our-columnists/did-last-summers-protests-change-anything

Thelen, P. D. (2020). Internal communicators' understanding of the definition and importance of employee advocacy. *Public Relations Review*, *46*(4), 101946. https://doi.org/10.1016/j.pubrev.2020.101946

Wakefield, M. A., Loken, B., & Hornik, R. C. (2010). Use of mass media campaigns to change health behaviour. *The Lancet*, *376*(9748), 1261–1271. https://doi.org/10.1016/s0140-6736(10)60809-4

Wallack, L. (1990). Media advocacy: Promoting health through mass communication. In K. Glanz, F. M. Lewis, & B. K. Rimer (Eds.), *The Jossey-Bass health series. Health behavior and health education: Theory, research, and practice* (pp. 370–386). San Francisco, CA: Jossey-Bass. https://doi.org/10.1097/00001416-199201000-00021

Wallack, L., Dorfman, L., Jernigan, D., & Themba, M. (1993). *Media advocacy and public health: Power for prevention*. Newbury Park, CA: Sage. https://doi.org/10.2307/3342596

Winett, L. B., & Wallack, L. (1996). Advancing public health goals through the mass media. *Journal of Health Communication*, *1*(2), 173–196. https://doi.org/10.1080/108107396128130

Yaeger, L. (2016, Nov 18). How to wear your politics on your sleeve. *Vogue*. https://www.vogue.com/article/protest-fashion-politics-safety-pin

7

CRISIS COMMUNICATION FOR SOCIAL GOOD

Lucinda Austin, LaShonda Eaddy,
Xuerong Lu, and Yan Jin

A crisis is defined as "a major occurrence with a potentially negative outcome affecting an organization, company or industry as well as its publics, products or good name" (Fearn-Banks, 2002, p. 1), which can lead to physical, emotional, and financial harms to organizations and publics (Sellnow & Seeger, 2020). Crisis communication is defined as "the collection, processing, and dissemination of information required to address a crisis situation" (Coombs, 2010, p. 20). The crisis communication research field has witnessed significant growth in the past two decades (Coombs, 2010; Manias-Muñoz et al., 2019), ranked third among emerging research areas in public relations (Ki et al., 2019; Pasadeos et al., 2010).

In light of the ongoing challenges of the COVID-19 pandemic, enhancing the effectiveness of communication management in times of public crises has become more critical than ever. As crisis scholars and practitioners have recently advocated, the challenges of crisis communication in a variety of settings from corporate to nonprofit to government affairs need to be investigated further (Jin & Austin, 2022; Jin et al., 2021), especially in areas such as public health crises (Coombs, 2022; Jin & Vijaykumar, 2022) and disasters (Liu et al., 2021), where crises can imperil the health and safety of large populations and severely threaten the physical, social, and economic well-being of individuals and communities. In managing a public crisis such as an outbreak, it is pivotal for government agencies, public and private organizations, communities, and other vital entities in the public ecosystem to collaborate so as to communicate more effectively (Jin & Vijaykumar, 2022). This provides unique challenges and opportunities for managing crisis information and motivating proactive crisis responses, as well as building and strengthening resilience in times of crisis.

DOI: 10.4324/9781003327189-9

As Liu and colleagues (2021) argued, it is essential for organizations and crisis communication practitioners to facilitate and enhance public crisis communication (including how to most effectively motivate publics to follow public authorities' instructions and take preventive/protective actions). As Jin and Vijaykumar (2022) emphasized, public health organizations need to

> (i) focus on providing information about protective actions individuals can take to keep themselves safe, especially through outlets enabling proactive information seeking; and (ii) consider disseminating information to news media and directly to the public, using renewal narratives, focusing on growth, learning, restoration, and healing if their credibility is called into question.

It is also essential for crisis scholars to continue bridging geographical and cultural gaps, as well as enhancing diversity and inclusiveness in theory and practice (Diers-Lawson & Meißner, 2021; Jin et al., 2021).

Major Crisis Communication Theories

According to the international Delphi study conducted by Manias-Muñoz et al. (2019), crisis scholars from different countries have identified several major crisis communication theories, including Image Repair Theory, Situational Crisis Communication Theory (SCCT), and the Contingency Theory of Strategic Conflict Management. Manias-Muñoz et al. also reported consensus among crisis scholars on the critical need to close the gap between crisis theory and practice: although these major crisis communication theories help answer basic, general questions in the field, these theories do not necessarily inform the practice of crisis communication. Beyond organizational crisis communication, other domains of practice, such as disaster and health, need further theoretical and practical advancement (Manias-Muñoz et al., 2019).

Echoing this need, Jin et al. (2021) published an edited volume, which aims to advance crisis communication practice by introducing research-vetted tools (including theory) to public relations professionals tasked with managing crisis communication. Four major crisis communication theories providing empirically tested methods and message types for crisis communication practitioners are included: SCCT; the Contingency Theory of Strategic Conflict Management; the Internalization, Distribution, Explanation and Action (IDEA) Model; and the Social-Mediated Crisis Communication (SMCC) Model, some of which were also integrated in Jin and Austin's (2022) *Social Media and Crisis Communication* with an emphasis on the role of social media and new technology in crisis management. Based on the two anchors (i.e., theory informing practice and theory essential to digital crisis communication) most relevant to crisis communication for social good, we focus on two major crisis communication theories in this chapter: the SCCT and SMCC models.

SCCT

The situational crisis communication theory (SCCT) originated as a response to a question of connecting crisis types to crisis strategies (Coombs, 2017). Three crisis type clusters are identified based on attribution theory and the assumed level and type of responsibility (Coombs, 2007, 2017): victim, accident, and preventable crisis clusters (Coombs, 2007). Crisis types range based on level of attributed responsibility: (1) minimal crisis responsibility, (2) low crisis responsibility, and (3) high crisis responsibility (Coombs, 2017).

Low-responsibility crises often include a focus on technological failings that result in accidents or product harm (Coombs, 2017). High-responsibility crises often include human-error accidents, human-error product harm, and organizational misdeeds or management misconduct. Crisis message strategy types (i.e., denial, diminish, rebuild, and bolster) are prescribed accordingly (Coombs, 2007, 2017). Coombs (2017) also extended the framework regarding social media crises suggesting that "social media have exposed to public view once-private efforts to manage certain crisis risks" (p. 21).

In the sixth edition of *Ongoing crisis communication: Planning, managing, and responding* (2022), Coombs discussed public health crises and how the SCCT can be extended to advance crisis research and practice, before, during, and after a health crisis or public emergency. Recently, SCCT has also been applied by scholars in examining COVID-19 pandemic crisis management. For example, in the context of Greece, Aspriadis (2021) applied SCCT to analyze the Greek government and health authorities' practice of crisis communication about the COVID-19 pandemic in their public briefings and public speeches. Macnamara (2021) used SCCT to analyze how organizations responded to stakeholders via communication when both the organization and stakeholders were threatened by the COVID-19 pandemic.

SMCC

The SMCC model (Austin & Jin, 2017) builds on aspects of SCCT, examining information flow and use in crisis among varying forms of media (e.g., digital, traditional, offline), publics, and organizations. SCCT is incorporated to inform crisis message considerations, and rumor psychology theory informs recommended responses at stages of rumor transmission.

Identified in the SMCC model are three key publics who contribute to information production, seeking, and sharing at different crisis stages: influential

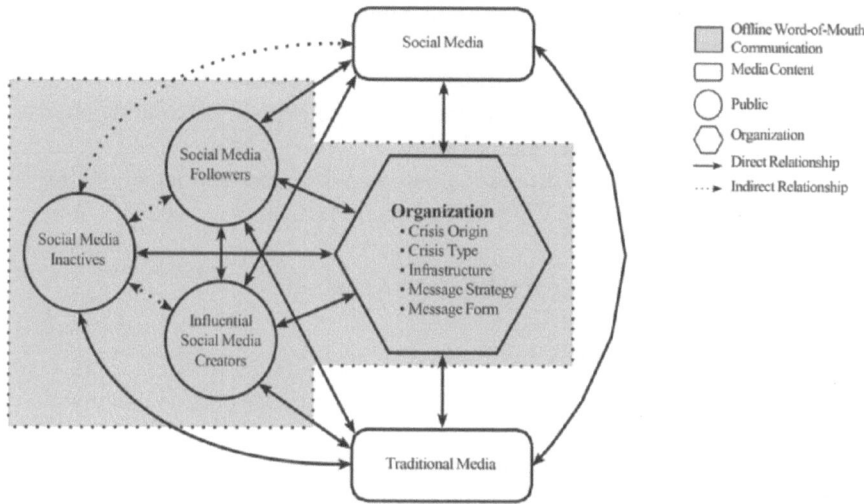

FIGURE 7.1   SMCC model.

social media creators, social media followers, and social media inactives (Jin, Liu, & Austin, 2014) (see Figure 7.1). Also represented in the model is information flow, including direct and indirect relationships. Five criteria are included for organizations to consider in their crisis communication response: (1) crisis origin, (2) crisis type, (3) organizational infrastructure, (4) message strategy, and (5) message form (see Austin & Jin, 2017; Jin, Liu, & Austin, 2014).

Prior SMCC research has suggested that the information channel (e.g., social media, word of mouth, etc.) matters, as well as the specific social media platform. These should be an important consideration for crisis messaging, as individuals turn to different mediums and different social media platforms to fulfill different functions during crisis (Austin & Jin, 2017). For example, social media has been used in crisis to obtain insider information and check in on family and friends during a crisis (Austin et al., 2012). In the specific context of natural disasters, social media can provide more timely information, allow affected community members to support each other, and facilitate emotional support and healing (Fraustino et al., 2017). In terms of information form, news media is still more credible for instructive information during crisis situations (Austin et al., 2012). SMCC research also suggests that different channels may be more or less effective during specific types of crises and with different audiences, and matching the communication to the appropriate platform and platform users can have differential crisis effects (e.g., Triantafillidou & Yannas, 2020).

Recent SMCC model research has incorporated big data analysis and social network perspectives to better contextualize complex information use and sharing during crisis and demonstrate how an individual's social network positioning and other factors affect their digital media influence during crisis (Zhao et al., 2019). Additionally, related research has examined a convergence framework theory discussed later in the chapter to explain how individuals' use of multiple media forms and sources works together to affect crisis-related perceptions (e.g., belief in and attitudes about a crisis event) and intentions for action (e.g., intention to take a COVID-19 vaccine) (Zhao et al., 2022).

Crisis as Applied to Public Health/Social Change

Disaster Communication

Overview

Disaster, defined by (Kreps, 1984), is an unplanned and socially disruptive event that might create harm to people and communities. Disaster is similar to crisis, as both happen suddenly and need immediate action taken to mitigate harm (Sellnow & Seeger, 2013). However, disasters focus on community while traditional crisis scholarship has focused on organizations and organizational reputation. Thus, community-focused questions, such as how to build community resilience, have become key topics in the disaster management field. Scholars point out that effective crisis and risk communication is key to building community resilience, as it can prepare the public and guide them before, during, and after a disaster (Chandra et al., 2013). However, factors such as uncertainty and rapidity surrounding disasters, limited information channels in times of disaster, and the need for teamwork among multiple governments and organizations provides a constant challenge for effective disaster communication. And the stakes are high: broken communication can further lead to the loss of life and other societal harms during disaster (e.g., Bharosa et al., 2010). Therefore, scholars and practitioners have discussed how to improve the effectiveness of communication during disaster to better protect the public and community at risk.

Disaster communication involves "information creation, seeking, and/or sharing among individuals, organizations, and the media surrounding an event involving largely damaging violations of publics' expectations" (Liu et al, 2018, p. 628). Like the three stages (pre-crisis, crisis, and post-crisis) discussed in crisis communication (Coombs, 2022), disaster communication includes three stages of disasters (i.e., disaster preparedness, disaster response, and disaster recovery) with different focal themes (Liu & Ni, 2022). Communication themes including information provision, inter-agency coordination, and community building are crucial (Liu and Ni, 2022).

The Case of Hurricanes

Government agencies have increasingly utilized social media to manage disasters at different stages. For example, local and federal government and emergency management organizations engaged heavily in social media conversation when Hurricane Harvey hit the Gulf Coast of Texas in August 2017 (Liu et al., 2018), changing the media landscape from previous disasters. Government and emergency management organizations also used Twitter to report and update disaster-related information, connect the public at risk to other resources, and boost community morale (Liu et al., 2018). Through a semantic network analysis of government organizations' tweets during Hurricane Harvey, Liu et al. (2018) found that government and emergency management organizations used Twitter to provide disaster-related information, such as weather information and preventive measures, to help the public prepare for the disaster, and to update rescue information during the Hurricane to facilitate disaster relief. At the post-disaster stage, government and emergency management organizations continued to engage in community building, such as praising partners and expressing solidarity, which helped with overall disaster recovery (Liu et al., 2018).

As argued by Quarantelli (2005), disaster not only impacts social systems and processes, but also facilitates social changes. Past disasters have also helped disaster responding officials realize the crucial role of social media in spreading emergency-related information. We can see the frequency of posting disaster-related information in a timely manner by local and federal government and emergency management organizations on social media has increased compared to previous disasters. For instance, in 2012 with Hurricane Sandy, the average of government organization tweets was around 5.66 tweets over 16 days, while response in 2017 to Hurricane Harvey was around 11.43 tweets over 23 days (Vera-Burgo & Padgett, 2020; Wang & Zhuang, 2017). Moreover, social media, such as the platform formerly known as Twitter, has been widely and expertly used by governments and officals in recent disasters to listen and respond to the community, correct misinformation, and allocate credible resources (Vera-Burgo & Padgett, 2020). Both scholars and practitioners have learned from previous experience that more frequent and timely posts on social meida helped maintain existing followers and avoid losing potential followers (Wang & Zhuang, 2017). Meanwhile, facilitating information sharing on social media helps capture attention and gathers different responding officials together to generate more impressions in a shorter time period (Wang & Zhuang, 2017). Recently, social media has been clearly incorporated into disaster management processes.

Health Crises

Overview

In response to the September 11, 2001 Word Trade Center attacks and ensuing anthrax bio terrorism attacks, Covello (2003) offered seven essential best practices for public health risk and crisis communication plans:

i) accept and involve stakeholders as legitimate partners;
ii) listen to people;
iii) be truthful, honest, frank, and open;
iv) coordinate, collaborate, and partner with other credible sources;
v) meet the needs of the media;
vi) communicate clearly and with compassion; and,
vii) plan thoroughly and carefully.

More than 20 years have since passed, but these fundamentals remain intact in the current public health risk and crisis communications landscape. As health risk communicators are tasked with relaying vital health information during far-reaching health crises, such as the global COVID-19 pandemic, additional complications have arisen, such as misinformation and disinformation and publics' lack of trust in governmental and health organizations. Van der Meer and Jin (2020) suggest that publics' exposure to factual elaboration regarding misinformation stimulates protective action intentions more than rebuttals. Moreover, the study offers that publics view news media and government health organizations as more reliable sources during crises. Thus, these organizations are able to rectify misperceptions and discredit misinformation more successfully, leading to improved belief accuracy compared to peer information sources.

Despite these encouraging results, health-risk communicators face increased challenges due to publics' eroding trust in government and health organizations. Edelman's 2021, 2022, and 2023 Trust Barometers indicate a shift in trust from government and health organizations to businesses. Governments and health organizations are no longer viewed as trusted social institutions; presenting a conundrum to these organizations that have information that is key to public health and safety. Concurrently, businesses have a newfound role as the most trusted social institution (Edelman, 2021), but oftentimes lack the expertise and infrastructure to help address public health risks and crises such as the COVID-19 pandemic. Moreover, businesses are faced with an ethical dilemma of continuing to focus on their organizations' "bottom line" and remaining good community partners or charting new courses to collaborate with government and health organizations to provide vital health information aimed to help the overall public good over profit. The role reversal of government/ health organizations and businesses is notable, especially considering customary social contracts between these entities.

The Case of COVID-19 Vaccines

As pharmaceutical companies raced to provide vaccines to combat the COVID-19 pandemic, their unprecedented collaborative efforts were illustrative of a new willingness to cooperate with competitors for the public good. While the industry's efforts allowed vaccines to be made available less than ten months after the pandemic's start, Pfizer was heavily criticized for taking advantage of the situation to gain profits without helping to alleviate the critical vaccine access issues in poor and developing countries. Pfizer's action could possibly undermine the pharmaceutical industry's progress to rise above previous perceptions of greed and lack of care for the public good. Moreover, Pfizer's actions could be perceived as unethical; possibly exacerbating hesitance to heed public health and safety guidance and precautions.

Nonprofit Crises

Overview of Literature

Nonprofit organizations offer a unique crisis context, given their organizational features (McKeever & Choi, 2022), namely: that their funding goes back into the organizational mission, they rely on volunteers and donations for support, and they differ in organizational structure and accountability. Nonprofit philanthropic organizations may face more scrutiny from a larger pool of potential stakeholders watching the organization given funding models and their philanthropic mission. As such, they may receive more criticism when making questionable decisions and communicating these decisions to the public (McKeever & Choi, 2022).

Although philanthropic organizations have a mission focused on social good, this does not provide them with immunity from advanced scrutiny. For example, high-profile nonprofit organizations such as Livestrong, Red Cross, and the Humane Society have all found themselves in the midst of controversy and reputational threats (Chronicle of Philanthropy, n.d.). Reputational threats can be particularly devastating for a nonprofit organization that relies on fundraising and the philanthropy of others to fund its organizational mission. Organizational reputation has been shown to directly influence donations, and collective or industry reputation also has a spillover effect for financial donations (Grant & Potoski, 2015).

Nonprofit organizations are not a monolith. Within nonprofit organizations, there are different types of organizational foci, each with its own contexts, opportunities, and challenges. For example, religious organizations, such as churches or faith-based associations, face unique crisis characteristics (Morehouse & Spaulding, 2022). With faith-based organizations, religion and spirituality may result in altered recognition, understanding, and acceptance of a crisis. An individual's religion and spirituality interacts with many other sectors and spheres of public life as well, including public health, politics, entertainment, and more. In religious organization crisis communication, the use of stakeholder-formed organizations and activist groups has been noted as a crisis communication difference (Morehouse, 2020). Other religious research has noted the different in the use of guilt in messaging, as it pertains to religious themes (Courtright & Hearit, 2002). Morehouse and Spaulding (2022) call for focus on prioritizing publics in the study of religious crisis communication and their wellbeing, including moralistic obligations in religious crises.

The Case of the 2022 World Cup

The Fédération Internationale de Football Association (FIFA) is a nonprofit organization that oversees, organizes, and promotes soccer worldwide. FIFA is best known for planning the World Cup and Women's World Cup. As a nonprofit organization, FIFA's costs are relatively low for planning and organizing the World Cup while host countries incur the more expensive infrastructure costs. According to FIFA, "The new FIFA is modernizing football to be global, accessible and inclusive in all aspects" (FIFA, n.d.). However, the nonprofit faced intense scrutiny regarding its selection of Qatar as the host site for the 2022 World Cup from the moment of the announcement in 2010.

The 2022 World Cup's first Middle Eastern location had many controversies over the prior 12 years. The biggest concerns were Qatar's human rights record, outlawing of same-sex relationships, and mistreatment of migrant workers. Qatar's stances on these issues seemed to directly contradict FIFA's inclusivity and accessibility pursuits, and media outlets were critical of this contradiction. Some soccer associations protested through uniform changes and other public statements. Even as the 2022 World Cup commenced, FIFA president Gianni Infantino failed to respond to the humanitarian issues proactively and constructively in a letter that he sent to the national soccer associations, instead imploring them to set politics aside and focus on football (Long, 2023). This was a missed opportunity to explain how allowing Qatar to host the World Cup was supportive of its intent for soccer to be global, accessible, and inclusive.

Emerging Trends and Future Directions in Crisis Communication in the Digital World

As crisis communication becomes increasingly digitized, emerging areas of focus have highlighted aspects of this digital media environment for further study and theoretical advancement, including misinformation, media affordances, and media convergence.

Misinformation

Misinformation is "explicitly false" information that cannot be supported by scientific consensus (Tan et al., 2015, p. 675). Such inaccurate and misleading information has "downstream consequences for health, social harmony, and political life" (Southwell et al. 2018, p. 2). Recent examples, including false information surrounding the COVID-19 pandemic and the myth that the measles, mumps, and rubella (MMR) vaccine causes autism, illustrate how powerful misinformation can disrupt public health and society.

Due to the complexity and uncertainty surrounding a crisis, the generation and spread of misinformation has become a characteristic phenomenon during crisis. Misinformation in crisis refers to "false information about any aspect of an ongoing crisis or any incorrect information that can lead to a crisis according to factual evidence from credible source(s) (e.g., the organization, news media, third-party experts, and government agencies, and internal/external witnesses)" (van der Meer & Jin, 2022, p. 131). During the COVID-19 pandemic, misinformation included topics related to the vaccine, prevention, treatment, and other conspiracy theories. In addition to being a feature of crisis, misinformation can also be the origin of a crisis and can compete with correct information shaping the public's understanding of emerging issues and threatening individuals and society. For example, because of exposure to misinformation, publics may fail to take protective behaviors during public health crises (Liu et al., 2020) or take risky behaviors, such as taking alternative untested medications (Nan et al., 2021). Moreover, the public trust in government agencies and mainstream media was also threatened due to the spread of misinformation, especially during the global financial crisis and pandemic (e.g., OECD, 2020). Unfortunately, the adverse impact of misinformation can be far more exacerbated as a growing population turns to the internet and social media for obtaining information (Pew Research Center, 2024). The lack of a gatekeeper on social media facilitates the spread of misinformation, compounded by the users' lack of knowledge to distinguish between misinformation and correct information (e.g., Lewandowsky et al. 2012).

The difficulty of correcting misinformation has been well documented. Cognitive bias predisposes individuals to keep these false beliefs and resist corrective information (Nyhan & Reifler, 2010). Emotional memory related to misinformation is easier to be evoked, especially during adverse and ambiguous events (Sangalang et al., 2019). As a result, scholars call for the development of communication strategies to (1) educate and sensitize individuals to misinformation, (2) discourage the discussion and sharing of misinformation while encouraging the sharing of corrective information, and (3) facilitate other positive information consumption behaviors, such as additional information seeking in a highly conflicting informational environment (e.g., Schwarz et al., 2016; Southwell et al., 2018).

Media Affordances

The media (both traditional and social media) play an increasingly complex role in crisis communication (Voges et al., 2022). As Sellnow and Seeger (2013) point out, "the media have no equal for rapidly distributing information to mass audiences during crises" (p. 139), which can be used as a way for organizations to communicate with publics and function as one of the main information-sharing platforms (Sellnow & Seeger, 2013). More than ever before, organizations have utilized social media in crisis communication in recent years (Jin & Austin, 2022) to engage publics, manage their expectations (Valentini et al., 2017), and optimize crisis communication outcomes for both organizations and stakeholders (Coombs, 2022).

As Eriksson (2018) pointed out, given that social media platforms are not homogeneous, it is essential to distinguish between the affordances of different platforms. Media affordances, defined as multidimensional relationships with varying possible outcomes when individuals interact with technology (Evans et al., 2017; Gibson, 1979), has recently reemerged as a promising framework for understanding how individuals engage with social media over time (Evans et al., 2017; Zhou & Xu, 2019). This framework includes how different publics use social media for different crisis outcomes, before, during, or after a crisis (Liu et al., 2023).

Prior studies have provided evidence that the affordances of some social media platforms have helped organizations (e.g., authorities) build credibility during crises. For instance, social media users tend to take organizational affiliations (Lin et al., 2016) and the number of followers on organizational social media accounts (Westerman et al., 2012) as these organizations' credibility cues. Some affordances were found to contribute to organizational–public dialogue during crises when social media platforms made certain mechanical affordances (e.g., openness, reach, networking capabilities, immediacy, back-and-forth communication, and affordability) available (Bruns, 2017; Ostertag & Ortiz, 2017). As Zhou and Xu (2019) advocated, media affordances can serve as an ideal framework for examining (1) fundamental differences among social media and digital platforms and (2) how these differences might generate varied organization–publics crisis communication outcomes.

As Liu et al. (2023) pointed out, there are several future directions to extend and refine the framework of media affordances to understanding digital crisis communication, including the need to: (1) have access to publics who are not active social media users during crises, (2) employ different affordances with consistent terminology, (3) be mindful about the possibility for negative affordances (e.g., rumor generation and spread, intimidation, or bullying) and link affordances (and their attributes) to crisis outcomes, and (4) examine how affordances might vary depending on the speed and magnitude of crisis information spread in different crisis situations.

Media Convergence

Recent scholarship in the area of media and crisis communication has also begun to examine convergence of media types (e.g., different mediums such as print or social media), in addition to various modalities including visual, text, or audio (e.g., Zhao et al., 2022). As individuals receive information within complex and changing media environments, they rely on multiple forms and formats of information to process risks and manage uncertainties. The initial concept of convergence (Jenkins, 2006) focused on shifts from old media types to new media, while acknowledging that new and old media forms are used simultaneously, but new media complicates the information transmission process.

Zhao et al. (2022) proposed a convergence framework to examine modality, source, and medium in crisis communication, along with antecedents and consequences of this convergence related to crises. Modality, as defined here, refers to format and characteristics (e.g., text, visual, audio). Source refers to the outlet sharing the information or the author of the information shared; message convergence theory states that individuals look for patterns in information shared from different sources to better understand risks (Anthony & Sellnow, 2016). Lastly, medium refers to the specific mediator of information (e.g., television, interpersonal, social media). Research suggests that individuals may turn to different mediums for different uses and gratifications, but in relation to convergence, complementary patterns in risk and crisis information received across these various platforms may help individuals to better understand and vet risk information. Research has also shown that message divergence can cause individuals to question crisis communication and ignore recommended protective actions (Anthony et al., 2017).

As media environments become more complicated related to crisis communication and risk information, frameworks such as media convergence provide a different way to examine source, medium, and modality combined. Zhao et al.'s (2022) framework provides four distinct archetypes of convergence behaviors in information seeking and processing during crises, and examines these in relation to demographics, motivations, and media affordances. While Zhao et al. found that level of convergence in these archetypes generally matched the level of situational risk awareness during crisis, more research is needed to understand protective action taking, as convergence levels did not align perfectly with action taking for each archetype.

Conclusion

Crises are unique communicative contexts with the potential for wide public impact. While the field of crisis communication in the public relations arena began its tradition with a focus on organizations—public and private organizations, including nonprofit and nongovernmental organizations—much of the recent crisis communication scholarship has also focused on areas of health (e.g., infectious disease threats) and natural disasters. These large-scale crises also have their own unique communication challenges and have the potential to endanger wellbeing and imperil lives. Understanding how to effectively and efficiently communicate during these crises helps to contribute to the greater social good and, sometimes, to social change.

As digital communication environments increase in complexity, theoretical understanding of digital social networks, artificial intelligence, and big data analytics will become increasingly important in understanding crisis communication for social good. And frameworks, such as media affordances, convergence, and network interconnectedness, can help us to better understand these complex media environments. For example, social networks may help to predict what kinds of information individuals will be exposed to during crisis but may also drive if individuals choose to engage in or avoid information in times of crisis and oversaturation of information (Qu et al., 2023). With misinformation rampant in times of crisis—from political crisis to infectious disease outbreaks and more—information vetting and further understanding of how to issue corrective misinformation in times of crisis (van der Meer & Jin, 2020), especially for politicized and controversial crises, will become increasingly important.

Discussion Questions

1. Using one of the crisis communication frameworks referenced in this chapter (SCCT, SMCC), what should organizations consider when communicating during a crisis?
2. What factors in the media environment affect crisis communication outcomes, and what should be taken into account, as a result?
3. How might crisis communication for social good (e.g., health/disaster communication, social causes, or with nonprofit organizations) differ from crisis communication in other context (e.g., corporate or business)?

Further Reading

Jin, Y., Austin, L., & Liu, B. F. (2022). Social-mediated crisis communication research: How information generation, consumption, and transmission influence communication processes and outcomes. In W. T. Coombs & S. Holladay (Eds.), *The handbook of crisis communication* (2nd ed., pp. 151–167). Wiley.

Liu, B. F., Jin, Y., & Austin, L. (2023). Digital crisis communication theory: Current land-scape and future trajectories. In C. Botan & E. Sommerefeldt (Eds.), *Public relations theory III* (3rd ed., pp. 191–212). Routledge.

Liu, B. F., Jin, Y., Austin, L., Kuligowski, E., & Young, C. (2021). The social-mediated crisis communication (SMCC) model: Identifying the next frontier. In Y. Jin, B. Reber, & G. Nowak (Eds.), *Advancing crisis communication eeffectiveness: Integrating public relations scholarship with practice* (pp. 214–230). Routledge.

Lu, X., Lee, Y. I, Austin, L., & Eaddly, L. L. (2022). Crisis information vetting: Extending the social-mediated crisis communication model. In Y. Jin & L. Austin (Eds.), *Social media and crisis communication* (2nd ed., pp. 142–154). Routledge.

McKeever, B. W., & Choi, M. (2022). Philanthropic crisis communication. In Y. Jin & L. Austin (Eds.), *Social media and crisis communication* (2nd ed., pp. 243–255). Routledge.

References

2021 Edelman Trust Barometer. (2021). https://www.edelman.com/trust/2021-trust-barometer

Anthony, K. E., & Sellnow, T. L. (2016). The role of the message convergence framework in medical decision making. *Journal of Health Communication, 21*, 249–256. https://doi.org/10.1080/10810730.2015.1064497

Anthony, K. E., Sellnow, T. L., Venette, S. J., & Fourney, S. P. (2017). Message convergence framework applied to health and risk messaging. *Oxford research encyclopedia of communication.* https://doi.org/10.1093/acrefore/9780190228613.013.540

Aspriadis, N. (2021). Managing COVID-19 pandemic crisis: The case of Greece. *Journal of International Crisis and Risk Communication Research, 4*, 387–412. https://doi.org/10.30658/jicrcr.4.2.8

Austin, L., & Jin, Y. (2017). Social media and crisis communication: explicating the social-mediated crisis communication model. In A. Dudo & L. A. Kahlor (Eds.) *Strategic Communication: New Agendas in Communication* (pp. 163–186). Routledge.

Austin, L., Liu, B. F., & Jin, Y. (2012). How audiences seek out crisis information: exploring the social-mediated crisis communication model. *Journal of Applied Communication Research, 40*(2), 188–207. 10.1080/00909882.2012.654498

Bharosa, N., Lee, J., & Janssen, M. (2010, January 1). Challenges and obstacles in sharing and coordinating information during multi-agency disaster response: Propositions from field exercises. *Information Systems Frontiers, 12*(1), 49–65. https://doi.org/10.1007/s10796-009-9174-z

Bruns, A. (2017). Conflict imagery in a connective environment: Audiovisual content on Twitter following the 2015/2016 terror attacks in Paris and Brussels. *Media, Culture & Society, 39*(8), 1122–1141. https://doi.org/10.1177%2F0163443717725574

Chandra, A., Williams, M., Plough, A., Stayton, A., Wells, K. B., Horta, M., & Tang, J. (2013). Getting actionable about community resilience: the Los Angeles County Community Disaster Resilience project. *American journal of public health, 103*(7), 1181–1189. https://doi.org/10.2105/AJPH.2013.301270

Chronicle of Philanthropy. (n.d.). Communicating in a crisis. https://www.philanthropy.com/package/communicating-in-a-crisis

Coombs, W. T. (2007). Protecting organization reputations during a crisis: The development and application of situational crisis communication theory. *Corporate Reputation Review, 10*(3), 163–176. 10.1057/palgrave.crr.1550049

Coombs, W. T. (2010). Parameters for crisis communication. In W. T. Coombs & S. J. Holladay (Eds.), *The handbook of crisis communication* (pp. 17–53). Blackwell.

Coombs, W. T. (2017). Revising situational crisis communication theory: The influences of social media on crisis communication theory and practice. In L. Austin and Y. Jin (Eds.), *Social media and crisis communication* (pp. 21–37). Routledge.

Coombs, W. T. (2022). *Ongoing crisis communication: Planning, managing, and responding* (6th ed.). SAGE.

Covello, V. (2003). Best practices in public health risk and crisis communication. *Journal of Health Communication*, 8, 3–5. https://doi.org/ 10.1080/10810730390224802

Courtright, J. L., & Hearit, K. M. (2002). The good organization speaking well: A paradigm case for religious institutional crisis management. *Public Relations Review*, 28(4), 347–360. https://doi.org/10.1016/S0363-8111(02)00166-2

Diers-Lawson, A. D., & Meißner, F. (2021). Editor's essay: The multi-disciplinary and diverse field of crisis and risk communication research. *Journal of International Crisis and Risk Communication Research*, 4(3), 439–450. https://doi.org/10.30658/jicrcr.4.3.0

Edelman Trust Barometer Archive. (n.d.) https://www.edelman.com/trust/archive

Eriksson, M. (2018). Lessons for crisis communication on social media: A systematic review of what research tells the practice. *International Journal of Strategic Communication*, 12(5), 526–551. https://doi.org/10.1080/1553118X.2018.1510405

Evans, S. K., Pearce, K. E., Vitak, J., & Treem, J. W. (2017). Explicating affordances: A conceptual framework for understanding affordances in communication research. *Journal of Computer-mediated Communication*, 22(1), 35–52. https://doi.org/10.1111/jcc4.12180

Fearn-Banks, K. (2002). *Crisis communications: A casebook approach*. Routledge.

FIFA. (n.d.). What we do. About FIFA. Retrieved February 8, 2023, from https://www.fifa.com/about-fifa

Fraustino, J. D., Liu, B. F., & Jin, Y. (2017). Social media during disasters: a research synthesis and road map. In L. Austin & Y. Jin (Eds.), *Social media and crisis communication* (pp. 283–295). Routledge.

Gibson, J. J. (1979). *The ecological approach to visual perception*. Houghton Mifflin.

Grant, L. E., & Potoski, M. (2015). Collective reputations affect donations to nonprofits. *Journal of Policy Analysis and Management*, 34(4), 835–852. https://doi.org/10.1002/pam.21868

Jenkins, H. (2006). *Convergence culture: Where old and new media collide*. New York University.

Jin, Y., & Austin, L. (2022). *Social media and crisis communication* (2nd ed.). Routledge.

Jin, Y., Liu, B. F., & Austin, L. (2014). Examining the role of social media in effective crisis management: the effects of crisis origin, information form, and source on publics' crisis responses. *Communication Research*, 41(1), 74–94. 10.1177/0093650211423918

Jin, Y., Choi, S. I., & Diers-Lawson, A. (2021). Special issue editor's essay: Advancing public health crisis and risk theory and practice via innovative and inclusive research on COVID-19 communication. *Journal of International Crisis and Risk Communication Research*, 4(2), 177–192. https://doi.org/10.30658/jicrcr.4.2.0

Jin, Y., & Vijaykumar, S. (2022). Crisis communication. In E. Ho, C. Bylund, & J. van Weert (Eds.), *The international encyclopedia of health communication*. Wiley.

Ki, E.-J., Pasadeos, Y., & Ertem-Eray, T. (2019). Growth of public relations research networks: A bibliometric analysis. *Journal of Public Relations Research*, 31(1–2), 5–31. https://doi.org/10.1080/1062726X.2019.1577739

Kreps, G. A. (1984). Sociological inquiry and disaster research. *Annual Review of Sociology*, 10(1), 309–330. https://doi.org/10.1146/annurev.so.10.080184.001521

Lewandowsky, S., Ecker, U. K., Seifert, C. M., Schwarz, N., & Cook, J. (2012). Misinformation and its correction: Continued influence and successful debiasing. *Psychological Science in the Public Interest, 13*(3), 106–131. https://doi.org/10.1177/1529100 612451018

Lin, X., Spence, P. R., Sellnow, T. L., & Lachlan, K. A. (2016). Crisis communication, learning and responding: Best practices in social media. *Computers in Human Behavior, 65*, 601–605. https://doi.org/10.1016/j.chb.2016.05.080

Liu, B. F., Jin, Y., & Austin, L. (2023). Digital crisis communication theory: Current landscape and future trajectories. In C. Botan & E. Sommerefeldt (Eds.), *Public relations theory III* (3rd ed., pp. 191–212). Routledge.

Liu, B. F., Jin, Y., Austin, L., Kuligowski, E., & Young, C. (2021). The social-mediated crisis communication (SMCC) model: Identifying the next frontier. In Y. Jin, B. Reber, & G. Nowak (Eds.), *Advancing crisis communication effectiveness: Integrating public relations scholarship with practice* (pp. 214–230). Routledge.

Liu, B.F., Austin, L., Lee, Y., Jin, Y.-I., & Kim, S. (2020). Telling the tale: the role of narratives in helping people respond to crises. *Journal of Applied Communication Research, 48*(3), 328–349. https://doi.org/10.1080/00909882.2020.1756377

Liu, B. F., Jin, Y., Briones, R., & Kuch, B. (2012). Managing turbulence online: Evaluating the blog-mediated crisis communication model with the American Red Cross. *Journal of Public Relations Research, 24*(4), 353–370. https://doi.org/10.1080/1062 726X.2012.689901

Liu, W., Lai, C.-H., & Xu, W. (2018). Tweeting about emergency: A semantic network analysis of government organizations' social media messaging during Hurricane Harvey. *Public Relations Review, 44*(5), 807–819. https://doi.org/10.1016/j.pubrev.2018.10.009

Liu W., & Ni, L. (2022). Natural disaster preparedness, response, and recovery crisis communication. In Austin L., Yan J. (Eds.), *Social media and crisis communication* (2nd ed, pp. 348–359). Routledge.

Long, M. (2023, January 11). 'Controversial, inorganic, the best ever': Grading Qatar's World Cup examination. SportsPro. Retrieved February 8, 2023, from https://www.sportspromedia.com/news/fifa-world-cup-qatar-2022-gianni-infantino-letter-protest-lgbtq-human-rights/

Macnamara, J. (2021). New insights into crisis communication from an "inside" emic perspective during COVID-19. *Public Relations Inquiry, 10*(2), 237–262. https://doi.org/10.1177/2046147X21999972

Manias-Muñoz, I., Jin, Y., & Reber, B. H. (2019). The state of crisis communication research and education through the lens of crisis scholars: An international Delphi study. *Public Relations Review, 45*(4), 101797. https://doi.org/10.1016/j.pubrev.2019.101797

McKeever, B. W., & Choi, M. (2022). Philanthropic crisis communication. In Y. Jin & L. Austin (Eds.), *Social media and crisis communication* (2nd ed., pp. 243–255). Routledge.

Morehouse, J. (2020). Stakeholder-formed organizations and crisis communication: Analyzing discourse of renewal with a non-offending organization. *Journal of International Crisis and Risk Communication Research, 3*(2), 243–274. https://doi.org/10.30658/jicrcr.3.2.5

Morehouse, J., & Spaulding, C. (2022). Advancing research on crisis communication and religion. In Y. Jin & L. Austin (Eds.), *Social media and crisis communication* (2nd ed., pp. 256–266). Routledge.

Naeem, S. B., Bhatti, R., & Khan, A. (2021). An exploration of how fake news is taking over social media and putting public health at risk. *Health Information & Libraries Journal, 38*(2), 143–149.

Nan, X., Wang, Y., & Thier, K. (2021). Health misinformation. In T. Thompson & N. Harrington (Eds.), *The Routledge handbook of health communication* (pp. 318–332). Routledge.

OECD (2020, July 3), Transparency, communication and trust: The role of public communication in responding to the wave of disinformation about the new Coronavirus. https://read.oecd-ilibrary.org/view/?ref=135_135220-cvba4lq3ru&title=Transparency-communication-and-trust-The-role-of-public-communication-in-responding-to-the-wave-of-disinformation-about-the-new-coronavirus

Ostertag, S. F., & Ortiz, D. G. (2017). Can social media use produce enduring social ties? Affordances and the case of Katrina bloggers. *Qualitative Sociology, 40*(1), 59–82. https://doi.org/10.1007/s11133-016-9346-3

Pasadeos, Y., Berger, B., & Renfro, R. B. (2010). Public relations as a maturing discipline: An update on research networks. *Journal of Public Relations Research, 22*(2), 136–158. https://doi.org/10.1080/10627261003601390

Pew Research Center. (2024, January 31). Americans' social media use. https://www.pewresearch.org/internet/2024/01/31/americans-social-media-use/

Qu, Y., Saffer, A., & Austin, L. (2023). What drives people away from COVID-19 information? Uncovering the influences of personal networks on information avoidance. *Health Communication, 38*(2), 216–227. https://doi.org/10.1080/10410236.2021.1944457

Quarantelli, E. L. (2005). *What is a disaster?: A dozen perspectives on the question.* Routledge. https://doi.org/10.4324/9780203984833

Sangalang, A., Ophir, Y., & Cappella, J. N. (2019). The potential for narrative correctives to combat misinformation. *Journal of Communication, 69*(3), 298–319. https://doi.org/10.1093/joc/jqz014

Schwarz, N., Newman, E., & Leach, W. (2016). Making the truth stick & the myths fade: Lessons from cognitive psychology. *Behavior Science & Policy, 2*(1), 85–95. https://doi.org/10.1353/bsp.2016.0009

Sellnow, T. L., & Seeger, M. W. (2013). *Theorizing crisis communication.* Wiley.

Sellnow, T. L., & Seeger, M. W. (2020). *Theorizing crisis communication* (2nd ed.). Wiley-Blackwell.

Southwell, B. G., Thorson, E. A., & Sheble, L. (2018). *Misinformation and mass audiences.* University of Texas.

Tan, A. S., Lee, C. J., & Chae, J. (2015). Exposure to health (mis) information: Lagged effects on young adults' health behaviors and potential pathways. *Journal of Communication,65*(4), 674–698. https://doi.org/10.1111/jcom.12163

Triantafillidou, A., & Yannas, P. (2020). Social media crisis communication in racially charged crises: Exploring the effects of social media and image restoration strategies. *Computers in Human Behavior, 106,* 106269. https://doi.org/10.1016/j.chb.2020.106269

Valentini, C., Romenti, S., & Kruckeberg, D. (2017). Handling crises in social media: From stakeholder crisis awareness and sense making to organizational crisis preparedness. In L. Austin & Y. Jin (Eds.), *Social media and crisis communication* (1st ed., pp. 57–67). Routledge.

van der Meer, T. G. L. A., & Jin, Y. (2020). Seeking formula for misinformation treatment in public health crises: The effects of corrective information type and source. *Health Communication, 35*(5), 560–575. https://doi.org/10.1080/10410236.2019.1573295

van der Meer, T. G. L. A., & Jin, Y. (2022). Crisis misinformation and corrective strategies in social-mediated crisis communication. In Y. Jin & L. Austin (Eds.), *Social media and crisis communication* (2nd ed., pp. 130–141). Routledge.

Vera-Burgos, C. M., & Griffin Padgett, D. R. (2020). Using Twitter for crisis communications in a natural disaster: Hurricane Harvey. *Heliyon, 6*(9), e04804. https://doi.org/10.1016/j.heliyon.2020.e04804

Voges, T. S., Jin, Y. Eaddy, L., &, Lu, X. (2022). *Responding to fire ignited from outside: Explicating "crisis spillover" through the multi-layered lens of organizational crisis communication.* Paper presented at the International Communication Association Conference, Paris, France.

Wang, B., & Zhuang, J. (2017). Crisis information distribution on Twitter: A content analysis of tweets during Hurricane Sandy. *Natural Hazards, 89*, 161–181. https://doi.org/10.1007/s11069-017-2960-x

Westerman, D., Spence, P. R., & Van Der Heide, B. (2012). A social network as information: The effect of system generated reports of connectedness on credibility on Twitter. *Computers in Human Behavior, 28*(1), 199e206. http://dx.doi.org/10.1016/j.chb.2011.09.001.

Zhao, X., Xu, S., & Austin, L. L. (2022). Medium and source convergence in crisis information acquisition: Patterns, antecedents, and outcomes. *New Media & Society,* 14614448221088866. https://doi.org/10.1177/14614448221088866

Zhao, X., Zhan, M. M., & Liu, B. F. (2019). Understanding motivated publics during disasters: Examining message functions, frames, and styles of social media influentials and followers. *Journal of Contingencies and Crisis Management, 27*(4), 387–399.

Zhou, X., & Xu, S. (2019). *Remaking dialogic principles for the digital age: The role of affordances in dialogue and engagement.* Paper presented at the International Communication Association Conference, Washington, D.C.

8

HEALTH JUSTICE FOR THE PAST, PRESENT, AND FUTURE

Exploring the Linkage between Social Movements and Public Relations

Candice L. Edrington and Sarah A. Aghazadeh

Introduction

For years, social movements and public health have remained separate in soci-etal conversations and academic literature (Brown & Fee, 2014). However, they are interconnected in that public health serves as both a focus and a consequence of various health social movements. This chapter explores the interrelatedness of these two in a way that centers public health, specifically physical and mental health, in the examination of behaviors for social change. Taking a historical ap-proach, this chapter will expose readers to past and present social movements, help them to conceptualize public health, and help them understand the role stra-tegic communication plays in improving public health and social conditions.

First, this chapter explores the many elements of social movements to pro-vide a concrete understanding and definition of the term. Public health is then conceptualized to provide a foundational connection between social movements and public health. Next, this chapter presents two case examples of social move-ments to highlight the use of strategic communication and relationship-building strategies to advance public health and social change. More specifically, this chapter details the health components of the Black Panther movement as well as the strategies and tactics used during the height of the AIDS epidemic in an effort to conceptualize the meaning of public health in society and how that meaning has changed over time. In doing so, it advances three central arguments: 1) social movements effect change for a variety of shared issues and concerns, and pub-lic relations provides a set of tools to strategically enact such change; 2) social movements help protect and advance public health as a form of physical, mental and social well-being; and 3) we must understand history to understand current

DOI: 10.4324/9781003327189-10

social movements and embrace a broader conceptualization of public relations. This chapter will conclude with definitions, key takeaways, discussion questions, and suggested readings that help prepare readers to be strategic communicators in the ever-changing field of public relations. Using the tools provided at the end of this chapter, readers should be able to clearly articulate the definition of social movements and develop actionable skills that enable them to participate in health advocacy and activism towards behavior change and social progress.

Conceptualizing Social Movements

Before we begin to define and conceptualize social movements, it is important to understand all that they encompass. We do this by tracing where the phrase social movements stems from. The study of social movements is centrally situated in three main areas: rhetorical studies, mediated communication, and public relations. By exploring the research/literature in these three areas, we can develop an understanding of social movements' organizational structure, appreciate their social aspects by viewing them as networks, and acknowledge how they have evolved with advancing media and technology. Social movement scholar Lucas (1980) suggested that "social movements arise out of and are shaped by" forces such as "objective material conditions, rhetorical discourse, and the perceptions, attitudes, and values" that participants share (p. 263). Continuing with the idea of networks, Diani (1992), another social movement scholar, contended that social movements are "networks of informal interactions between a plurality of individuals, groups, and/or organizations, engaged in political or cultural conflicts, on the basis of shared collective identities" (p. 1). Four very important aspects of social movements emerge from these definitions: "a) networks of informal interaction; b) shared beliefs and solidarity; c) collective action on conflictual issues; d) action which displays largely outside the institutional sphere and the routine procedures of social life" (Diani, 1992, p. 7).

It is easy to think of social movements as forms of collective action, but what separates them from other instances of phenomena such as protests, boycotts, and coalitions? In their text, Stewart et al. (2012) made the delineation of social movements from other forms of collective action by proposing that social movements are required to meet six criteria if they are to be classified as such. These criteria include 1) being organized, 2) remaining separate from institutions, 3) being large in scope, 4) promoting or opposing changes in societal norms and values, 5) encountering opposition in moral struggle, and 6) relying primarily on persuasion to bring about or resist change (p. 23). While protests, boycotts, coalitions, and other forms of collective action highlight the ability to mobilize everyday citizens, these occurrences only represent collective action as a visible form. Oftentimes, these instances are only singular in occurrence. Social movements, on the other hand, require much more organization, preparation, strategy, communication, and relationship building. In addition to requiring mobilization and visibility, social movements also require funding and dedicated participation to sustain long-term.

Mediated communication has maintained an essential role throughout the history of social movements. For example, print media such as newspapers reported on the Women's Suffrage Movement and television broadcasted news during the Civil Rights Movement. In this way, media was used as the vehicle to share information with mass audiences, build relationships with potential supporters, and encourage calls to action from their publics. Media became necessary for social movements to scale up by providing reach that would not have been possible through interpersonal communication alone. Media continues to play a pivotal part in social movements today. Specifically, social media have created an opportunity for movement organizers and their participants to reach mass audiences almost instantly, which helps to mobilize direct action in real time. In addition to rapid reach and mobilization, social media have generated a means of connectedness despite spatial and temporal limitations through hashtag usage. Hashtags on social media are used as a way to organize, link, and archive conversations (Kuo, 2018). In addition to hashtags being used for message content and creation, people use them to break communication silos and build relationships and "any participation in the discussion aids the messages' ability to spread quicker and wider across multiple clusters and generate a larger network" (p. 511). By integrating the concepts found in rhetorical studies, public relations and media communication, we can define *social movements* as "an occurrence of collective action, born out of confrontation, and communicatively mobilized to implement change" (Edrington, 2020, p. 27).

So, then, what role does *public relations* play in social movements? While public relations is often framed as a corporate activity, framing it as such misses key elements of its history (Byerly, 1993). Activists and social movement organizations have used and still use public relations for a range of social movement ends (Byerly, 1993; Ciszek, 2015). For instance, Byerly (1993) explains how public relations entangles with activist work in the Suffrage and Women's Rights Movements by strategically organizing events, creating networks of change agents, and banding with other social movements to enact change. Specifically, these activists of the late nineteenth century applied "a coherent strategy to shape public opinion about women's inherent human value and their rights to enjoy the same privileges as their male counterparts" (Byerly, 1993, p. 16). Thus, for the purposes of this chapter, we take on Edwards' (2012) definition of public relations as "the flow of purposive communication" that happens among and between a variety of people and groups within society (p. 21) that is not limited to corporations or even colloquial understandings of organizations. Over time, social movements help effect change for a variety of shared issues and concerns, including those that affect our collective health and wellbeing. Public relations provides a set of tools to enact such change.

Conceptualizing Public Health

Health is considered by many people to be a basic human right (World Health Organization (WHO), 2020; Nelson, 2011). As such, leaders, governments, and public entities are expected to protect the welfare of society, and activists have held society and institutions to those responsibilities. We often use the term *public health* to represent those efforts of an entity (e.g., government body, health system) to promote health within communities, organizations, societies, and even the world. Importantly, contemporary public health aspires to be preventative rather than responsive, seeking to keep people from poor health rather than treat health problems after they arise (Jarvis et al., 2020). The health of a public also involves social determinants of health, which acknowledge that individuals are parts of larger communities and systems that influence their health rather than individual behaviors alone. In other words, "nonmedical and nonbehavioral characteristics" of people's living situations influence their health (Raphael, 2006, p. 651).

This definition of public health brings us to another important question— what is health? While we may think of health as the opposite of illness, there is more to it. Health involves the holistic wellbeing of people in a "physical, mental and social" sense (WHO, 2020, p. 1). Looking at health in such a way means that health involves having safe living conditions, obtaining human and civil rights, preventing violence, among many other seemingly tangential components. Furthermore, health entails the holistic well-being of individuals and their communities, which includes mental and emotional health. While mental health issues have been a major contributor to global disease for decades (Sowers et al., 2009), COVID-19 has thwarted mental well-being for many people and corresponds with increased rates of mental health conditions such as anxiety and depression (Santomauro et al., 2021). Mental health also faces a host of stigma and discrimination related barriers to care. For instance, people may not have access to quality mental health care and institutions have traditionally treated patients in a punitive fashion (Sowers et al., 2009). Thus, realizing comprehensive public health is not an easy task and requires orchestrated efforts from multiple organizations and collectives within society.

The responsibility of public health often falls under the purview of government agencies at a variety of levels (local, state, national, and global), because of its communal and shared nature. In the United States, the Centers for Disease Control and Prevention (CDC) and the National Institutes of Health (NIH) are some of the most well-known and respected public health agencies at the national level; however, local county and state health departments help carry out similar missions. While there are a variety of ways that governments contribute to public health, the Minnesota Department of Health (n.d.) outlines six key areas from its state's legislation that mirror government onus throughout the United States:

(1) assuring an adequate local public health infrastructure, (2) promoting healthy communities and healthy behaviors, (3) preventing the spread of communicable disease, (4) protecting against environmental health hazards, (5) preparing for and responding to emergencies, and (6) assuring health services. *(para. 5)*

Since its 1948 establishment, the World Health Organization (WHO) has built relationships and taken on health issues that challenge humankind globally, including contagious diseases such as smallpox (Tulchinsky & Varavikova, 2014). However, many of the health challenges that people experience today are chronic and non-communicable. For instance, mental health issues, obesity, diabetes, and even climate change comprise some of the most pressing health problems that people and government agencies are faced with today (Tulchinsky & Varavikova, 2014).

The range of public health challenges exemplify how public health, public relations, and social movements are inherently intertwined. First, public relations and social movements help prioritize health issues within society, determining which issues are central to the vitality of the public or group at hand. Second, public relations helps both public health agencies and activists translate those pressing issues into specific strategies, tactics, and messages that can improve health and prevent health issues for populations. For instance, health agencies use media releases, social media, and other communication and relationship building materials to share recent studies, health tips, and other actionable ways people can be informed to make decisions that improve or protect their health. Social movements help ensure that public health is accessible, equitable, and sometimes reimagined to speak to people's lived experiences. Public relations helps public health bodies, "achieve their organizational goals with respect to providing essential health services" (Wise, 2001, p. 477) and the same holds true for social movements. Social movement organizations may use media relations, social media, protests, and collective organizing to draw attention to and promote solutions for a variety of public health problems. While many well-known social movements center racial justice, disability rights, and LGBTQIA rights, often these efforts are intricately interwoven with a variety of health issues because of the interconnections between health and human rights.

Black Panthers and Health Activism

An example that showcases how social movements embody public health includes the activism of the Black Panther Party (BPP) to inspire social change and racial justice. As with other parts of U.S. life, medical treatment and access to health care were segregated in the United States throughout history, and the consequences of such inequity remains today. Much of the United States had separate hospital systems for white and Black communities throughout the 1900s (Smith, 2005). Even though the Civil Rights Act of 1946 showed promise in making health care more equitable and accessible by withholding federal funds from entities that discriminate against people, inequity and implicit segregation still exist (Chandra et al., 2017). A history of slavery, oppression and injustice, implicit bias and stereotyping, and inaccessible or infeasible health services coalesce and continue the lineages of unequal health for Black people. For instance, Black communities typically experience worse maternal health outcomes (Crear-Perry et al., 2021) and higher rates of morbidity/mortality related to communicable diseases such as COVID-19 (Johnson-Agbakwu et al., 2022) than their white counterparts. While these health injustices still challenge our societies today, social movements and activists from both historic and contemporary perspectives have inspired meaningful ideals and social changes.

History and Background of the Black Panther Party

The BPP emerged in the 1960s to resist oppression of Black people in America, and this group took a different approach to civil rights by way of self-protection and an unapologetic push for equality, health, and freedom (Joseph, 2016). As both a political party and a social movement known for its revolutionary tone and controversiality (Joseph, 2016), the Black Panthers resisted police brutality and protected Black communities (Nelson, 2016). Their ways of communicating and building relationships that inspired social change were varied and specific to the geographic and political contexts where different BPP members lived. For instance, they wrote and shared party newspapers, participated in community canvassing, contacted people in their networks to build relationships, organized protests or boycotts, and a host of other creative public relations endeavors to inspire the change they wanted to see and build trust in the communities they wanted to serve (Jennings, 2016; Shih & Williams, 2016).

Ten points comprised their platform in the 1960s, and broadly the BPP demanded essential resources such as employment, food, education, and housing, an end to oppression from the justice system and police, exemption from military service for Black communities, and opportunities to self-govern (National Archives, 2021). While the Ten Point Platform and Program of the 1960s did not use the words "health" or "public health" specifically, its holistic view of human and civil rights incorporated important efforts to look at the various social determinants of health and encourage full agency and support in pursuit of well-being. Over time, the Black Panthers revised its platform to include health as a specific, and explicit, component of its social movement and community activism.

Health as Racial Justice

In an important way, the movement for racial justice was and still is intimately related to health. Nelson (2011) argued that the party faced a "paradox" of health because Black communities were "medically underserved but also overexposed to the worst jeopardies of medical practice and bioscientific research" (p. xii–xiii). Thus, as the movement for racial justice evolved and grew, so did the Black Panthers' mission for health equity. By the 1970s, the Black Panthers had started the People's Free Medical Clinics (PFMC) (Nelson, 2016) and incorporated expectations of health services broadly as "'serve the people'" or "'survival'" programs (Nelson, 2011, p. 52) that were formed to keep Black communities alive by protecting them from racial violence and other injustices. The Black Panthers also engaged in ambulatory services (Waxman & Aneja, 2021), free children's breakfasts, and other community services (Shih & Williams, 2016) that prioritized health as a necessary piece of human rights and a form of activism that supported the larger social movement for racial equity.

Along with providing health services, the group revised its Ten Point Program in 1972 to explicitly include health (Bassett, 2016). The Black Panther Party's (1972) rationale for its health specific points included the following:

> We believe that the government must provide, free of charge, for the people, health facilities which will not only treat our illnesses, most of which have come about as a result of our oppression, but which will also develop preventive medical programs to guarantee our future survival.
>
> *(p. 21; cited by Bassett, 2019)*

Because of the ways in which civil rights and health advocacy intertwine, "the Panther health 'turn' was an extension of the long civil rights movement rather than a strategic about-face" (Nelson, 2011, p. 49). Through its activism, the BPP presented powerful alternatives to national initiatives that they believed would not properly serve Black communities, due to racial bias and oppressive health systems, and they prioritized preventive health, free health care, health literacy, and other health options to replace racist health institutions (Nelson, 2011, 2016).

The work to secure civil and human rights for Black communities is not over and the legacy of the Black Panthers lives on for future generations. As Bassett (2019) explained, although the Black Panther Party dissolved in the early 1980s, "it popularized a set of beliefs that identified health as a social justice issue for Blacks and the poor that has influenced public health to this day," and Black Lives Matter echoes related demands for change (p. 361). In summary, the Black Panthers represent a revolutionary political and social movement that explicitly integrated not only traditional forms of health activism and advocacy but also community services and innovative alternatives to inspire social change.

ACT UP and AIDS Activism

Public Relations Efforts in the Past for Venereal Diseases

In the United States, public relations strategies and tactics have been used widely to share information as it relates to sexually transmitted diseases. For example, the American Social Hygiene Association (ASHA) partnered with the Commission on Training Camp Activities (CTCA) during World War I to implement an anti-venereal disease campaign. The purpose of this campaign was to "educate recruits and soldiers about the new social ideal for manhood" (Anderson, 2017, p. 511) through the use of pamphlets, posters, film, and the vilification of disease carriers. Again, in the 1930s during the Great Depression, U.S. Surgeon General Thomas Parran Jr. implemented a public health education campaign on venereal diseases such as syphilis and gonorrhea. During this campaign, Parran used persuasive communication, brochures, and media relations to "generate awareness of the dangers of VD, ameliorate the social stigma associated with those diseases, and receive more funding for VD control" (Anderson, 2018, p. 63). Later, governmental and health officials used some of these same strategies and tactics to inform the public about the AIDS epidemic of the 1980s. However, information shared at that time was often not timely or completely accurate causing panic and misinformation. This prompted grassroots efforts from activist groups such as the AIDS Coalition to Unleash Power (ACT UP). Participants in organizations such as ACT UP that formed the AIDS movement were "broad based and diverse, ranging from grassroots activists and advocacy organizations to health educators, journalists, writers, service providers, people with AIDS or HIV infection and other members of the affected communities" (Epstein, 1995, p. 413).

Overview of the AIDS Pandemic at Its Height in the 1980s

AIDS was first said to have appeared in the United States in the early 1980s. Before being identified as acquired immunodeficiency syndrome (AIDS), doctors reported cases of strange pneumonia and rare skin cancer in gay men. By the end of 1981, over 100 gay men had died from this disease. Given the name AIDS in 1982, the information shared publicly about this disease was mainly geared towards gay men (Geiling, 2013). Because the disease was initially attributed to a certain community, little media attention and information to others were given causing those with AIDS to be stigmatized. This in fact led to misinformation that AIDS could only be contracted by gay men engaging in sexual acts (Geiling, 2013). The first few years of the AIDS epidemic were also met with a lack of institutional response. According to AIDS activist Monica B. Pearl (2021), "homophobia—and its many attendant aversions—made the AIDS epidemic" (p. 217). It wasn't until infants and people with hemophilia were reported to have the disease that Americans began to panic (CDC, 2021). The realization that people other than the gay male population could contract this disease increased media attention and educational efforts. In 1982 historical writer Natasha Geiling (2013) notes, "two gay men living with AIDS in New York City, published *How to Have Sex in an Epidemic*, which helped spread the idea that safe sex could be used as protection against spreading the epidemic—an idea that hadn't yet become prevalent in the medical community" (para. 5). Soon after, the government and many health organizations began releasing information through posters and educational campaigns to combat the confusion and anxiety that many Americans faced. In 1986, then U.S. Surgeon General, C. Everett Koop, issued his report on AIDS where he advocated for the widespread use of condoms and sex/AIDS education campaigns (Specter, 1987). However, grassroots activist groups and organizations felt this information was a little too late and still, not enough.

ACT UP Organization Strategies and Tactics Used by This Organization

Founded in 1987, ACT UP emerged "with a primary focus on advocating for changes in the processes of scientific investigation, drug development, and regulatory procedures that would make it possible to more rapidly develop new treatment options" (Parker, 2011, p. 25). According to ACT UP's (n.d.) website,

> ACT UP—the AIDS Coalition to Unleash Power—is a diverse, non-partisan group of individuals, united in anger and committed to direct action to end the AIDS crisis. We meet with government officials, we distribute the latest medical information, we protest and demonstrate. We are not silent.

The organization focused, and continues to focus, on three main areas of advocacy: 1) research for new medicines and AIDS/HIV treatments, 2) prevention and care access for all, and 3) dismantling institutionalized discrimination, stigmas, and poverty (ACT UP, n.d.). To do this, the organization used(s) several public relations strategies and tactics. The members of ACT UP were very cohesive, despite their many differences (race, diagnosis, sexuality, gender, etc.). The agenda was simple: end the AIDS crisis. Meetings were planned and ideas strategically thought out to make the biggest impact. Activist Sarah Schulman (2021) recalls ACT UP creating solutions to the problem that the government couldn't or wouldn't solve. She writes, "ACT UP became the experts on their issues, creating reasonable, winnable and doable solutions. ACT UP then presented them to the authorities" (para. 9). As an action-based organization, ACT UP members employed fundraising efforts such as selling t-shirts and artwork. The funds raised then went on to help the organization and its members perform efforts such as condom distribution and other educational campaigns. They also distributed information via various forms of accessible media. Social movement strategies and tactics were also used to make a statement. Some of these social movement strategies came from members who were already members of other social movements. With their knowledge and learned tactics, they were able to leverage their social capital and help guide other members in the creation of highly visible demonstrations (Schulman, 2021). Rabkin et. al. (2018) highlights that "ACT UP was loud; it was confrontational; it was effective" (p. 2). Members used the media to their advantage, often crossing social and cultural boundaries through activities such as speaking openly about sexual orientation and anal sex and attending public (and some private) events like mass at the Catholic Church and the Republican National Convention with banners. They also participated in protests and marches. Some of ACT UP's most remarkable achievements during the peak of their activity were summarized by Jolly (2022) as:

- changing the FDA's drug approval process
- compiling and disseminating lifesaving information in clear and accessible form
- challenging the exclusion of women from experimental drug trials
- advocating for clean needle exchange
- pushing the CDC to revise its definition of the disease in order to include the symptoms faced by women
- and creating social services for people who did not have family networks or who were excluded by the AIDS surveillance definition

(p. 171)

ACT UP represents an action-based organization that used both public relations and social movement strategies and tactics to educate and advocate. The fight to end the AIDS epidemic is still not over, as evidenced by ACT UP still being a very active organization.

Intersections of Black Panther Party and ACT UP Social Movements

There are obvious differences between the social movements explained in this chapter. For instance, BPP was/is not often framed as a health movement, while ACT UP had/has an explicit focus that speaks to colloquial notions of health. Each movement's activism privileged different marginalized groups. Furthermore,

ACT UP still exists today and continues its work through a range of actions such as protests, partnering with other activist organizations (e.g., GLAAD), and garnering attention from the media and society about injustices (Aaron, 2023). The BPP does not exist today as it once did but lives on through new manifestations, such as Black Lives Matter (Basset, 2019).

However, there are also important points where these social movements and their activism overlap to complement the arguments we have made thus far. In both cases, health was imperative to the underlying human rights issues that activists and their movements strived to uphold (ACT UP, n.d.; Nelson, 2011) because opportunities for freedom, acceptance, and justice are meaningless without the requisite health and wellbeing to enjoy such liberation. Both movements attack deep, historic oppressions that are interconnected. The consequences of injustices such as racism, incarceration, and inequitable health care mean that Black Americans grapple with HIV/AIDS disproportionately to other groups in the United States (CDC, 2017; Lewis & Boykin, 2021). Both movements also made tangible changes and offered real-world alternatives for communities in need of quality services and essential resources. Lastly, both social movements relied on a variety of public relations and communication tools to enact change, build solidarity, and articulate the shape of the society they imagined.

Conclusion

Social movements have a profound effect on how we understand and communicate about our health and vice-versa. This chapter explicated the important relationships between social movements, collective health and well-being, and the role that strategic communication plays in advancing social change and health topics. To achieve this, it reviewed the many elements of social movements to provide a concrete understanding and definition of the term, conceptualized public health, and presented two case studies of social movements to highlight strategic communication and relationship-building strategies used to advance public health and social change. Three central arguments are woven through this chapter: 1) social movements effect change for a variety of shared issues and concerns, including those that affect our collective health and well-being, and public relations provides a set of tools to strategically enact such change; 2) social movements help protect and advance public health as a form of physical, mental, and social well-being; and 3) we must understand history to understand current social movements and embrace a broader conceptualization of public relations. The Black Panther Party and the ACT UP organization during the AIDS epidemic exemplified the inextricability of public health and social movements. Ultimately, this chapter provides readers with the information and tools to equip them for debates and action for health-related social change efforts.

Key Definitions

Public relations: "the flow of purposive communication" that happens among and between a variety of people and groups within society (Edwards, 2012, p. 21)

Social movements: an occurrence of collective action, born out of confrontation, and communicatively mobilized to implement change.

Public health: efforts of an entity or institution to promote health within communities, organizations, societies, and around the globe.

Discussion Questions

1. How might we differentiate between social movements and other forms of collective action?
2. What role does public relations play in advancing social change?
3. In what ways do you see social movements integrating health topics? Provide examples that you have seen or see in your daily life.
4. How did your perception of the Black Panthers change by reading this chapter, if at all?
5. Think about the social movements of today. What are some of the public relations strategies and tactics used in these movements?

Further Reading

Diani, M. (1992). The concept of social movement. *The Sociological Review*, *40*(1), 1–25. https://doi.org/10.111/j.1467-954X.1192.tb02943.x.

McKeever, B. W. (2021). Public relations and public health: The importance of leadership and other lessons learned from "Understanding AIDS" in the 1980s. *Public Relations Review, 47*, 1–9. https://doi.org/10.1016/j.pubrev.2020.102007

Nelson, A. (2011). *Body and soul: The Black Panther Party and the fight against medical discrimination*. University of Minnesota Press.

References

Aaron, D. (2023). GLAAD, ACT UP NY unite in protest at Simon & Schuster headquarters over AIDS denialism book release. GLAAD. https://glaad.org/glaad-act-ny-unite-protest-simon-schuster-headquarters-over-aids-denialism-book-release/

ACT UP. (n.d.). About. ACT UP. https://actupny.com/contact/

Anderson, W. B. (2017). The great war against venereal disease: How the government used PR to wage an anti-vice campaign. *Public Relations Review*, *43*, 507–516. https://doi.org/10.1016/j.pubrev.2017.03.003

Anderson, W. B. (2018). The next plague to go: How the U.S. Surgeon General used public relations to fight venereal disease during the Great Depression. *Journalism History*, *44*(2), 63–69. https://doi.org/10.1080/00947679.2018.12059195

Bassett, M. T. (2016). Beyond berets: The Black Panthers as health activists. *American Journal of Public Health*, *106*(10), 1741–1743. https://doi.org/10.2105/AJPH.2016.303412

Bassett, M.T. (2019). No Justice, No Health: The Black Panther Party's fight for health in Boston and beyond. *Journal of African American Studies*, *23*, 352–363. https://doi. org/10.1007/s12111-019-09450-w

Black Panther Party. (1972). People's free medical research and health clinics. In D. Hillard (Ed.), *The Black Panther Party: Service to the People Programs* (pp. 21–23). University of New Mexico Press.

Brown, T., & Fee, L. (2014). Social movements in health. *Annual Review of Public Health*, *35*, 385–398. https://doi.org/10.1146/annurev-publhealth-031912-114356

Byerly, C. M. (1993, August 11–14). Toward a comprehensive history of public relations. [Conference presentation]. Annual Meeting of the Association for Education in Journalism and Mass Communication, Kansas City, MO, United States. https://files.eric. ed.gov/fulltext/ED361812.pdf

Centers for Disease Control and Prevention (2017, February 2). CDC fact sheet: HIV among African Americans. https://www.cdc.gov/nchhstp/newsroom/docs/factsheets/ cdc-hiv-aa-508.pdf

Centers for Disease Control and Prevention. (2021, March 26). The AIDS epidemic in the United States, 1981–early 1990s. David J. Sencer CDC Museum. https://www.cdc. gov/museum/online/story-of-cdc/aids/index.html

Chandra, A., Frakes, M., & Malani, A. (2017). Challenges to reducing discrimination and health inequity through existing civil rights laws. *Health Affairs (Project Hope)*, *36*(6), 1041–1047. https://doi.org/10.1377/hlthaff.2016.1091

Ciszek, E. L. (2015). Bridging the gap: Mapping the relationship between activism and public relations. *Public Relations Review*, *41*, 447–455. https://doi.org/10.1016/j. pubrev.2015.05.016

Crear-Perry, J., Correa-de-Araujo, R., Johnson, T. L., McLemore, M. R., Neilson, E., & Wallace, M. (2021). Social and structural determinants of health inequities in maternal health. *Journal of Women's Health*, *30*(20), 230–235. http://doi.org/10.1089/ jwh.2020.8882

Diani, M. (1992). The concept of social movement. *The Sociological Review*, *40*(1), 1–25. https://doi.org/10.111/j.1467-954X.1192.tb02943.x.

Edrington, C. L. (2020). Identification and relationships: How social movements use and articulate identification across digital platforms to build relationships [Doctoral dissertation. North Carolina State University]. NCSU Campus Repository. https://repository. lib.ncsu.edu/bitstream/handle/1840.20/37347/etd.pdf?sequence=1

Edwards, L. (2012). Defining the 'object' of public relations research: A new starting point. *Public Relations Inquiry*, *1*(1), 7–30. https://doi.org/10.1177/2046147X114 22149

Epstein, S. (1995). The construction of lay expertise: AIDS activism and the forging of credibility in the reform of clinical trials. *Science, Technology, & Human Values*, *20*(4), 408–437.

Geiling, N. (2013, December 4). The confusing and at-times counterproductive 1980s response to the AIDS epidemic. *Smithsonian Magazine*. https://www.smithsonianmag. com/history/the-confusing-and-at-times-counterproductive-1980s-response-to-the- aids-epidemic-180948611/

Jarvis, T., Scott, F., El-Jardali, F., & Alvarez, E. (2020). Defining and classifying public health systems: a critical interpretive synthesis. Health research policy and systems, *18*(1), 68. https://doi.org/10.1186/s12961-020-00583-z

Jennings, B. X. (2016). Block-by-block, door to door: Building community support by serving the people—Billy X Jennings. In B. Shih & Y. Williams, *The Black Panthers: Portraits from an unfinished revolution* (pp. 112–117). Nation Books.

Johnson-Agbakwu, C. E., Ali, N. S., Oxford, C. M., Wingo, S., Manin, E., & Coonrod, D. V. (2022). Racism, COVID-19, and health inequity in the USA: A call to action. *Journal of Racial and Ethnic Health Disparities*, *9(*1), 52–58. https://doi.org/10.1007/ s40615-020-00928-y

Jolly, J. (2022). Theorizing agency: New directions in research on HIV/AIDS activism. *American Quarterly*, *74*(1), 169–180. https://doi.org/10.1353/aq.2022.0008

Joseph, P. E. (2016). Introduction: The Black Panthers and Black power. In B. Shih & Y. Williams, *The Black Panthers: Portraits from an unfinished revolution* (pp. 1–7). Nation Books.

Kuo, R. (2018). Racial justice activist hashtags: Counterpublics and discourse circulation. *New Media & Society*, *20*(2), 495–514. https://doi.org/10.1177/14614448 16663485

Lewis, T. J., & Boykin, M. (2021). We the People: A Black strategy to end the HIV epidemic in the United States of America. *Journal of Healthcare, Science and the Humanities*, *11*(1), 173–192. https://www.ncbi.nlm.nih.gov/pmc/articles/ PMC9930506/#b3-jhsh-11-173

Lucas, S. E. (1980). Coming to terms with movement studies. *Central States Speech Journal*, *31*(4) 255–266. https://doi.org/10.1080/10510978009368065

Minnesota Department of Health. (n.d.). Government's responsibility for public health. https://www.health.state.mn.us/communities/practice/resources/chsadmin/mnsystem-responsibility.html

National Archives. (2021, March 22). African American heritage: The Black Panther Party. https://www.archives.gov/research/african-americans/black-power/black-panthers# bpintro

Nelson, A. (2011). *Body and soul: The Black Panther Party and the fight against medical discrimination.* University of Minnesota Press.

Nelson, A. (2016). The longue durée of Black Lives Matter. *American Journal of Public Health*, *106* (10), 1734–1737. https://doi.org/10.2105/AJPH.2016.303422

Parker, R. (2011). Grassroots activism, civil society mobilization, and the politics of the global HIV/AIDS epidemic. *The Brown Journal of World Affairs*, *17*(2), 21–37. https://www.jstor.org/stable/24590789

Pearl, M. B. (2021). A thousand kindred spirits: Reflections on AIDS activism and representations of AIDS in US culture and conversation. *Radical History Review*, *140*, 217–225. https://doi.org/10.1215/01636545-8841814

Rabkin, J. G., McElhiney, M. C., Harrington, M., & Horn, T. (2018). Trauma and growth: Impact of AIDS activism. *AIDS Research and Treatment*, *2018*, 1–11. https://doi. org/10.1155/2018/9696725

Raphael, D. (2006). Social determinants of health: Present status, unanswered questions, and future directions. *International Journal of Health Services*, *36(4)*, 651–677. https://doi.org/10.2190/3MW4-1EK3-DGRQ-2CRF

Santomauro, D. F., Mantilla Herrera, A. M., Shadid, J., Zheng, P., Ashbaugh, C., Pigott, D. M., Abbafati, C., Adolph, C., Amlag, J. O., Aravkin, A. Y., Bang-Jensen, B. L., Bertolacci, G. J., Bloom, S. S., Castellano, R., Castro, E., Chakrabarti, S., Chattopadhyay, J., Cogen, R. M., Collins, J. K., . . . Ferrari, A. J. (2021). Global prevalence and burden of depressive and anxiety disorders in 204 countries and territories in 2020 due to the COVID-19 pandemic. *The Lancet*, *398*(10312), 1700–1712. https://doi. org/10.1016/S0140-6736(21)02143-7

Schulman, S. (2021, June 8). What ACT UP's successes can teach today's protest movements. *The Guardian.* https://www.theguardian.com/commentisfree/2021/jun/08/ act-up-protest-movements-us-direct-action

Shih, B. & Williams, Y. (2016). *The Black Panthers: Portraits from an unfinished revolution.* Nation Books.

Smith, D. B. (2005). The politics of racial disparities: Desegregating the hospitals in Jackson, Mississippi. *The Milbank Quarterly*, *83*(2), 247–269. https://doi. org/10.1111/j.1468-0009.2005.00346.x

Sowers, K. M., Rowe, W. S., & Clay, J. R. (2009). The intersection between physical health and mental health: A global perspective. *Journal of Evidence-based Social Work*, *6*(1), 111–126. https://doi.org/10.1080/15433710802633734

Specter, M. (1987, October 13). Koop asks doctors to back condom use. *The Washington Post*. https://www.washingtonpost.com/archive/politics/1987/10/13/koop-asks-doctors-to-back-condom-use/6c75afbf-5765-4632-b074-51c89a138754/

Stewart, C. J., Smith, C. A., & Denton, R. E. (2012). *Persuasion and social movements*. Long Grove, IL: Waveland Press.

Tulchinsky, T. H., & Varavikova, E. A. (2014). *The new public health*. https://doi.org/10.1016/B978-0-12-415766-8.00001-X

Waxman, O. B., & Aneja, A. (2021, February 25). What school didn't teach you about the Black Panthers. *TIME*. https://time.com/5937647/black-panther-medical-clinics-history-school-covid-19/

Wise, K. (2001). Opportunities for public relations research in public health. *Public Relations Review, 27*(4), 475–487. https://doi.org/10.1016/S0363-8111(01)00102-3

World Health Organization. (2020). Basic documents: forty-ninth edition (including amendments adopted up to 31 May 2019). Geneva: World Health Organization. https://apps.who.int/gb/bd/pdf_files/BD_49th-en.pdf#page=6

PART 3
Places and Spaces

9

NONPROFIT ORGANIZATIONS

A Force for Good

Brooke W. McKeever

In 2022, U.S. nonprofit organizations received more than $499 billion in donations. Much of this goes to religious and educational organizations, including churches and colleges and universities, some of which are considered nonprofit, but following those two categories, a great deal of funding goes toward health-related nonprofit organizations. Approximately $51 billion went to health organizations in 2022, providing support for nonprofit health facilities, specific diseases, disorders, or conditions, and scientific research for medical prevention and treatment options or cures (Giving USA Foundation, 2023). Healthcare has been called the most resource-intensive domain of U.S. nonprofit activity (Schlesinger & Gray, 2006). The health industry is also where many of the largest nonprofit organizations, including nonprofit hospitals, are located. Nonprofit health organizations are vital in our society, providing "the necessary funding for biomedical research, free from federal, state and institutional politics, to not only save lives and improve health, but also lower health care costs" (Kiessling, 2008, p. 5). Simply put, nonprofit health organizations and health-related philanthropy save lives (Falk, 2005).

This chapter focuses on nonprofit organizations as a place where public relations and other forms of strategic communication are carried out to benefit both public health and other forms of social good. Almost every cause you can think of has nonprofit organizations associated with it. These organizations raise awareness and money, provide services, and often engage in advocacy or activism related to their cause. As Frumkin (2002) noted, one of the key features that differentiates nonprofit organizations is that they are voluntary. This does not mean that everyone working for nonprofit organizations is a volunteer, of course. Nonprofit organizations have paid staff, and you can make a living

DOI: 10.4324/9781003327189-12

working in the nonprofit industry. What it does mean, however, is that a lot of the funding and work contributed to help make nonprofits successful are given and done voluntarily. Nonprofits are dependent upon volunteers (in addition to staff) to carry out their work and provide services; they are also dependent upon donations to fulfill their mission. Most nonprofits would not exist without donations from the public or from their many stakeholders, and much of the work they do could not happen without volunteers. Because of this, relationship building and communication are key. In fact, one could argue that public relations is *more important* for nonprofit organizations than for other entities. Think about it: you could go your entire life without ever giving to or volunteering with a nonprofit. However, you could not go through life without engaging with corporations or government entities. We have to buy products, like food, clothing, and shoes. We also have to pay taxes and for water and other goods that come from local government entities. However, one does not have to volunteer or donate to a nonprofit. Thankfully, many do, but the voluntary nature of nonprofits is what makes them so dependent upon the goodwill of others, and this goodwill is often because of relationship-building, communication, and storytelling done by nonprofits.

Of course, nonprofits are partially dependent upon economic conditions. In 2008–2009, during the Great Recession, donations to nonprofit organizations declined. Contributions to the largest nonprofit organizations decreased by 11 percent in 2009, the largest drop the industry had seen in 20 years (Poole, 2010). The 2022 statistics from Giving USA show a decrease in giving as well, although there were many years of increases in giving in between these two time periods. In 2022, nonprofits saw a 3.4 percent decline in giving over 2021; however, adjusted for inflation, total giving declined by 10.5 percent. The COVID-19 pandemic and the highest rates of inflation in 40 years, which came in the pandemic's wake, meant that individuals had less disposable income to contribute to nonprofit organizations (Biever, 2023).

Nonprofit health organizations provide not only treatment, but also important support programs for patients and their families. They fund vital research that may not be conducted otherwise, and they engage in advocacy efforts that help change social, economic, political, and environmental factors affecting health. Wallack et al. (1993) and others have described these factors as the "upstream" elements that influence the health of people "downstream." Research suggests that these broad, upstream efforts to improve public health may be more effective than those focused on health behavior change of individuals downstream, and communication campaigns should focus on larger social, political, and economic conditions to create healthier environments (Cho & Salmon, 2007; Niederdeppe, 2009). In other words, upstream influences need to be connected to downstream conditions to improve public health. Nonprofit health organizations help make these connections, illuminating causes for problems through advocacy and communication, and raising funds to provide research, treatment, and other solutions for important health problems.

Advocacy and Fundraising: Elements of Nonprofit Success

Advocacy and fundraising are two ways nonprofit organizations work to improve public health, influence social change, and support public good. Both concepts, and the various strategies involved in each, are essential to carry out nonprofit organizations' missions and serve constituents' needs. Of course, communication with various publics is essential to advocacy and fundraising efforts. Without mobilizing key stakeholders, advocacy and fundraising would not be possible, and nonprofit organizations' efforts to improve public health or influence social change would be fruitless. This chapter explores advocacy, fundraising, and communication related to nonprofits because, as mentioned, these are key elements supporting the success of many nonprofits.

McCarthy and Castelli (2002) described nonprofit organizational advocacy as collective action aimed at influencing public policy. Much like upstream and downstream efforts to improve public health, nonprofit advocacy can be divided into two categories: direct and indirect advocacy. The authors explain: "Organizations may operate through a wide array of direct advocacy strategies aimed at shaping public opinion and policy, but they may also operate indirectly, through the mobilization of advocacy by individual citizens" (p. 104). When citizens are encouraged to participate in an organization's advocacy activities as individuals, rather than as formal representatives of the organization, the tactics are referred to as grassroots lobbying, indirect advocacy (Hrebenar, 1997; McCarthy & Castelli, 2002), or more commonly in recent years, grassroots advocacy.

Indirect or grassroots advocacy is often carried out though routine contact between organizations and their stakeholders (e.g., donors, volunteers), and it is successful when citizens directly, yet seemingly independently, build constituencies that apply pressure to bring about change in favor of their issue or position (McCarthy & Castelli, 2002). Similarly, Palfrey (2006) described the importance of group advocacy (i.e., the bringing together of different stakeholders for one purpose or cause), which can be effective for increasing health or social funding because "policymakers and philanthropists often respond positively to appeals for financial support to resolve particular, well-defined, categorical problems" (p. 12). This approach is how many nonprofit health and social organizations operate, through grassroots and/or group advocacy and fundraising that mobilizes multiple constituents around a health or social issue. Indeed, some of the tactics that fall under the umbrella of advocacy include activities practiced by many nonprofit organizations, including grassroots organizing and mobilization of volunteers, lobbying, mass communication campaigns, media relations—and fundraising (McKeever, 2013; McKeever et al., 2016; Wallack et al., 1993).

Nonprofit Philanthropy and Fundraising

As part of the "upstream" approach to influencing public health or social change, philanthropy and fundraising are essential to nonprofit organizations and are important but often overlooked components of nonprofit advocacy efforts. Although advocacy and philanthropy are separate concepts, nonprofit organizations rely on both strategies, and it could be argued that they are related and equally integral parts of a nonprofit organization's efforts to improve public health or to influence social change. Fundraising is a function of philanthropy, and both are crucial to the health of nonprofit organizations.

Fundraising has been described as "an organizational function unique to that sector of our democratic society alternatively referred to as nonprofit, voluntary or independent" (Kelly, 1998, p. 1). While Kelly's definition is more than 25 years old, it applies today, and while fundraising tactics have changed dramatically over the years, the importance of fundraising remains stable for nonprofits. Fundraising involves "soliciting financial support and is an essential way for most nonprofits to bring in revenue for their organization's mission" (*Nonprofit Quarterly*, 2017, para. 1). However, as noted by the editors of *Nonprofit Quarterly* (2017, para. 1): "Fundraising is about so much more than just asking for money. It also consists of ways for charitable organizations to build relationships, bring in foundation support, and attract new donors." Fundraising is part of the broader term and function of "development," which can include research, institutional planning, and more (Drozdowski, 2003).

It has been argued that fundraising and philanthropy are necessary for providing many of the services people rely upon in the U.S., particularly as many public needs previously fulfilled by government entities are now (since the late 1980s/early 1990s) provided by nonprofit organizations (Boris & Steuerle, 2006; Clemens, 2006; Hall, 2006a). Increasingly, nonprofit organizations are working with corporate and government entities to raise funds and provide services to the public (Frumkin, 2002; Galaskiewicz & Colman, 2006). However, the majority of nonprofit contributions still come from individuals (64 percent), rather than foundations (21 percent) and corporations (6 percent) (Giving USA Foundation, 2023). Thus, the necessity of fundraising in the U.S. has been described this way: "Fundraising is an essential part of American philanthropy; in turn, philanthropy—as voluntary action for the public good—is essential to American democracy" (Rosso, 1991, p. 4). As noted, the healthcare industry includes multiple nonprofit entities that rely on fundraising. In these instances, the generosity or philanthropy expressed through fundraising ultimately helps nonprofit health organizations provide services to the sick, information to those in need, and research into illnesses with ineffective treatment options, vaccines, or cures. In this way, nonprofit organizations are vital to public health.

Types of Nonprofit Organizations

It is important to note that the nonprofit sector works differently outside of the U.S., and in fact most of the world does not refer to "nonprofit" organizations but rather "nongovernmental" organizations or NGOs. The term nongovernmental organization originated with the United Nations to differentiate between government bodies and mission-driven or service-oriented organizations in the nonprofit sector (Harvard Law School, 2022). NGOs are a type of nonprofit organization, and most international or multinational nonprofit organizations are NGOs. NGOs can operate in the U.S. and abroad, and foreign NGOs can operate in the U.S., if they file through the Internal Revenue Service (IRS) as a nonprofit organization (U.S. Department of State, 2021). There are also multiple types of nonprofit or charitable organizations, according to the IRS, based on federal tax obligations and exempt status. For more information, visit the IRS website.

One of the most common types of nonprofit organizations in the U.S. is a 501(c)3 organization, because these organizations are considered tax-exempt under section 501(c)3 of the Internal Revenue Code. Such organizations "may not attempt to influence legislation as a substantial part of its activities and may not participate in any campaign activity for or against political candidates" (IRS, 2023, para. 1). However, some 501(c)3 organizations that seek to influence legislation as part of their mission form separate organizations to participate in such efforts. An example in the health sector is the American Cancer Society (ACS) and its Cancer Action Network (ACS CAN). The ACS is a 501(c)3, while the ACS CAN is a 501(c)4 organization according to the IRS, which means it can participate in legislative advocacy efforts. According to its website, the federal government is the largest funder of medical research in the U.S.; thus, lobbying Congress to increase funding to support cancer research is an important part of the work of organizations like ACS CAN (2023). The fact that mammograms and other cancer screenings are covered by medical insurance is because of the work of organizations like ACS CAN; tobacco control policies and other legislative issues have also been influenced by advocacy efforts on the part of nonprofit organizations over the years (ACS CAN, 2023).

Nonprofits Benefiting Public Health

Nonprofit organizations have made real differences in helping people in myriad ways; some have made a difference in terms of health outcomes. St. Jude Children's Research Hospital is a nonprofit hospital in Memphis, Tennessee. The hospital has affiliate clinics in other locations, and it conducts research on multiple forms of pediatric cancer, pediatric HIV, sickle cell disease, and other illnesses affecting children. The hospital opened in 1962, and since that time, its focus on acute lymphoblastic leukemia (ALL), the most common form of childhood cancer, has led to a 94 percent survival rate for patients diagnosed with ALL (St. Jude, 2023a). St. Jude has been able to make such strides because of tremendous public support, which has been cultivated over years of stewardship and fundraising programs. In St. Jude's case, it does not hurt that they have also been the beneficiaries of support from numerous celebrities (Weberling, 2010). The funds raised have led to more facilities being built to treat more patients, more researchers being hired to conduct investigations into more illnesses, and more sharing and translation of research to other hospitals and doctors around the world.

In recent years, St. Jude has gotten involved in promoting vaccination for the human papilloma virus (HPV), which causes six types of cancer in both men and women. HPV vaccination is recommended for everyone, aged 9–26 years, yet it has not been part of routine school vaccinations. Misinformation and myths surrounding the HPV vaccine (among other vaccines) have led to some people forgoing vaccinations. As a leader in researching and treating various forms of cancer, St. Jude aimed to increase vaccination rates to help prevent some forms of cancer. The organization created the Path to a Bright Future campaign, to increase public awareness and ultimately increase on-time HPV vaccination. Through a combination of this campaign, community interventions (particularly in rural areas or other places where HPV vaccination rates are lower), and public policy and advocacy work, St. Jude is aiming to increase HPV vaccine uptake and help meet the goal put forth by the national Healthy People plan of having 80 percent of the eligible population vaccinated against HPV by 2030 (St. Jude, 2023b).

Of course, St. Jude is just one of many nonprofit hospitals and organizations working to improve public health. There are also nonprofit foundations, associations, and other types of organizations working to improve health outcomes. For example, de Beaumont foundation has a mission "to advance policy, build partnerships, and strengthen public health to create communities where people can achieve their best possible health" (de Beaumont, 2023a). By working with associations such as the American Public Health Association (APHA), foundations like de Beaumont leverage research, expertise, and funding to support major public health initiatives. For instance, in 2020 and 2021, de Beaumont partnered with an individual pollster named Frank Luntz and a data intelligence company called Morning Consult to develop a series of polls and focus groups to identify the messaging and language most likely to build support for public health measures and confidence in COVID-19 vaccines (de Beaumont, 2023b). They created the Changing the COVID Conversation page on their website as a repository for this information and share(d) the information freely with the numerous individuals and organizations that were trying to understand and communicate about this issue during the height of and since the onset of the COVID-19 pandemic (de Beaumont, 2023b).

Nonprofits Benefiting Social Change

Other nonprofit organizations lead or help organize social change movements, some of which also affect public health. Gun violence is an issue that has seen a lot of activity in recent years. In America, deaths by gun violence have reached record numbers. In 2021, more Americans died of gun-related injuries than in any other year on record (thus far), according to data from the Centers for Disease Control and Prevention (CDC). Almost 50,000 people died from gun-related injuries that year, including murder, suicides, accidental shootings, mass shootings, and more (Gramlich, 2023). This is not a new problem in America, of course, but it is one that has gained more recognition and momentum in recent years in terms of media advocacy, awareness, and policy-related efforts. This momentum is thanks in part to nonprofit organizations.

Some of the organizations involved in this movement include Everytown for Gun Safety, March for our Lives, Moms Demand Action, and more. These organizations were born out of various groups of people who were tired of gun violence incidents. For example, Everytown for Gun Safety is a combined movement of what initially started as a group called Mayors Against Illegal Guns, founded in 2006, and Moms Demand Action, a nonprofit founded in 2012 by stay-at-home mom Shannon Watts in response to the Sandy Hook Elementary School shooting that took place in Newtown, Connecticut (Everytown for Gun Safety, 2023). Everytown for Gun Safety formed in 2013 and, as of 2023, the group had almost 10 million supporters. The group works to combine research, policy, litigation, grassroots advocacy, and more to try to prevent more gun violence. Its website tracks changes that have taken place over time, thanks in part to some of the work done by this and other organizations and individuals (Everytown for Gun Safety, 2023).

March for Our Lives is a youth-led movement and organization started after the shooting at Marjory Stoneman Douglas High School in Parkland, Florida. After the shooting, which took place on February 14, 2018, students and others affected by the school shotting organized the largest single day of protest against gun violence in history and subsequently worked to register new voters. According to the organization's website, there was a 47 percent increase in youth voter turnout in the 2018 midterm election (over the last midterm election), and that was the highest percentage of youth voter turnout in history. The website summarizes the results of that election: "Voters made it clear that the status quo was no longer acceptable—a record 46 NRA-backed candidates lost their elections that November" (March for Our Lives, 2023). Organizations like Everytown and

March use many public relations tactics to communicate their mission to the public, and because they are nonprofit organizations, they use advocacy, fundraising, and rely on the support of volunteers, donors, advocates, media, and more to build and maintain support for their mission.

Gun violence is a public health and social change issue around which we are seeing media advocacy. Other nonprofit organizations such as the American Public Health Association have acknowledged the extreme effects gun violence is having on society at large, and mainstream and legacy media such as *The New York Times*, *The Washington Post*, and *Fortune* magazine have written about gun violence as a public health crisis (McKeever et al., 2022). This type of media attention makes people aware of the issue and helps change the framing of the issue, which eventually changes the conversation and sometimes inspires legislation or other real-world consequences that can help quell the problem. Recent research has investigated social media advocacy strategies that might help nonprofit organizations better communicate about the issue of gun violence and highlights the importance of individuals amplifying organizational messages and helping to raise the volume on the public health rationale for curbing gun violence (Choi & McKeever, 2022). More work is needed on this issue, of course, and more research is needed to help us understand nonprofit communication surrounding this and other important issues.

Research on Public Relations and Nonprofit Organizations

An article in the *Journal of Public Relations Research* in 2013 noted the paucity of published research on nonprofit PR in public relations research over time, but it also noted the increase in this type of research in the six years leading up to 2013. Indeed, many scholars have noted the importance of the nonprofit sector in recent years, and some have studied important aspects of nonprofit PR, such as philanthropy and fundraising (e.g., Das, Kerkhof, & Kuiper, 2008; Hall, 2006b; Madden et al., 2022). Prior to recent decades, much of the research in public relations focused on corporations or the agency side of PR. Bridging from traditional PR research, leading scholars studying nonprofit organizations began by focusing on relationship management. Kathleen Kelly, one of the first scholars to study fundraising as it relates to public relations, described fundraising as "the management of relationships between a charitable organization and its donor publics" (Kelly, 1998, p. 8). Richard Waters, who studied with Kathleen Kelly, applied relationship management theory to fundraising and found that donors who gave multiple times to a nonprofit hospital evaluated their relationship to be stronger than did one-time donors (Waters, 2008). The same author found that the four strategies of stewardship—reciprocity, responsibility, reporting, and relationship nurturing—were viewed favorably by donors and affect multiple dimensions of the donor–organization relationship, including trust, satisfaction, commitment, and control mutuality or perceived balance of power (Waters, 2009a, 2009b). Another study by Waters (2009c) examined the role of cognitive dissonance in crisis fundraising and found that individuals who donated to the American Red Cross following the 2004 Asian tsunami felt better or more balanced after making a donation; they also avoided news to reduce additional negative feelings during that time. Like many scholars, nonprofit public relations researchers attempt to understand the underlying causes or relationships behind phenomena we see happening around us. Fundraising following a natural disaster is one example where researchers look to build or expand theory. Because of the unique nature of nonprofits, much of the more recent research in nonprofit PR has attempted to build upon and expand theory in public relations research more broadly, to help explain the unique nature of nonprofit PR.

Theory Building in Nonprofit PR

It is important to understand *how* nonprofit organizations communicate with various stakeholders to affect public health and social change. How do people become aware of and communicate about particular health or social issues or organizational efforts? From research, we know this can partially be explained by some of the variables involved in some longstanding theories in communication. For example, the theory of situational support was proposed as a blend of variables from the situational theory of problem solving (STOPS) and the theory of reasoned action (TRA) or theory of planned behavior (TPB). In four different instances, the theory of situational support was found to predict involvement in nonprofit fundraising events, such as Relay for Life benefiting the American Cancer Society, and in communicating about these events (McKeever, 2013; McKeever et al., 2016). In short, the theory of situational support involves the independent variables of problem recognition, constraint recognition, involvement, attitudes, and subjective norms predicting communication behaviors and intentions to support nonprofit organizations (see Figure 9.1). Other research found support for this theory in China, where the nonprofit landscape and fundraising are different than in the United States (Zheng, McKeever, & Xu, 2016); however, this study highlighted some key differences between donors in the U.S. and China, noting cultural characteristics like collectivism that may help explain some of the differences in variables such as subjective norms. More research is needed on the nonprofit and NGO landscape in various international cultures.

As noted, one of the purposes of social science research is to explain phenomena we see in the real world. Research in nonprofit PR aims to do this as well. In 2016, following the election of President Donald Trump, there was a trend noticed and written about by nonprofit trade publications as well as media outlets such as the *Boston Globe*: rage donations. The *Boston Globe* article describes how the American Civil Liberties Union of Massachusetts saw a

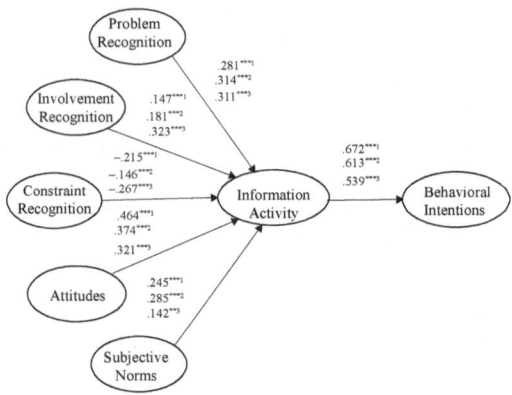

Mediation model for emerging theory of situational support with path coefficients from studies 1–3.
Note: Unstandardized path coefficients are reported. *$p<.05$. **$p<.01$. ***$p<.001$. R^2 -.676, .689, and .722 for the model of behavioral intentions regressed on all independent and mediator variables in studies 1–3, respectively. Numbers in superscripts denote the study number. Study 1-Relay for Life. Study 2-Race for the Cure. Study 3-March for Babies.

FIGURE 9.1   Theory of situational support model.

500 percent increase in the number of contributions from individuals who were angry following Trump's election. In an attempt to try to understand this new phenomenon, a group of public relations researchers (including the author of this chapter) conducted a survey and applied the Anger Activism Model (AAM) to explore these donation behaviors. The AAM posits that anger and efficacy, or feelings of empowerment, can combine to influence behaviors. In this study, we found support for the AAM influencing financial donations and advocacy-related communication behaviors (Austin et al., 2020). This was an unusual application of the AAM model, and the results of the study help to build theory in public relations, generally, and in nonprofit PR, more specifically.

Other research has explored when nonprofits partner with corporations on corporate social responsibility (CSR) or corporate social advocacy (CSA) efforts. Interviews with practitioners in charge of such partnerships revealed areas of overlap and key distinctions in the way the organizations view and manage such initiatives (Remund & McKeever, 2018). This research was summarized for public relations practitioners on a blog post via the Institute for Public Relations (McKeever & Remund, 2019). In short, to benefit the public interest and the communities they serve, it was suggested that nonprofits and corporations work together toward clarity, consistency, and being comprehensive or "going deep" in their efforts. In choosing partners, interviewees highlighted the importance of putting communities first, having shared values, and remembering reputation so that appropriate partnerships are entered into in the first place. When organizations work well together, achieving these gold standards and benefiting communities in compelling ways, we believe these initiatives can be called "public interest partnerships," as they begin with the public interest in mind rather than thinking about PR first followed by what might be achieved for various important publics (McKeever & Remund, 2019). The term public interest partnerships was coined, in part, based on scholarship related to public interest communication (PIC), which has been building as its own field, unique from but somewhat related to public relations. Fessman (2016, p. 16) defined PIC this way: "the development and implementation of science-based, planned strategic communication campaigns with the main goal of achieving significant and sustained positive behavioral change on a public interest issue that transcends the particular interests of any single organization."

Some of the most well-known health communication campaigns have grown into multi-faceted partnerships. The Heart Truth campaign is one such example. It started with the National Heart, Lung, and Blood Institute, was aided by a public relations agency (Ogilvy), and now includes countless nonprofit organizations such as the American Heart Association. The Heart Truth Campaign aims to inform women that heart disease is the leading cause of death in women, and does so using a red dress symbol, events, media coverage, and more. The results of such partnerships can include positive health outcomes, such as more people being aware that heart disease has a major impact on women, and steps can be taken to prevent the disease (National Heart, Lung, and Blood Institute, 2023). More research is needed on these types of partnerships. As our world continues to grow and evolve, partnerships are more likely to make an impact in terms of awareness, communication, public health, and social change.

Conclusion

There is a famous quote by American anthropologist Margaret Mead that (to this author) sums up what nonprofit organizations have meant to society: "Never doubt that a small group of thoughtful committed individuals can change the world. In fact, it's the only thing that ever has." While this quote does not apply to nonprofit organizations alone, it encapsulates the work that nonprofits do and the ways in which they tend to do it. Most nonprofit organizations start with one individual or a group of individuals who inspire others to make a difference related to an issue or cause. This chapter has provided an overview of some of the ways in which nonprofit organizations do their work; namely, through fundraising and advocacy. In these ways, nonprofit organizations have helped make a difference by funding research that increased treatment options and survival rates for diseases such as cancer. They have influenced awareness and changed policy related to issues like gun violence. In short, they bring people together to raise awareness and funds, and to advocate for causes that people care about; and our society is better for it. There has been research into how these organizations work, and how public relations helps these organizations achieve their goals, but more research is needed. More people working in these important entities will likely always be needed, too.

Discussion Questions

1. This chapter highlights nonprofit organizations as a force for good. While most nonprofit organizations do good, or strive to do good, not all nonprofits do good all the time. Can you think of examples of nonprofits that have not done good or that have had an issue or crisis that you can recall? What happened in those instances? How did you find out about it? If you're able to think of what the organization could have done differently from a public relations perspective, please discuss.
2. Knowing what you know from this chapter (and/or from other readings) about research on nonprofit organizations and public relations, what do you think we still need to know? Where should current or future scholars and students focus their energy in terms of research in these areas?
3. There are fine lines between nonprofit public relations, public interest communication, health communication, and other similar terms or areas of study. How would you delineate these terms or areas of focus in scholarly research? How important is it to name them differently or to categorize instances or case studies under one term or another?

Further Reading

Barone-Rosanio, G. (2020). *Getting started in health care public relations*. Kendall Hunt Publishing Company.
Capozzi, L., & Spector, S. (2016). *Public relations for the public good: How PR has shaped America's social movements*. Business Expert Press.
Johnston, J., & Pieczka, M. (Eds.). (2018). *Public interest communication: Critical debates and global contexts*. Routledge.
Powell, W. W., & Bromley, P. (Eds.). (2020). *The nonprofit sector: A research handbook*. Stanford University Press.

References

American Cancer Society Cancer Action Network (2023). Frequently asked questions. Retrieved from https://www.fightcancer.org/about-our-organization/frequently-asked-questions
Austin, L., Overton, H., McKeever, B. W., & Bortree, D. (2020). Examining the rage donation trend: Applying the anger activism model to explore communication and donation behaviors. *Public Relations Review*, *46*(5), 101981. https://doi.org/10.1016/j.pubrev.2020.101981
Biever, S. (2023). Giving USA 2023 Report Insights. Bentz, Whaley, Flessner & Associates, Inc. Retrieved from https://www.bwf.com/giving-usa-2023-report-insights/?utm_referrer=https%3A%2F%2Fwww.google.com%2F

Boris, E.T. & Steuerle, C.E. (2006). Scope and dimensions of the nonprofit sector. In W.W. Powell, & R. Steinberg (Eds.), *The nonprofit sector: A research handbook*. New Haven, CT: Yale University Press.

Cho, H., & Salmon, C. T. (2007). Unintended effects of health communication campaigns. *Journal of Communication, 57,* 293–317. https://doi.org/10.1111/j.1460-2466.2007.00344.x

Choi, M., & McKeever, B. (2022). Social media advocacy and gun violence: Applying the engagement model to nonprofit organizations' communication efforts. *Public Relations Review, 48*(2), 102173. https://doi.org/10.1016/j.pubrev.2022.102173

Clemens, E.S. (2006). The constitution of citizens: Political theories of nonprofit organizations. In W.W. Powell, & R. Steinberg (Eds.), *The nonprofit sector: A research handbook*. New Haven, CT: Yale University Press.

Das, E., Kerkhof, P., & Kuiper, J. (2008). Improving the effectiveness of fundraising messages: The impact of charity goal attainment, message framing, and evidence on persuasion. *Journal of Applied Communication Research, 36*(2), 161–175. https://doi.org/10.1080/00909880801922854

De Beaumont (2023a). Programs. https://debeaumont.org/programs/

De Beaumont (2023b). Changing the COVID conversation. https://debeaumont.org/changing-the-covid-conversation/

Drozdowski, M. J. (2003, April 7). Development and fund raising: What's the difference? *The Chronicle of Higher Education*. Retrieved from https://www.chronicle.com/article/development-and-fund-raising-whats-the-difference-45139/?sra=true&cid=gen_sign_in

Everytown for Gun Safety (2023). Our history. https://www.everytown.org/about-everytown/history/

Falk, S.C. (2005). Maximizing fundraising's strategic contribution. In W. C. McGinly, & K. Renzetti (Eds.), *Expanding the role of philanthropy in health care*. Hoboken, NJ: John Wiley & Sons.

Fessmann, J. (2016). The emerging field of public interest communications. In E. Oliveira, A. D. Melo, & G. Goncalves (Eds.), *Strategic communication in non-profit organizations: Challenges and alternative approaches* (pp. 13–34). Wilmington, NC: Vernon.

Frumkin, P. (2002). *On being nonprofit: A conceptual and policy primer*. Cambridge, MA: Harvard University Press.

Galaskiewicz, J., & Colman, M. S. (2006). Collaboration between corporations and nonprofit organizations. In W. W. Powell, & R. Steinberg (Eds.), *The nonprofit sector: A research handbook*. New Haven, CT: Yale University Press.

Giving USA Foundation (2023). Giving USA 2023: The annual report on philanthropy. https://store.givingusa.org/products/2023-infographic?variant=44055760109792

Gramlich, J. (2023, April 26). What the data says about gun deaths in the U.S. Pew Research Center. https://www.pewresearch.org/short-reads/2023/04/26/what-the-data-says-about-gun-deaths-in-the-u-s/

Hall, P. D. (2006a). A historical overview of philanthropy, voluntary associations, and nonprofit organizations in the U.S., 1600–2000. In W. W. Powell, & R. Steinberg (Eds.), *The nonprofit sector: A research handbook*. New Haven, CT: Yale University Press.

Hall, M. R. (2006b). Corporate philanthropy and corporate community relations: Measuring relationship-building results. *Journal of Public Relations Research, 18*(1), 1–21. https://doi.org/10.1207/s1532754xjprr1801_1

Harvard Law School (2022). Nongovernmental organizations (NGOs). Retrieved from https://hls.harvard.edu/bernard-koteen-office-of-public-interest-advising/about-opia/what-is-public-interest-law/public-service-practice-settings/international-public-interest-law-practice-setting/nongovernmental-organizations-ngos/

Hrebenar, R.J. (1997). *Interest group politics in America*. Armonk, NY: M.E. Sharpe.

Internal Revenue Service (2023). Exemption Requirements – 501(c)(3) Organizations. Retrieved from https://www.irs.gov/charities-non-profits/charitable-organizations/exemption-requirements-501c3-organizations

Kelly, K. S. (1998). *Effective fund-raising management*. Mahwah, NJ: Lawrence Erlbaum Associates.

Kiessling, A. A. (2008). Philanthropy is key to rapid life science innovation. *Journal of Biolaw and Business*, *11*(3), 1–5. https://www.bedfordresearch.org/wp-content/uploads/2015/03/Kiessling_Philanthropy08.pdf

Madden, S., Harrison, V., & Vafeiadis, M. (2022). Relational care in communication as the basis of nonprofit fundraising: Theorizing professional ethics based in stewardship and ethics of care. *Journal of Philanthropy and Marketing, 28*(4), e1762. https://doi.org/10.1002/nvsm.1762

March for Our Lives (2023). On elections. Retrieved from https://marchforourlives.org/on-elections/

McCarthy, J. D., & Castelli, J. (2002). The necessity for studying organizational advocacy comparatively. In P. Flynn & V. A. Hodgkinson (Eds.), *Measuring the impact of the nonprofit sector* (pp. 103–121). New York: Kluwer Academic/Plenum Publishers.

McKeever, B. W. (2013). From awareness to advocacy: Understanding nonprofit communication, participation, and support. *Journal of Public Relations Research, 25*(4), 307–328. http://dx.doi.org/10.1080/1062726X.2013.806868

McKeever, B. W., Pressgrove, G., McKeever, R., & Zheng, Y. (2016). Toward a theory of situational support: A model for exploring fundraising, advocacy and organizational support. *Public Relations Review, 42*(1), 219–222. https://doi.org/10.1016/j.pubrev.2015.09.009

McKeever, B. W., Choi, M., Walker, D., & McKeever, R. (2022). Gun violence as a public health issue: Media advocacy, framing and implications for communication. *Newspaper Research Journal, 43*(2), 138–154. https://doi.org/10.1177/07395329221090497

McKeever, B. W., Remund, D. (2019, Oct. 22). Partnerships in the public interest: Best practices for building successful corporate–nonprofit relationships. Institute for Public Relations. https://instituteforpr.org/partnerships-in-the-public-interest-best-practices-for-building-successful-corporate-nonprofit-relationships/

National Heart, Lung, and Blood Institute (2023). About the heart truth. https://www.nhlbi.nih.gov/health-topics/education-and-awareness/heart-truth/about

Niederdeppe, J. (2009) On the role of public communication campaigns in reducing, maintaining, or widening socioeconomic health behavior disparities. Paper presented at the International Communication Association Annual Convention in Chicago, May.

Nonprofit Quarterly (2017). What is fundraising? https://nonprofitquarterly.org/what-is-fundraising-definition/

Palfrey, J.S., M.D. (2006). *Child health in America: Making a difference through advocacy*. Baltimore, MD: The Johns Hopkins University Press.

Poole, S.M. (2010). Donation cuts hit Georgia's biggest nonprofits. *The Atlanta Journal-Constitution*. https://www.ajc.com/news/local/donation-cuts-hit-georgia-biggest-non-profits/0qPdKjIFvFwYxKHKcpuTON/

Remund, D., McKeever, B. W. (2018). Forging effective corporate–nonprofit partnerships for CSR programs. *Journal of Communication Management, 22*(3), 309–326. https://doi.org/10.1108/JCOM-08-2017-0084

Rosso, H. A., & Associates (1991). *Achieving excellence in fund raising: A comprehensive guide to principles, strategies, and methods*. San Francisco, CA: Jossey-Bass.

Rothman, A., Bartels, R., Wlaschin, J., & Salovey, P. (2006). The strategic use of gain- and loss-framed messages to promote healthy behavior: How theory can inform practice. *Journal of Communication, 56,* 202–220. https://doi.org/10.1111/j.1460-2466.2006.00290.x

Schlesinger, M. & Gray, B. H. (2006). Nonprofit organizations and health care: Some paradoxes of persistent scrutiny. In W. W. Powell, & R. Steinberg (Eds.), *The nonprofit sector: A research handbook.* New Haven, CT: Yale University Press.

St. Jude Children's Research Hospital (2023a). Our history. https://www.stjude.org/about-st-jude/history.html

St. Jude Children's Research Hospital (2023b). HPV Cancer Prevention Program. https://www.stjude.org/research/comprehensive-cancer-center/hpv-cancer-prevention-program.html

U.S. Department of State (2021, Jan. 20). Non-governmental organizations (NGOs) in the United States. Retrieved from https://www.state.gov/non-governmental-organizations-ngos-in-the-united-states/

Wallack, L., Dorfman, L., Jernigan, D., & Themba, M. (1993). *Media advocacy and public health: Power for prevention.* Newbury Park, CA: Sage Publications.

Waters, R. D. (2008). Applying relationship management theory to the fundraising process for individual donors. *Journal of Communication Management, 12*(1), 73–87. https://doi.org/10.1108/13632540810854244

Waters, R. D. (2009a). Increasing fundraising efficiency through evaluation: Applying communication theory to the nonprofit organization-donor relationship. *Nonprofit & Voluntary Sector Quarterly, 31*(3), 429–436. https://doi.org/10.1177/0899764009354322

Waters, R. (2009b). Measuring stewardship in public relations: A test exploring impact on the fundraising relationship. *Public Relations Review, 35*(2), 113–119. https://doi.org/10.1016/j.pubrev.2009.01.012

Waters, R. (2009c). Examining the role of cognitive dissonance in crisis fundraising. *Public Relations Review, 35*(2), 139–143. https://doi.org/10.1016/j.pubrev.2008.11.001

Weberling, B. (2010). Celebrity & charity: A historical case study of Danny Thomas and St. Jude Children's Research Hospital, 1962–1991. *PRism, 7*(2). https://www.prism-journal.org/uploads/1/2/5/6/125661607/v7-no2-a4.pdf

Zheng, Y., McKeever, B.W., Xu, L. (2016). Nonprofit communication and fundraising in China: Exploring the theory of situational support in an international context. *International Journal of Communication, 10,* 4280–4303. https://ijoc.org/index.php/ijoc/article/view/4271

10

HIGH STAKES, LOW TRUST

Government Public Relations

Abbey Blake Levenshus

Government communication with citizens, other governments, and other nations' citizens is critically important given today's high-stakes risk and crisis context (Horsley & VanDyke, 2022). Yet government communication challenges exist, such as declining trust and even legal and regulatory restrictions rooted in fears of government propaganda. For example, researchers and practitioners have called for a repeal of the 1913 Gillett Amendment that prohibits U.S. government spending on "publicity experts" among other communication limitations (Taylor & Kent, 2016). A relational approach to government communication shows promising possibilities for ethically and effectively managing communication between governments and the publics they serve—particularly for public health aims. To explore these ideas, the chapter first lays the foundation for government public relations. It then explores government communication in public health and crisis communication contexts. Intersecting themes of trust, relationships, and social media surface related to successful and mutually beneficial government public relations for public health and social good. The chapter concludes with a teaching prompt and discussion questions that point to future challenges and opportunities for scholars and practitioners interested in these topics.

Laying the Conceptual Foundation

Progress has been made in the last ten years, but the government public relations context has been under-studied compared to other sectors (Sanders, 2020), and political elected government has received more attention than the non-elected side (Lee, 2022). That political emphasis can show up in how the concept of government public relations is defined. For example, Sanders (2011) points out a key

DOI: 10.4324/9781003327189-13

omission in Strömbäck and Kiousis' (2011) otherwise comprehensive definition of political public relations:

> the management process by which an organization or individual actor for political purposes, through purposeful communication and action, seeks to influence and to establish, build, and maintain beneficial relationships and reputations with its key publics to help support its mission and achieve its goals.
>
> *(p. 8)*

Sanders (2011) notes that the definition fails to encompass government's civic purposes and suggests amending the definition with "political and civic purposes" in order to clearly distinguish "between communication managed to achieve a government's political goals and communication managed in line with overarching government obligations in relation to the common civic good" (p. 266). Such obligations, including public health ones, are rooted in government's public nature. Canel and Sanders (2012, p. 4) carve out government communication as "usually managed communication directed to key publics and pursuing both political and civic purposes, carried out by executive politicians and officials working for public institutions with a political rationale." They further note that government institutions exist based on citizens' "direct or indirect consent and are charged to enact their will" (Canel & Sanders, 2012, p. 4).

Within the public sector context, scholars have identified several attributes that influence government public relations (e.g., Canel & Sanders, 2012; Liu et al., 2010; Sanders, 2020). For example, differences between government and corporate communication include greater political influence, public and media scrutiny, and impacts of legal and regulatory frameworks (Liu et al., 2010). Yet government is not monolithic. It is multilayered and complex. For example, the Government Communication Decision Wheel (GCDW) identified four micro-environments for public sector communication: intragovernmental, intergovernmental, multilevel, and external (Liu & Horsley, 2007). Government communication professionals may operate in any or all of those four micro-environments when addressing public health. For example, a single agency may make all of the communication decisions for an upcoming public health campaign (i.e., *intragovernmental*). The *intergovernmental* micro-environment includes two or more communicators from the same level of government making decisions and communicating together. Complex or widespread public health issues may require a *multilevel* operating micro-environment with cooperation and dissemination among multiple levels of government entities. Often when it comes to public health, government communicators work in an *external* micro-environment where they cooperate with at least one private sector, nonprofit, or international organization to communicate more comprehensively and expansively about an issue.

All of these micro-environments exist within a larger government operating environment. And communication scholars have identified publicness and public good obligations as key hallmarks of the public sector (e.g., Avery & Graham, 2013; Canel & Sanders, 2012; Lee, 2015; Sanders, 2020). For example, while many institutions seek to influence public health and social change, government entities are uniquely positioned in both power and potential consequences given their missions, resources, and authority. Governments cannot pick and choose their publics the way other entities can (Lee, 2015). In theory (and hopefully in practice), governments must ensure the public health, safety, and overall well-being of *all* of their citizens. In the face of risk, crisis and emergency, governments are more likely than private sector organizations to be responsible for ensuring citizens' preparation and safety (e.g., Horsley, 2010; Sanders, 2020). They are also most often the ones responsible for issuing and disseminating warnings and instructing information (Houston et al., 2015). Whether or not people take government-recommended actions can have lethal consequences. The fragmented digital communication landscape has increased the importance of the public's ability to identify, access, and trust credible scientific and health information (Chon & Park, 2021). Governments often find themselves in the role of myth buster as minformation circulates (van der Meer & Jin, 2020), but government efforts to correct misinformation are made harder by the trust deficit discussed next.

The Trust Crisis in Government Communication

In the U.S., trust in the government has generally been in decline since the 1960s when it eroded due to the federal government's handling of the Vietnam War. While it has recovered at times, including a short-lived spike immediately following the September 11, 2001 terrorist attacks, the boosts have not lasted. In a 2022 survey by the Pew Research Center, just 20 percent of Americans reported that they can trust the federal government to do what is right (Bell, 2022). On a brighter note, 70 percent of people gave the government highly positive ratings for responding to natural disasters.

In the U.S., public and media scrutiny and distrust of politics have undoubtedly contributed to that legal and regulatory environment. For example, Taylor and Kent (2016) called for the repeal of the 1913 Gillett Amendment that prohibits U.S. government spending on "publicity experts" among other communication limitations. They note the negative unintended impacts of the law, such as a lack of clarity and transparency about the practice of government public relations and a limit on public information available to the public on issues (Taylor & Kent, 2016). Public reporting and responsiveness to the public "are not luxuries in the context of a democratic governance" (Lee, 2022, p. 14). Yet there are gray areas between what one person may consider public reporting and another would consider publicity (Gelders & Ihlen, 2010; Lee, 2022).

Propaganda is a term associated with government lies and deceit (Gelders & Ihlen, 2010). Misunderstandings of public relations as self-serving publicity or propaganda show up in unique places. A 2011 U.S. Food and Drug Administration report titled "Communicating Risks and Benefits: An Evidence-Based User's Guide" includes the following language in its introduction (Fischoff et al., 2011, p. 1):

> Risk communication is the term of art used for situations when people need good information to make sound choices. It is distinguished from public affairs (or public relations) communication by its commitment to accuracy and its avoidance of spin. Having been spun adds insult to injury for people who have been hurt because they were inadequately informed.

Indeed, there is a long history of distrust, cynicism, and perception of government communication as spin and propaganda in many countries (e.g., Chang & Lin, 2014; Kim & Krishna, 2018; Lee, 2022). Lee described a "hostility" to government public relations "buried deep in the DNA of American political culture" coming from "suspicion of government, dislike of bureaucracy, and opposition to supposedly self-serving public relations" (Lee, 2015, p. 110). Beyond a healthy skepticism, this hostility can also be reflected as cynicism. In their study of citizens' perceptions of government communication strategies, Kim and Krishna (2018) used Miller's (1974) understanding of public cynicism: "the degree of negative affect toward the government," and "a statement of the belief that the government is not functioning and producing outputs in accordance with individual expectations" (Miller, 1974, p. 218).

Can government persuasion about policies ever be ethical? Scholars say yes (Gelders & Ihlen, 2010; Taylor & Kent, 2016). As Taylor and Kent (2016, p. 7) argue:

> Government agencies should conduct public information campaigns that make us healthier and safer. Government offices should be allowed to use persuasion—once considered the same as propaganda, but now understood as one of the features that makes us uniquely human—to help raise awareness of government policies.

While it is unfair and inaccurate to categorize all government communication as propaganda, it would also be inaccurate and unrealistic to say that government propaganda activities do not exist. All countries, to some degree and at some point, have engaged in propaganda to win over public opinion in their favor (Chang & Lin, 2014). Propaganda can happen within a country and also as a form of mediated diplomacy. Anderson (2020) wrote about the U.S. president and congressional leaders electing to use "mass persuasion over mass coercion" that leveraged Americans' patriotism in order to convince people to pay personal income taxes in support of World War II (p. 5). More recently, Russia placed advertorials (paid newspaper advertising supplements that look like news stories, editorials, op-eds, etc.) in a U.S. newspaper to communicate an underlying government social responsibility message that framed the country as a trustworthy partner on important global issues (Golan & Viatchaninova, 2013, p. 405). The key to balancing persuasion and education motives may lie in effective public relations that is participatory, transparent, and hopefully trust-building.

Government public relations practitioners need to account for low trust and interest in politics in their public segmentation and relationship management efforts. Low trust in government can serve as a barrier for citizens' willingness to adopt online government communication tools such as a public health data dashboard—even ones designed to benefit citizens and improve transparency and effectiveness of citizen-government communication (Park & Lee, 2018). Hong et al. (2012) used data from the U.S. and 19 European countries to segment publics based on salient characteristics (perceptions of government, media use, demographic characteristics, etc.). The lowest level of trust in government institutions was associated with the largest segment, the underserved inactive majority. This segment was characterized by low levels across several factors, including income, education, interest in politics, citizenship standards (i.e., how important it is to vote, obey laws, volunteer), social participation (i.e., amount of participation in voluntary civic organizations), and trust in others (Hong et al., 2012). Some of these same factors (e.g., low income, limited education, weak community ties) can put individuals at higher risk for poor health outcomes and increased vulnerability during any crisis or disaster. As such, these vulnerabilities make it important to engage the underserved inactive majority, but doing so will be difficult work. The next section considers the pros and cons of using social media to improve government communication, including with the distrusting and disengaged public.

The Advantages and Disadvantages of Government Social Media Communication

Just as in other sectors, digital and social media have disrupted and evolved government's traditional communication processes—bringing new challenges, channels, and complexities for engaging with the public, including about public health (e.g., Avery et al., 2010; Kavanaugh et al., 2012; Wang, 2022). Kavanaugh et al. (2012)'s definition of social media remains relevant despite how these media have evolved. To that end, social media are "internet-based applications designed to facilitate social interaction and for using, developing and diffusing information through society" (p. 482). A key distinction of social media is that they facilitate user-generated content (Kavanaugh et al., 2012). Social media present a double-edged sword for government communication. Social media platforms operate outside of government, which can result in cybersecurity risks and a lack of control over the technology and its changes (Mergel, 2016).

They also generate an overwhelming amount of data for government to monitor, analyze, and act upon when issues or crises are identified—from traffic accidents to disease outbreaks (Chon & Kim, 2022; Kavanaugh et al., 2012). While they create more opportunities to improve government listening, crisis management, relationship management, and other functions, government cannot always use social media to its full potential. Significant staff, budget, and content resources are required to *be* social online and not all government organizations, particularly local ones, have the teams, resources and expertise to maintain effective social media communication, especially in health (e.g., Avery & Graham, 2013) or crisis contexts (Graham et al., 2015).

Distrusting citizens may not want to use digital or social media platforms to communicate with government entities (Park & Lee, 2018). Such efforts require a relational posture and activities such as organizational listening and ongoing engagement (Gelders & Ihlen, 2010; Sanders, 2020). While social media are not always used effectively, they can offer an accessible strategy for government transparency and participatory approaches—especially at the local level (Avery & Graham, 2013; Kavanaugh et al., 2012). These tools and strategies have the potential to enhance public trust and satisfaction in government, which are hallmarks of strong organization–public relationships (Hong, 2013; Porumbescu, 2016). However, social media also constantly evolve, making it risky for governments to develop long-term strategies and plans for particular platforms (Rooksby & Sommerville, 2012). The next section considers government public relations in the public health context.

The Public Health Context

COVID-19 put government public relations on display in highly visible ways—especially in the early months of the pandemic. In most countries, governments served as the main source of official communication for COVID-19 (Arcila-Calderón et al., 2021). Local, state, national, and global health agencies and their executives and experts found themselves center stage, essentially becoming Public Health Communicators in Chief overnight in their jurisdictions. Many lessons learned reinforce the critical role of government public relations in ensuring public health and social good—including around public trust and social media—that have important theoretical and practical applications for government public relations.

Much government public health research has focused on risks, crisis, and emergency management—and the response stage in particular for various crises like HIV/AIDS (e.g., McKeever, 2021), influenza (e.g., Paek et al., 2008; Vos & Buckner, 2016), MERS (e.g., Kang et al., 2018); Zika (Ali et al., 2019), and most recently COVID-19 (e.g., Chang, 2022; Chon & Kim, 2022; Ortega & Orsini, 2020; Wang, 2022). Disasters have significant impacts on public health, including immediate risks to health and safety that can be worsened if communication or transportation infrastructure are damaged (Sledge & Thomas, 2019). Other potential public health complications can include disruptions in access to patient care, worsening social and economic conditions for the already vulnerable, and other risks. In the face of risk and crisis, governments are more likely than are private sector organizations to be responsible for ensuring citizens' preparation and safety (e.g., Graham et al., 2015; Horsley, 2010). In the U.S., this responsibility is complicated by the byzantine nature of bureaucracy. Local, state, and federal governments must each play their respective and coordinated roles in the face of a widespread public health disaster. To provide context, the U.S. Centers for Disease Control and Prevention (CDC) sits as one of 12 operating divisions within the larger U.S. Department of Health and Human Services.

Governments must sometimes take measures that can be life-changing with little time for public input as was the case during the COVID-19 pandemic (Hyland-Wood et al., 2021; Sutton et al., 2015). It is crucial that publics follow government instructions when facing a public health crisis (Chon & Park, 2021). People are most likely to heed local government officials' warnings about protective actions following a crisis (Liu et al., 2106)—even if they hold the government accountable for the crisis (Bakker et al., 2018). In a survey of U.S. adults, participants with positive perceived relationships with the CDC were more likely to express intentions to take and share CDC information after reading a description of an infectious disease (Chon & Park, 2021). Additionally, these individuals were also more likely to *follow* CDC instructions during an outbreak.

Unfortunately, not all governments are credible disaster managers or communicators. The authoritarian Brazilian president and his central government failed to play an effective role in disaster management, and its public health leadership collapsed in what Ortega and Orsini (2020) call "non-governance of COVID-19" (p. 1259). In the absence of that leadership, local, informal leadership emerged but not without catastrophic loss of life. In Spain, distrust in the government undermined publics' willingness to follow government mitigation recommendations (Arcila-Calderón et al., 2021).

The communication landscape in which governments are communicating about risks has grown more complex. Credible scientific and health information and sources are needed today more than ever (Chon & Park, 2021). In public health crises, governments use communication for multiple purposes such as communicating accurate, credible, important information about the emergency or crisis and how the public can protect themselves (e.g., Wang, 2022). The crisis and emergency risk communication (CERC) framework and CDC training module helps explain and plan communication during a health crisis (Hewitt et al., 2008; Seeger & Reynolds, 2008). The CERC approach involves communicators providing messages that help individuals make sense of what is happening (reduce uncertainty) and also give them information on how to respond effectively (Reynolds & Seeger, 2005). In addition to serving as an information source, government communication can help debunk misinformation (van der Meer & Jin, 2020) and signal leadership and competency at managing the emergency or crisis (Wang, 2022).

In some cases, though, government mismanagement of a crisis can decrease organizational legitimacy and trust. This decrease can result in lower compliance with government warnings and recommendations. It can also fuel additional crises. For example, the U.S. federal government response to Hurricane Katrina in 2005 was largely considered and portrayed as a failure by the public, news media, and researchers. Even the Federal Emergency Management Agency describes on its own website: "The federal government's response to the extensive and disruptive impacts of Hurricane Katrina faced criticism, which caused a significant reevaluation of the execution of federal disaster response efforts and resource allocation." FEMA's website notes that Congress passed the Post-Katrina Emergency Management Reform Act of 2006 in order to clarify and strengthen the agency's mission and establish its central advisory role related to emergency management in the U.S. (FEMA, n.d.).

One compounding crisis during Katrina studied by Veil and Anthony (2017) involved temporary housing trailers provided by FEMA with heightened levels of the cancer-causing chemical formaldehyde. The discovery resulted in a compounding environmental and health crisis. Compounding crises occur in "close succession to another (potentially unrelated) crisis before an organization has the opportunity to rebuild legitimacy" (Veil & Anthony, 2017, p. 154). In this case, FEMA also found itself facing a pariah effect, where other government agencies typically responsible for responding to environmental and health crises like the Environmental Protection Agency and the CDC were reluctant to get involved. FEMA was then forced to set formaldehyde standards for the travel trailers it was willing to buy (Veil & Anthony, 2017).

When publics hold government accountable for a crisis, they may still follow government instructions and advice in the crisis response stage, but there can be damage done to the government–public relationship (Bakker et al., 2018). This makes it more critical for governments to focus on organization–public relationships before and after a crisis hits, so that trust is there when it is needed. Hyland-Wood et al. (2021, p. 7) reviewed research in public health, risk communication, cognitive and social psychology, sociology, and public policy and offered ten summative recommendations for effective government communication strategies in a post-COVID environment that can help bolster trust, transparency and engagement:

- Engage in clear communication
- Strive for maximum credibility
- Communicate with empathy
- Communicate with openness, frankness, and honesty
- Recognize that uncertainty is inevitable
- Account for audience's different levels of health literacy and ability to work with math and numbers
- Empower people to act
- Appeal to social norms, expectations, and standards
- Consider diverse community needs
- Be proactive in combating misinformation

Those recommendations reference "community" and otherwise focus most on the general public. But emergencies and crises, as discussed next, are inherently multivocal, meaning many organizational voices and sources are involved, not just the government (Heath et al., 2009).

Government Crisis Communication

In a crisis context, official government sources are often preferred by the public, though people also depend on family and friends for information sharing (e.g., Liu et al., 2016; Tang & Zou, 2021). Liu et al. (2016) found that people use a mix of sources for different purposes such as finding out about a crisis, seeking additional information, and following mitigation instructions. Television was the first choice for seeking additional information about crises followed by face-to-face interpersonal communication and then local government websites (Liu et al., 2016). In countries like China where government censors communication, publics were more likely to report sharing information about COVID-19 with family through private channels versus public social media (Tang & Zou, 2021).

Even without censorship concerns, Liu et al. (2016) found people prefer to share crisis information interpersonally, through text messages, phone calls, face-to-face conversations, and emails. Social media also fulfill emotional needs such as social connection and help share information to mobilize resources (Tang & Zou, 2021). Social media provide outlets for citizens to share or amplify negative messages and blame about the government's handling of a crisis (e.g., Arcila-Calderón et al., 2021; Chon & Kim, 2022). When citizens perceived the U.S. president or the federal government as poorly handling the COVID-19 crisis, they were more likely to share negative tweets and retweets about the federal government. These negative social media messages attributing blame to President Trump and the federal government dominated the platform formerly known as Twitter (Chon & Kim, 2022).

Government agencies have typically initiated and distributed warnings through mass broadcast channels like newspapers, radio, and television, though there were unique examples of direct messaging as detailed in McKeever's (2021) case study of the U.S. Surgeon General's highly unusual direct mailing about HIV/AIDS in 1988 to 107 million U.S. households. Given the need to quickly and widely disseminate information to the public, media represent a key stakeholder group for government communicators in a public health context. In countries like China, state media are government sources (Tang & Zou, 2021). In democratic countries, tensions often exist between journalists and government information officers and emergency managers, but their ability to work together effectively is critical to publics receiving credible, timely, accurate information (e.g., Avery et al., 2010; McLean & Power, 2014). McLean and Power describe the tensions between both the media and emergency managers (2014, pp. 310–311):

> They operate in a constant state of distrustful wariness, fearful of trusting those who, from the journalists' perspective, may be slow in giving them access to information, and, from the emergency managers' view, may be seizing the chance to get behind the scenes and gather information they will later use in allocating blame for what journalists judge to be inadequacies in how the emergency or disaster was handled.

While media still play a critical role in the information ecosystem, crisis and disaster communication messages are also disseminated through social media channels (e.g., Graham et al., 2015; Liu et al., 2016; Houston et al., 2015; Vos & Buckner, 2016). Social media may be rising to the "channel of choice" for government emergency warnings (Sutton et al., 2015, p. 135). While social media's speed can be helpful, the Internet is a highly competitive communication environment. Messages are often fraught with misinformation (van der Meer & Jin, 2020) and fear-arousing, sensationalist appeals and messages with minimal efficacy information (Ali et al., 2019). In a U.S.-based experiment on misinformation, both government agencies and news media sources were found to be more successful than social peers at improving belief accuracy when participants held incorrect beliefs based on misinformation (van der Meer & Jin, 2020). When debunking misinformation, government communicators should go beyond providing corrective information and provide factual elaboration if they want to increase people's intention to take desired protective actions in a public health crisis (van der Meer & Jin, 2020).

To increase public trust and lower anxiety during complex crises like a pandemic, public health messaging efforts should centralize, unify, and streamline delivery of information (Van Scoy et al., 2021). Otherwise, audiences begin a self-fueling anxiety cycle that drives further consumption of media that can then further confuse, overwhelm and deepen distrust. While trusted government information sources can reduce anxiety, that effect is undermined by inconsistent messaging or information overload (Van Scoy et al., 2021).

Information must also be communicated quickly. A 2020 survey of Spanish citizens identified overall poor perceptions of Spain's COVID-19 management with the national government's failure to communicate quickly as one of the most negatively rated items in the survey (Ancila-Calderón et al., 2021). While not utilizing social media's dialogic attributes, platforms like Twitter/X can be used effectively by governments to communicate direct and brief emergency warnings that provide information about the hazard, its impacts, as well as any recommended preventive measures (Sutton et al., 2015). Data dashboards provide a mechanism that can quickly aggregate, synthesize, and visually display updated data in an interactive, comprehensible way. Ireland's government used COVID-19 dashboards to accurately and rapidly report to the public and media, shape decision-making and policy, as well as justify difficult mitigation decisions to the public (Gleeson et al., 2022). Dashboards could help fulfill Hyland-Wood et al.'s (2021) recommendation to translate public health data in accessible, visual ways that account for publics' various levels of health literacy and numeracy (Hyland-Wood et al., 2021).

Taking a Relational Approach

State and local government communicators may hold the key to effective government public relations in a public health crisis (e.g., Arcila-Calderón et al., 2021; Bakker et al., 2018; Chang, 2022; Graham et al., 2015). Media and non-governmental entities must be part of the larger government–public relationship equation. Internal government employees are often forgotten stakeholders, and future research should examine inter-governmental and intra-government relationship management efforts (Sanders, 2020). Intra-departmental communication, coordination, and internal relationship building may be key to effective communication, and even more important when there is a lack of trust or when the media and political context are contentious (e.g., Rice & Somerville, 2013; Wolf-Fordham, 2020).

Relationship management must include "trust-building practices and policies" to help build communication transparency, reliability, accessibility and accountability (Sanders, 2020, p. 181–182). Trust building and personalization of risks beyond education or publicity can strengthen support for controversial mitigation actions (Paek et al., 2008). Digital and social media have the potential to carry out those activities (e.g., Avery & Graham, 2013; Chon & Park, 2021), but the rest of the media mix should not be abandoned in the process (Liu et al., 2016). Relational communication and social media efforts may help bridge the gap between propaganda and public relations around policy development and communication by engaging the public in ongoing ways (Gelders & Ihlen, 2010).

Relationships are multidirectional and multilayered. The relationship management approach aligns with the U.S. "whole of government" approach to emergency management as defined by the U.S. Department of Health and Human Services' National Health Security Strategy Implementation Plan that seeks to leverage the "full range of public and private sector tools, academia, NGOs, resources, and capabilities to save lives and safeguard people's health" (2019, p. 2). Non-government entities may be able to serve as intervening publics and partners to reach marginalized populations (Sledge & Thomas, 2019). In a study of public health communication in India during COVID-19, engagement was found to be the key ingredient to empowering and involving the public in joining together to fight the pandemic (Venkatraman & Manoharan, 2023). When government communicators encourage active public engagement and involvement in risk communication, the public may be more likely to comply with recommendations and more quickly end the health crisis. The authors write, "Engagement (to empower) occurs as an off-spin from empathy and can be viewed as the highest form of empathy, ideally when the public feels that they are given the power to act in the situation" (Venkatraman & Manoharan, 2023, p. 293).

Conclusion

Unlike for-profit corporate entities, governments are, at their core, tasked with doing social good. Yet governments face a complex public health communication ecosystem that includes a persistent and pernicious distrust of governments and their communication as propaganda, publicity, and spin (e.g., Taylor & Kent, 2016; Waymer, 2013). Unfortunately, not all distrust is unfounded. Political motives that outweigh civic ones can deepen distrust and disrupt ethical and effective government communication. Future research should study the impact of politically appointed government leaders and tensions that emerge between long-serving scientists, health experts, or government public relations professionals and the political appointees or elected officials they serve. Ultimately, as Chang (2022) noted, "The battle is not merely a matter of who can better contain the outbreak; it will be won by actors that communicate better with the public"

(p. 484). Communicating better with the public also means communicating ethically. Relational government public relations approaches that integrate strategies and tools like social media in order to build trust, transparency, and engagement with internal and external stakeholders may be key to winning that battle for public health and social good.

Discussion Questions

1. Research a public health agency in your area. Review its website and any social media channels it uses. Pick a particular issue, risk, or crisis discussed by the agency. Review the Government Communication Decision Wheel's four micro-environments. Practice mapping the organization's micro-environments in which it may need to plan and disseminate communication about the issue, risk, or crisis.
2. Consider the key research findings described in the chapter and the list of communication best practices suggested by Hyland-Wood et al. (2021). Audit the public health communication around the issue you identified in Question 1 against these principles.
3. Government communicators have to decide when to warn. On September 15, 2022, the U.S. Food and Drug Administration issued a consumer update warning about a TikTok trend challenging people to cook chicken in NyQuil cold medicine. Review the FDA's update and YouTube video about the trend and read the *New York Times* story to get more background. If you worked for the FDA, what would have guided your decision-making about the risks versus benefits of when to warn and how?

   U.S. Food and Drug Administration. (2022, September 15). A recipe for danger: Social media challenges involving medicines [Consumer Update]. https://www.fda.gov/consumers/consumer-updates/recipe-danger-social-media-challenges-involving-medicines

   Victor, D., & Holpuch, A. (2022, September 21). F.D.A. warning on NyQuil chicken alerts many to existence of NyQuil chicken. *The New York Times*. https://www.nytimes.com/2022/09/21/technology/nyquil-chicken-tiktok-fda.html

Further Reading

Avery, E. J., Graham, M., & Park, S. (2016). Planning makes (closer to) perfect: Exploring United States' local government officials' evaluations of crisis management. *Journal of Contingencies & Crisis Management, 24*(2), 73–81. https://doi.org/10.1111/1468-5973.12109

Guttman, N., & Lev, E. (2021). Ethical issues in COVID-19 communication to mitigate the pandemic: Dilemmas and practical implications. *Health Communication, 36*(1), 116–123. https://doi.org/10.1080/10410236.2020.1847439

Hyland-Wood, B., Gardner, J., Leask, J., & Ecker, U. K. H. (2021). Toward effective government communication strategies in the era of COVID-19. *Humanities and Social Sciences Communications, 8*(1), 1–11. https://doi.org/10.1057/s41599-020-00701-w

Strömbäck, J., & Kiousis, S. (Eds.). (2020). *Political public relations: Concepts, principles, and applications* (2nd ed.). Routledge.

References

Ali, K., Zain-ul-abdin, K., Li, C., Johns, L., Ali, A. A., & Carcioppolo, N. (2019). Viruses going viral: Impact of fear-arousing sensationalist social media messages on user engagement. *Science Communication, 41*(3), 314–338. https://doi.org/10.1177/1075547019846124

Anderson, W. B. (2020). "I paid my income tax today": How the U.S. government used public relations to persuade its citizens to accept a mass tax during World War II. *Public Relations Review, 46*(4), 101945. https://doi.org/10.1016/j.pubrev.2020.101945

Arcila-Calderón, C., Blanco-Herrero, D., & Oller-Alonso, M. (2021). Trusting communication of the pandemic: The perceptions of Spanish citizens regarding government information on Covid-19. *El Profesional de La Información, 30*(6). https://doi.org/10.3145/epi.2021.nov.06

Avery, E. J., & Graham, M. W. (2013). Political public relations and the promotion of participatory, transparent government through social media. *International Journal of Strategic Communication, 7*(4), 274–291. https://doi.org/10.1080/1553118X.2013.824885

Avery, E., Lariscy, R., Amador, E., Ickowitz, T., Primm, C., & Taylor, A. (2010). Diffusion of social media among public relations practitioners in health departments across various community population sizes. *Journal of Public Relations Research, 22*(3), 336–358. https://doi.org/10.1080/10627261003614427

Bakker, M. H., van Bommel, M., Kerstholt, J. H., & Giebels, E. (2018). The influence of accountability for the crisis and type of crisis communication on people's behavior, feelings and relationship with the government. *Public Relations Review, 44*(2), 277–286. https://doi.org/10.1016/j.pubrev.2018.02.004

Bell, P. (2022, June 6). Public trust in government: 1958–2022. *Pew Research Center—U.S. Politics & Policy.* https://www.pewresearch.org/politics/2022/06/06/public-trust-in-government-1958-2022/

Canel, M. J., & Sanders, K. (2012). Introduction: Mapping the field of government communication. K. Sanders & M. J. Canel (Eds.), *Government communication: Cases and challenges* (pp. 1–26). Bloomsbury Academic.

Chang, C. (2022). Cross-country comparison of effects of early government communication on personal empowerment during the COVID-19 pandemic in Taiwan and the United States. *Health Communication, 37*(4), 476–489. https://doi.org/10.1080/10410236.2020.1852698

Chang, T.-K., & Lin, F. (2014). From propaganda to public diplomacy: Assessing China's international practice and its image, 1950–2009. *Public Relations Review, 40*(3), 450–458. https://doi.org/10.1016/j.pubrev.2014.04.008

Chon, M.-G., & Kim, S. (2022). Dealing with the COVID-19 crisis: Theoretical application of social media analytics in government crisis management. *Public Relations Review, 48*(3), 476–486. https://doi.org/10.1016/j.pubrev.2022.102201

Chon, M.-G., & Park, H. (2021). Predicting public support for government actions in a public health crisis: Testing fear, organization–public relationship, and behavioral intention in the framework of the Situational Theory of Problem Solving. *Health Communication, 36*(4), 476–486. https://doi.org/10.1080/10410236.2019.1700439

FEMA. (n.d.). *Historic Disasters.* https://www.fema.gov/disaster/historic

Fischoff, B., Brewer, N. T., & Downs, J. S. (2011). *Communicating risks and benefits: An evidence-based user's guide* (pp. 1–242). U.S. Food and Drug Administration. https://www.fda.gov/about-fda/reports/communicating-risks-and-benefits-evidence-based-users-guide

Gelders, D., & Ihlen, Ø. (2010). Government communication about potential policies: Public relations, propaganda or both? *Public Relations Review, 36*(1), 59–62. https://doi.org/10.1016/j.pubrev.2009.08.012

Gleeson, J., Kitchin, R., & McCarthy, E. (2022). Dashboards and public health: The development, impacts, and lessons from the Irish government COVID-19 dashboards. *American Journal of Public Health, 112*(6), 896–899. https://doi.org/10.2105/AJPH.2022.306848

Golan, G. J., & Viatchaninova, E. (2013). Government social responsibility in public diplomacy: Russia's strategic use of advertorials. *Public Relations Review, 39*(4), 403–405. https://doi.org/10.1016/j.pubrev.2013.09.011

Graham, M. W., Avery, E. J., & Park, S. (2015). The role of social media in local government crisis communications. *Public Relations Review, 41*(3), 386–394. https://doi.org/10.1016/j.pubrev.2015.02.001

Heath, R. L., Lee, J., & Ni, L. (2009). Crisis and risk approaches to emergency management planning and communication: The role of similarity and sensitivity. *Journal of Public Relations Research, 21*(2), 123–141. https://doi.org/10.1080/10627260802557415

Hewitt, A. M., Spencer, S. S., Ramloll, R., & Trotta, H. (2008). Expanding CERC beyond public health: Sharing best practices with healthcare managers via virtual learning. *Health Promotion Practice, 9*(4_suppl), 83S–87S. https://doi.org/10.1177/1524839908319090

Hong, H. (2013). Government websites and social media's influence on government-public relationships. *Public Relations Review, 39*(4), 346–356. https://doi.org/10.1016/j.pubrev.2013.07.007

Hong, H., Park, H., Lee, Y., & Park, J. (2012). Public segmentation and government-public relationship building: A cluster analysis of publics in the United States and 19 European countries. *Journal of Public Relations Research, 24*(1), 37–68. https://doi.org/10.1080/1062726X.2012.626135

Horsley, S. (2010). Crisis-adaptive public information: A model for reliability in chaos. In W. T. Coombs & S. J. Holladay (Eds.), *The handbook of crisis communication* (pp. 550–567). Wiley-Blackwell.

Horsley, J. S., & VanDyke, M. S. (2022). Crisis communication: Challenges in the public sector. In M. Lee, G. Neely, & K. B. Stewart (Eds.), *The practice of government public relations* (2nd ed., pp. 72–98). Routledge.

Houston, J. B., Hawthorne, J., Perreault, M. F., Park, E. H., Goldstein Hode, M., Halliwell, M. R., Turner McGowen, S. E., Davis, R., Vaid, S., McElderry, J. A., & Griffith, S. A. (2015). Social media and disasters: A functional framework for social media use in disaster planning, response, and research. *Disasters, 39*(1), 1–22. https://doi.org/10.1111/disa.12092

Hyland-Wood, B., Gardner, J., Leask, J., & Ecker, U. K. H. (2021). Toward effective government communication strategies in the era of COVID-19. *Humanities and Social Sciences Communications, 8*(1), 1–11. https://doi.org/10.1057/s41599-020-00701-w

Kang, M., Kim, J. R., & Cha, H. (2018). From concerned citizens to activists: A case study of 2015 South Korean MERS outbreak and the role of dialogic government communication and citizens' emotions on public activism. *Journal of Public Relations Research, 30*(5/6), 202–229. https://doi.org/10.1080/1062726X.2018.1536980

Kavanaugh, A. L., Fox, E. A., Sheetz, S. D., Yang, S., Li, L. T., Shoemaker, D. J., Natsev, A., & Xie, L. (2012). Social media use by government: From the routine to the critical. *Government Information Quarterly, 29*(4), 480–491. https://doi.org/10.1016/j. giq.2012.06.002

Kim, S., & Krishna, A. (2018). Unpacking public sentiment toward the government: How citizens' perceptions of government communication strategies impact public engagement, cynicism, and communication behaviors in South Korea. *International Journal of Strategic Communication, 12*(3), 215–236. https://doi.org/10.1080/15531 18X.2018.1448400

Lee, M. (2015). Government is different. In B. St. John, M. O. Lamme, & L'Etang (Eds.), *Pathways to public relations: Histories of practice and profession* (1st ed., pp. 108–127). Routledge.

Lee, M. (2022). Government public relations: What is it good for? In M. Lee, G. Neely, & K. B. Stewart (Eds.), *The practice of government public relations* (2nd ed., pp. 72–98). Routledge.

Liu, B. F., Fraustino, J. D., & Jin, Y. (2016). Social media use during disasters: How information form and source influence intended behavioral responses. *Communication Research, 43*(5), 626–646. https://doi.org/10.1177/0093650214565917

Liu, B. F., & Horsley, J. S. (2007). The government communication decision wheel: Toward a public relations model for the public sector. *Journal of Public Relations Research, 19*(4), 377–393. https://doi.org/10.1080/10627260701402473

Liu, B. F., Horsley, J. S., & Levenshus, A. B. (2010). Government and corporate communication practices: Do the differences matter? *Journal of Applied Communication Research, 38*(2), 189–213. https://doi.org/10.1080/00909881003639528

McKeever, B. W. (2021). Public relations and public health: The importance of leadership and other lessons learned from "Understanding AIDS" in the 1980s. *Public Relations Review, 47*(1), 102007. https://doi.org/10.1016/j.pubrev.2020.102007

McLean, H., & Power, M. R. (2014). When minutes count: Tension and trust in the relationship between emergency managers and the media. *Journalism, 15*(3), 307–325. https://doi.org/10.1177/1464884913480873

Mergel, I. (2016). Social media institutionalization in the U.S. federal government. *Government Information Quarterly, 33*(1), 142–148. https://doi.org/10.1016/j. giq.2015.09.002

Miller, A. H. (1974). Political issues and trust in government: 1964–1970. *American Political Science Review, 68*(3), 951–972. https://doi.org/10.2307/1959140

Ortega, F., & Orsini, M. (2020). Governing COVID-19 without government in Brazil: Ignorance, neoliberal authoritarianism, and the collapse of public health leadership. *Global Public Health, 15*(9), 1257–1277. https://doi.org/10.1080/17441692.2020.17 95223

Paek, H.-J., Hilyard, K., Freimuth, V. S., Barge, J. K., & Mindlin, M. (2008). Public support for government actions during a flu pandemic: Lessons learned from a statewide survey. *Health Promotion Practice, 9*(4_suppl), 60S–72S. https://doi. org/10.1177/1524839908322114

Park, H., & Lee, T. (2018). Adoption of e-government applications for public health risk communication: Government trust and social media competence as primary drivers. *Journal of Health Communication, 23*(8), 712–723. https://doi.org/10.1080/1081073 0.2018.1511013

Porumbescu, G. A. (2016). Linking public sector social media and e-government website use to trust in government. *Government Information Quarterly, 33*(2), 291–304. https://doi.org/10.1016/j.giq.2016.04.006

Reynolds, B., & Seeger, M. W. (2005). Crisis and emergency risk communication as an integrative model. *Journal of Health Communication, 10*(1), 43–55. https://doi. org/10.1080/10810730590904571

Rice, C., & Somerville, I. (2013). Power-sharing and political public relations: Government–press relationships in Northern Ireland's developing democratic institutions. *Public Relations Review*, *39*(4), 293–302. https://doi.org/10.1016/j.pubrev. 2013.07.014f

Rooksby, J., & Sommerville, I. (2012). The management and use of social network sites in a government department. *Computer Supported Cooperative Work (CSCW)*, *21*(4), 397–415. https://doi.org/10.1007/s10606-011-9150-2

Sanders, K. (2011). Political public relations and government communication. In J. Strömbäck & S. Kiousis (Eds.), *Political public relations: Principles and applications* (pp. 254–273). Taylor & Francis.

Sanders, K. (2020). Government communication. In J. Strömbäck & S. Kiousis (Eds.), *Political public relations: Concepts, principles, and applications* (2nd ed., pp. 165–186). Routledge.

Seeger, M. W., & Reynolds, B. (2008). Crisis communication and the public health: Integrated approaches and new imperatives. In M. W. Seeger, T. L. Sellnow, & R. R. Ulmer (Eds.), *Crisis communication and the public health* (pp. 3–20). Hampton Press.

Sledge, D., & Thomas, H. F. (2019). From disaster response to community recovery: Nongovernmental entities, government, and public health. *American Journal of Public Health*, *109*(3), 437–444. https://doi.org/10.2105/AJPH.2018.304895

Strömbäck, J., & Kiousis, S. (2011). Political public relations: Defining and mapping an emergent field. In J. Strömbäck & S. Kiousis (Eds.), *Political public relations: Principles and applications* (pp. 1–32). Taylor & Francis.

Sutton, J., League, C., Sellnow, T. L., & Sellnow, D. D. (2015). Terse messaging and public health in the midst of natural disasters: The case of the Boulder floods. *Health Communication*, *30*(2), 135–143. https://doi.org/10.1080/10410236.2014.974124

Tang, L., & Zou, W. (2021). Health information consumption under COVID-19 lockdown: An interview study of residents of Hubei Province, China. *Health Communication*, *36*(1), 74–80. https://doi.org/10.1080/10410236.2020.1847447

Taylor, M., & Kent, M. L. (2016). Towards legitimacy and professionalism: A call to repeal the Gillett Amendment. *Public Relations Review*, *42*(1), 1–8. https://doi. org/10.1016/j.pubrev.2015.09.012

U.S. Department of Health and Human Services. (2019). *National health security strategy implementation plan 2019–2022*. https://aspr.hhs.gov/ResponseOperations/legal/NHSS/Documents/2019-2022-nhss-ip-v508.pdf

van der Meer, T. G. L. A., & Jin, Y. (2020). Seeking formula for misinformation treatment in public health crises: The effects of corrective information type and source. *Health Communication*, *35*(5), 560–575. https://doi.org/10.1080/10410236.2019.1573295

Van Scoy, L. J., Snyder, B., Miller, E. L., Toyobo, O., Grewel, A., Ha, G., Gillespie, S., Patel, M., Reilly, J., Zgierska, A. E., & Lennon, R. P. (2021). Public anxiety and distrust due to perceived politicization and media sensationalism during early COVID-19 media messaging. *Journal of Communication in Healthcare*, *14*(3), 193–205. https://doi.org/10.1080/17538068.2021.1953934

Veil, S. R., & Anthony, K. E. (2017). Exploring public relations challenges in compounding crises: The pariah effect of toxic trailers. *Journal of Public Relations Research*, *29*(4), 141–157. https://doi.org/10.1080/1062726X.2017.1355805

Venkatraman, K., & Manoharan, A. (2023). Public engagement as the fifth dimension of outbreak communication: Public's perceptions of public health communication during COVID-19 in India. *Health Communication*, *38*(2), 285–297. https://doi.org/10.1080/10410236.2021.1950294

Vos, S. C., & Buckner, M. M. (2016). Social media messages in an emerging health crisis: Tweeting bird flu. *Journal of Health Communication*, *21*(3), 301–308. https://doi.org/10.1080/10810730.2015.1064495

Wang, Q. (2022). Using social media for agenda setting in Chinese government's communications during the 2020 COVID-19 pandemic. *Journal of Communication Inquiry*,
46(4), 373–394. https://doi.org/10.1177/01968599221105099

Waymer, D. (2013). Democracy and government public relations: Expanding the scope of
"Relationship" in public relations research. *Public Relations Review*, *39*(4), 320–331.
https://doi.org/10.1016/j.pubrev.2013.07.015

Wolf-Fordham, S. (2020). Integrating government silos: Local emergency management
and public health department collaboration for emergency planning and response.
The American Review of Public Administration, *50*(6–7), 560–567. https://doi.org/
10.1177/0275074020943706

11

PROVING IT WITH ACTION

Embracing a Responsibility to Advocate for Social Change

Holly Overton and Nicholas Eng

Global events, social movements, and controversial issues in recent years have transformed our society and the way we perceive the world. The COVID-19 pandemic has affected every aspect of life, raising challenging questions about how to protect public health while testing the limits of organizations' capabilities and responsibilities. Tragedies such as the killing of George Floyd and mass shootings in schools have led to powerful movements such as the Black Lives Matter (BLM) movement and the formation of several organizations advocating for public safety measures related to gun violence. Recent legislation such as the overturning of *Roe v. Wade* has created more controversy in an already polarized society divided over issues including immigration, climate change, and human rights such as voting, health care, and marriage rights.

A common theme that resonates with each of these examples is the need to rethink social change and the role of business in society. For years, the Edelman Trust Barometer has highlighted in its annual survey that stakeholder expectations for business have changed. A key takeaway from the Edelman (2022) Trust Barometer Global Report is that societal leadership is now a core business function—a notion that highlights a fundamental shift in the role of business in society. Similar arguments have emerged from USC Annenberg's (2022) Global Communication Report. For example, the report indicates that 83 percent of those surveyed feel that business has a powerful platform it can use to speak from on important issues, while 78 percent agree that business has a responsibility to support causes and speak out on issues that align with their brand purpose/mission. With regard to stakeholder expectations, the most recent Cone Communications CSR Study (2017) highlighted how even more than five years ago, 63 percent of Americans were hopeful businesses would be a leader in efforts to

DOI: 10.4324/9781003327189-14

drive social change, 78 percent want companies to address social justice issues, and 87 percent would purchase a company's product because they engaged in advocacy efforts.

While it has become clear that the role of business in society has shifted, guidance for how organizations can most effectively inspire social change has been tentative in light of the need to balance public expectations with organizational values, identity, and performance. Furthermore, the question remains as to whether/how businesses can drive social change without further polarizing society. In this chapter, we discuss examples of how organizations have attempted to influence prosocial behaviors through the examination of three timely, controversial topics/issues: COVID-19, women's rights, and gun violence. Through a discussion of current academic literature in corporate social responsibility (CSR) and corporate social advocacy (CSA) communication, we integrate and apply arguments from scholarship to illustrate how organizations can effectively inspire social change. We offer case examples of how organizations have engaged in prosocial behaviors to varying degrees, including examples highlighting CEO actions. We conclude with recommendations for the profession and a discussion about emerging research trends in strategic communications.

Contributing to Societal Change through Social Responsibility and Advocacy

Companies have long made efforts to contribute to societal good by donating to charitable causes, partnering with nonprofit organizations, and facilitating or supporting employee volunteerism in local communities, as some examples. Such efforts have been commonly accepted as falling under the umbrella of CSR, which scholars have broadly defined as a company or organization's voluntary efforts to improve society (David et al., 2005). Some companies with strong reputations for consistent engagement in socially responsible efforts include Toms, which is known for being built on the model of giving away a pair of shoes for every pair sold, and Patagonia, with its longstanding support of environmental causes. Other companies such as Google, Levi's, and the LEGO Group, have become well known for their dedication to social impact through commitments to using carbon-free energy and reducing water waste. Health-care companies such as Pfizer have also embraced CSR and sustainability as part of their mission and made significant charitable donations to help combat the global health effects of COVID-19. These examples illustrate organizational efforts to influence prosocial behaviors and to align organizational missions with contributing to societal good. Extant literature has consistently pointed to the importance of authentic (not cosmetic) CSR efforts (Mombeuil & Zhang, 2020) and how perceptions of organizations' motives for engaging in CSR can impact attitudes and behavioral intentions (Vlachos et al., 2017). Furthermore, engaging in CSR activities is often seen as necessary for organizations to be perceived as socially valid or legitimate (Seele & Lock, 2015) in the eyes of the public.

While organizations have sharpened their focus on CSR, another shift in societal expectations has become evident in recent years with stakeholders looking to organizations to take a public stance on controversial social-political issues. This concept, which scholars have termed corporate social advocacy (CSA; Dodd & Supa, 2014), extends beyond the definition of CSR. CSA broadly refers to company efforts to contribute to societal good. As it is a relatively new concept, scholars have not yet agreed on a clear demarcation line between CSR and CSA, or a singular definition for either of the terms. However, recent scholarship has attempted to identify similarities and differences between the terms that most agree are tangentially related but separate, distinctive concepts. A few examples include Dodd & Supa (2014), who emphasize that CSA is a company taking a public stance on a controversial social-political issue and that the issue itself is "outside the company's normal sphere of CSR interest" (Dodd & Supa, 2015, p. 288). This is further highlighted in Rim et al.'s (2020) attempt to distinguish CSR by noting that "unlike CSR, the social-political issues that the organization advocates for or against are not directly related to the organization's core business" (p. 2). Finally, Browning et al. (2020) define "the taking of a stance on a controversial sociopolitical issue that risks alienating some stakeholders while signaling to others a shared commitment to values or ideals important to both parties" (p. 1030) as organizational advocacy.

Some well-known examples of CSA include Nike's 30th Anniversary Campaign featuring former 49ers quarterback Colin Kaepernick, who is known for kneeling in protest of racial injustice; DICK's Sporting Goods speaking out in favor of gun reform in response to gun violence; and Ben & Jerry's frequent stance-taking on several social-political issues such as voting, climate change, and various controversial issues related to human rights. These bolder, riskier attempts to inspire social change are in alignment with what stakeholders today are demanding from companies. Softer efforts such as donating to societal causes are still expected, but they no longer meet public expectations of the role of business in society. Arguably, this is a new era of CSR in which the expectations and boundaries for company actions are tested.

The notion of organizations inspiring social change through stance-taking creates an unprecedented opportunity yet an enormous responsibility for businesses today. Organizations are inherently challenged to balance stakeholder expectations to take action with the risks involved with stance-taking. However, while the boundaries between CSR, CSA, and other related terms continue to be tested, one thing is clear: organizations need to find meaningful ways to embrace a responsibility to inspire social change, whether through socially responsible actions and/or more explicit advocacy efforts. In the next section, we discuss three timely, controversial topics/issues: COVID-19, women's rights, and gun violence, and how various organizations have attempted to inspire social change through social responsibility and advocacy efforts.

Case Topic 1: COVID-19, Vaccine Mandates, and Protecting Public Health

The coronavirus disease 2019 (COVID-19) pandemic dramatically changed the lives of millions around the world. Referred to as pneumonia of unknown cause, the World Health Organization (WHO, 2020) Country Office in China was informed about the spread of COVID-19 in Wuhan City, China, on December 31, 2019. The virus quickly made its way to the U.S., with the first laboratory-confirmed case of COVID-19 reported by the Centers for Disease Control and Prevention (CDC, 2023) on January 20, 2020. As of March 2024, there have been over 103.4 million confirmed cases of COVID-19 in the U.S., and over 1.2 million deaths (WHO, n.d.).

When a public health crisis like COVID-19 emerges, individuals often look to businesses to provide aid and solutions to mitigate the threats of the pandemic. At the onset of the pandemic in early 2020, news headlines such as "50 Ways Companies Are Giving Back during the Coronavirus Pandemic" (Morgan, 2020) were commonplace, suggesting that not only are corporations seeing a need to champion social change, but that their initiatives are considered to be newsworthy also indicates public expectations for corporate action. In the following sections, we highlight some of the ways in which companies have contributed to COVID-19 efforts, ranging from uncontroversial charitable efforts (i.e., CSR), to more controversial actions that have the potential to alienate stakeholders (i.e., CSA).

Numerous companies have taken action to aid with the pandemic, especially when it became evident that health-care workers were not only overwhelmed by the uptick in COVID cases and hospitalizations, but they were also putting themselves at heightened risks for contracting the virus. Companies like Crocs and Allbirds targeted their CSR efforts at health-care workers. Crocs shares that: "Since the spring of 2020, we've donated nearly 1M free pairs of shoes to health-care heroes on the frontlines of COVID-19" (Crocs, n.d., para. 1). Allbirds made a similar claim that the company was able to "supply over 50,000 pairs of Wool Runners to healthcare professionals in need" through their buy-one-give-one initiative (Allbirds, n.d., para. 2).

Apart from charitable efforts targeted at health-care workers, some corporations also have broader initiatives aimed at curbing the spread of the virus. For instance, Nike (2020) tweeted an image with the text, "If you ever dreamed of playing for millions around the world, now is your chance. Play inside, play for the world" (n.d.). Similarly, Lego's #LetsBuildTogether campaign was aimed at families to encourage them to stay home during the pandemic, while also providing educational tips and resources on how to play well at home (Lego, n.d.).

Both Nike and Lego's messaging encourage the public to stay home and socially distance to prevent virus spread. Other companies have also gone one step further to encourage the public to get vaccinated. In 2021, Walgreens launched two vaccination campaigns, one in April (i.e., "This Is Our Shot" campaign, and another in September (i.e., "Before You Go There, Start Here") to boost vaccination rates in their pharmacies (Collings, 2021). To incentivize vaccinations, patrons of Krispy Kreme (n.d.) who presented their vaccination record card in-store could redeem a free doughnut. Notably, while Walgreens may have financial benefits to reap from higher vaccination rates and Krispy Kreme does not, both corporations' social responsibility efforts attempt to increase vaccination rates for public health.

Thus far, we have described cases of companies' CSR efforts to aid with the pandemic. Now, we turn to vaccine mandates as an example of bolder, more controversial corporate advocacy efforts.

Mandating vaccinations for their employees is one form of corporate advocacy. Whether to mandate vaccinations to prevent the spread of COVID remains a contentious issue in the U.S. According to a Pew Research Center survey, 82 percent of Republicans agree that employers that have vaccine mandates should allow employees with religious objections to keep their jobs despite refusing to get vaccinated, while 52 percent of Democrats share the same sentiment (Nortey, 2022). When Carhartt, an American apparel company, required employees to be vaccinated before returning to work, the company received tremendous backlash, particularly from conservatives, on social media with consumers vowing to boycott the company for their decision (Dean, 2022). However, when Starbucks reversed its decision to enforce the same mandate, #BoycottStarbucks started trending on social media, driven primarily by liberal users (Suciu, 2022). This form of advocacy targeted at internal publics can also influence external stakeholders even though the decisions do not directly influence the consumers.

Because advocating for a vaccine mandate for employees can have reputational risks for a corporation, companies have varying levels of corporate advocacy. In a survey of 500 top corporations and their COVID policies, *The New York Times* (2022a) reported that of the 129 respondents, 18 companies (e.g., The Home Depot, P&G, and Bank of America) did not have plans to require employees to be vaccinated prior to returning to the office, 36 companies (e.g., Starbucks, JetBlue, and Coca-Cola) reported that their plans are dependent on federal, state, or local vaccine mandates, while 75 employers (e.g. Walmart, Uber, and American Express) planned to require vaccinations for some workers. On one end of the spectrum, companies that do not have plans for employees to be vaccinated are considered to *not* be engaging in corporate advocacy since no controversial action is taken by the organization. On the other end of the spectrum, companies that plan to have vaccine mandates, despite the Supreme Court's decision to block a vaccine mandate for large corporations (Liptak, 2022), are potentially alienating their stakeholders (e.g., employees or customers) and yet are still advocating for vaccinations for public good. Such forms of voluntary compliance go above and beyond the advocacy efforts of companies like Starbucks, where decisions are made merely in accordance with federal, state, or local guidelines. In so doing, Starbucks may be seen as taking a more neutral and less "controversial" stance towards vaccinations. However, as COVID guidelines are constantly evolving, Starbucks' Chief Operating Officer John Culver wrote in an open letter on January 4, 2022, to their partners that following the Occupational Safety & Health Administration's guidelines, employees would have to be fully vaccinated against the virus, or submit weekly COVID tests (Starbucks, 2022). Less than a month later, Starbucks reversed the decision citing the Supreme Court's ruling against vaccine mandates, sparking outrage from both consumers and employees (Romero, 2022).

Case Topic 2: Roe v. Wade and the Battle for Women's Rights

In 1973, the U.S. Supreme Court ruled that the Fourteenth Amendment of the U.S. Constitution would protect an individual's fundamental right to privacy, which extends to an individual's right to abortion (*Roe v. Wade*, 1973). However, almost 50 years later, in a leaked draft ruling published by news outlet *Politico*, news about the overruling of *Roe v. Wade* made waves (Gerstein & Ward, 2022). Following the overturning of *Roe v. Wade* in June 2022, tensions regarding women's rights have become increasingly heated. Research conducted by the Yale Chief Executive Leadership Institute found that 118 companies publicly responded to the Supreme Court's decision in support of abortion rights (Sonnenfeld et al. 2022). With at least 14 states in the U.S. banning abortion procedures as of March 2024 (Choi & Cole, 2024), some companies like Yahoo, Apple, Johnson & Johnson, and UnitedHealth Group have announced that they would either reimburse or cover abortion-related travel (Goldberg, 2022) for employees. BuzzFeed's chief executive, Jonah Peretti, went as far as to call the Supreme Court's decision "regressive and horrific for women" (Goldberg et al., 2022, para. 25), while Levi Strauss & Co. issued a strong statement condemning the decision. However, standing up for abortion rights is a risky affair. In fact, prior to the overturning of *Roe v. Wade*, when Citigroup offered to cover the travel costs for their employees seeking abortions, Republican lawmakers responded by urging the U.S. to cancel government contracts with the bank (Gibson, 2022). Such response explains why so many companies have kept mum on the issue, choosing not to advocate publicly (Daniels, 2022).

Despite the high risk, some companies' actions are reflective of corporate America reckoning with its role in this issue (Hodges, 2022) and the need to support and retain employees. However, several companies offering to pay for employees' abortion-related coverage are also those that had made political donations to lawmakers who supported these laws—an action many deem as hypocritical. This raises questions about company motives and authenticity in their advocacy efforts. That is, how can a company condemn abortion law yet fund the very politicians advocating for it? This question is loaded with implications about a company's role in society and just how much they walk the talk by backing up their words with actions. Furthermore, it raises questions about just how much companies' social responsibility and/or advocacy efforts align with the bottom line vs. how much they are genuinely committed to protecting public health and human rights.

This issue also hit home in the sport sector, with several female athletes speaking out about the Supreme Court's decision, which was announced just after the 50th anniversary of Title IX. Athletes and sports legends such as Megan Rapinoe and Billie Jean King, among many others, condemned the ruling as "cruel," "sad," and "a step backwards" for the country (ESPN, 2022). Several sports organizations also released statements condemning the ruling, and calls for banning states that criminalize abortion have grown louder. The Supreme Court ruling and the abortion law issue have heightened discussions about women's rights, as well as the level of controversy surrounding the issue. Furthermore, this example illustrates the complexities of organizations' role in the issue and the potential dangers of speaking out when words don't always align with actions.

Case Topic 3: Gun Violence, Corporate America, and Athlete Activism

According to the nonprofit research group Gun Violence Archive (2023), there were 656 cases of mass shootings in the U.S. in 2023. Gun violence in the U.S. has been characterized by *The New York Times* (2023) as an "epidemic of mass shootings" (para. 1). Despite this "epidemic," support for stricter gun laws still remains deeply divided down political party lines (Brenan, 2022). With the increasing number of mass shootings around the U.S, some corporations have been vocal in their advocacy for reduced gun violence. One of the most prominent cases in the academic literature on CSA is Dick's Sporting Goods' advocacy for gun reform (Gaither et al., 2018). Not only did Dick's stop selling assault-style weapons and raised the minimum age of gun sales to 21 (prior to the passing of the *Protecting Our Kids Act* in 2021), then Chairman and CEO Edward Stack also called on elected officials to seriously consider gun reforms (Gaither et al., 2018). However, Dick's is not the only company to have engaged in CSA for gun violence. In 2019, Doug McMillon (2019), President and CEO of Walmart, released the following statement: "It's clear to us that the status quo [present gun laws] is unacceptable," announcing the company's decision to discontinue sales of short-barrel rifle ammunition and handguns. Like McMillon, 228 CEOs from companies like Unilever, Levi Strauss & Co., and Lyft co-signed a letter to members of the U.S. Senate to reduce gun violence in the country (Huddleston Jr., 2022). Addressing members of the Senate using first-person language, the letter brings attention to the "more than 110 people [that] are shot and killed in the United States every day" and an impassioned plea that, "Our country needs you to take bold urgent action to address our gun violence epidemic" (CEOs for Gun Safety, 2022). However, governmental efforts in Republican states like Texas to force companies to remain neutral on the issue have raised challenges and further raised questions about when companies are going to challenge the gun lobby (Moran and Albright, 2022).

Calls for action to reduce gun violence were also prominent in the sport sector. Particularly after mass shootings in 2022 such as those in Uvalde, Texas and Buffalo, N.Y., athletes, teams, and even coaches took a stand on the issue and engaged in various efforts to improve safety measures across the nation. In a pre-game press conference, Warriors coach Steve Kerr made a passionate speech criticizing the lack of action and senators who refuse to support legislation for stricter gun laws (Poole, 2022). He chose to devote the full time of his nationally televised press conference to calling for change. San Francisco Giants manager Gabe Kapler refused to come out of the dugout for the national anthem in protest of gun violence (Miller, 2022).

Several sports teams also took action, such as the New York Yankees and Tampa Bay Rays intentionally using their Twitter platforms to tweet facts about the impacts of gun violence in lieu of game coverage. The Rays also pledged to donate $50,000 to a group supporting gun control—a move dubbed as supporting societal efforts but also taking a stance by supporting gun control. In Chicago, five professional sports teams announced a $300,000 donation to several organizations with a mission to end school shootings. They also released a powerful statement as the Chicago Sports Alliance, stating: "It is our responsibility to those innocent lives lost to do more. We are committed to making a difference through the resources in our power to solving this gun violence epidemic. Lives depend on it. This is not a game" (Sheinin, 2022, para. 4).

These examples are reflective of what scholars have called a resurgence of athlete activism (Hurley, 2017) that is characterized by unprecedented technological power that enables athletes to speak more directly and publicly to audiences (Cooper et al., 2019). Furthermore, individual athletes have taken vocal stances on issues—something perhaps even more impactful and riskier than sports teams entering the conversation. For example, basketball star LeBron James has long spoken out against gun violence. Recently, he tweeted his outrage about the 2022 mass shooting in Uvalde, Texas:

> My thoughts and prayers goes out to the families of love ones loss & injured at Robb Elementary School in Uvalde, TX! Like when is enough enough man!!! These are kids and we keep putting them in harms way at school. Like seriously "AT SCHOOL" where it's suppose to be the safest!
>
> *(James, 2022)*

Another example is Chicago Cubs pitcher Marcus Stroman, who has called out politicians for not taking more action to prevent tragedies in the future. "America continuing to go backward!" (Stroman, 2022) is among his many tweets about the issue.

Some scholars have argued that athletes and sports teams can serve as agents of social change (Pelak, 2005) while others have even suggested that sport has an *obligation* to inspire social change, given its position of power and wealth in society (Godfrey, 2009). However, others are more critical of the politicization of sports (Kim et al., 2020), suggesting that politically charged discussions don't belong in this space. Furthermore, some question the notion of sports teams, athletes, and/or coaches speaking out on social-political issues that undoubtedly risks alienating fan bases. However, as controversial social-political issues continue persisting and our nation becomes further polarized, it seems almost impossible for even the sport sector to remain apolitical—or even to expect that it wants to.

Shifting Societal Roles and Expectations: Reflections and Future Directions

This chapter has discussed examples of how organizations have engaged in prosocial behaviors to varying degrees related to three controversial topics/issues: COVID-19, women's rights, and gun violence. We highlighted examples of organizational efforts to improve public health through initiatives to curb the spread of COVID-19 and other charitable efforts, as well as bolder actions such as company statements condemning Supreme Court actions. The case examples also illustrate how athletes and sports teams have engaged in social-political issues and can serve as agents of social change. However, organizational actions (or lack thereof) can come with costs—the potential to alienate stakeholders, a blow to the bottom line, or government-imposed pressure or penalties, to name a few. For example, Richard Edelman, CEO of the public relations firm Edelman, is quoted in a *Wall Street Journal* article saying, "we better be careful here because there's starting to be a pushback against wokeness" (The Editorial Board, 2022, para. 6). Edelman's warning suggests that organizations and CEOs need to be cautious about stance-taking or take the approach that some organizations have long taken: touting themselves as apolitical organizations. For this reason, many companies continue to be reticent to speak out and/or take action, especially when even a well-intentioned effort such as supporting employees' health care can cause reputational damage because of previous support efforts the organization extended to political candidates that ultimately positioned the organization as hypocritical. Despite progress in scholarly literature, we still lack clear guidance on how companies can meaningfully engage in social-political issues without further polarizing society.

Balancing Public Expectations with Organizational Values, Identity, and Performance

Companies considering whether to take a bold stance on socio-political issues should be prepared for the potential backlash, but can also take the opportunity to become stewards for social change. For example, by taking a bold stance on protective COVID measures like a vaccine mandate for employees, companies can instill confidence in consumers, especially for corporations like Starbucks with public-facing storefronts. While this may initially invite backlash from the public, being fickle and changing guidelines for employees can be even more detrimental to the reputation of the corporation (Suciu, 2022). After all, Dodd and Supa (2014) argue that "engagement in and stances on social-political issues may differ among stakeholder groups and across individuals, ultimately impacting organizational goals" (p. 3); hence, certain groups of individuals are bound to be unhappy with whatever decision is being made by the corporation. Considering that many large organizations have operations across the U.S., where guidelines and laws are different, corporations need to decide if and how they want to become stewards of social change.

If companies wish to truly embrace the idea of inspiring change, they should also embrace the need to balance public expectations with organizational values, identity, and performance. While there certainly isn't a cookie-cutter approach on how to successfully navigate these murky waters, scholars have offered some suggestions such as Argenti's (2020) three questions to guide an organization's approach: Does the issue align with your company's strategy? Can you meaningfully influence the issue? Will your constituencies agree with speaking out? When constituencies disagree, Argenti (2020) recommends weighing their relative importance to the organization. In a recent blog post, scholar Melissa Dodd discussed the role of public relations in gun violence prevention. Among many suggestions, Dodd offered advice for companies to engage authentically and for leaders to be courageous and to lead with purpose (Dodd, 2022). While it is important to be cognizant of the potential for organizational actions to lead to more polarization, which some warn is a "lose-lose proposition" (Penning, 2022, para. 8), organizations and CEOs can inspire change if they are thoughtful about their approach and align their actions with their words and their values.

Making Purpose Our DNA

Much like how organizations have found that consistent, proactive engagement with social responsibility efforts has often led to more favorable reception, we argue that companies taking stances on social issues are more likely to be successful in their efforts to inspire change without further adding to the polarization problem if they embrace the notion of leading with purpose and making advocacy and activism part of their organizational DNA. For example, Ben & Jerry's is a company that has long been known for its efforts to influence change. Along those lines, several companies have taken steps to create activism departments and/or positions dedicated to values-driven engagement on societal issues. While it would be unrealistic to expect organizations to speak up and take action on every issue, it is important for them to stand for something and to proactively and consistently take action when appropriate. At times, organizational involvement may be best conducted in the form of social responsibility, but other times, it is important for organizational leaders to be courageous and to embrace a moral, ethical responsibility to proactively take action and not bow to stakeholder (e.g., consumers and governments) pushback.

The proliferation of athlete activism and sports teams' involvement in societal issues is worthy of continued examination in scholarly literature and in practice. Sports teams and athletes have very large, public platforms and a loyal fan base that is likely to continue watching games and purchasing tickets and merchandise even if an athlete or team takes a stance that does not align with a fan's values. While some will always take issue with the politicization of sports, others have acknowledged that no organization—even those in entertainment—can or should tout itself as completely apolitical and remain silent on every issue. Continued research about the role of sport in this conversation is necessary, as are scholarly investigations that will advance our understanding of the role of business in society and how to measure organizational effectiveness in this area. Furthermore, we need more scholarly research that can offer meaningful contributions to the profession through tangible, actionable insights. Now, more than ever, it is important for organizations to embrace a responsibility to be agents of social change in our ever-changing society.

Questions for Discussion

1. In your opinion, when should organizations focus on social responsibility efforts vs. engaging in advocacy efforts regarding social-political issues?

2. What are the benefits and drawbacks that come with an organization's vocal advocation for controversial socio-political issues?
3. In your opinion, are the public's expectations for organizations to be drivers of social change misplaced? If so, how? If not, why not?
4. How do you feel about sports teams and athletes' involvement in controversial social-political issues?

Further Reading

Austin, L., Gaither, B., & Gaither, T. K. (2019). Corporate social advocacy as public interest communications: Exploring perceptions of corporate involvement in controversial social-political issues. *The Journal of Public Interest Communications*, *3*(2), 3–3.

Hong, C., & Li, C. (2020). To support or to boycott: A public segmentation model in corporate social advocacy. *Journal of Public Relations Research*, *32*(5–6), 160–177.

Waymer, D., & Logan, N. (2021). Corporate social advocacy as engagement: Nike's social justice communication. *Public Relations Review*, *47*(1), 102005.

References

Allbirds. (n.d.). Better together. https://www.allbirds.com/pages/better-together

Argenti, P.A. (2020, Oct. 16). When should your company speak up about a social issue? *Harvard Business Review*. https://hbr.org/2020/10/when-should-your-company-speak-up-about-a-social-issue

Brenan, M. (2022, November 21). Diminished majority supports stricter gun laws in U.S. Gallup. https://news.gallup.com/poll/405260/diminished-majority-supports-stricter-gun-laws.aspx

Browning, N., Lee, E., Park, Y.E., Kim, T., & Collins, R. (2020). Muting or meddling? Advocacy as a relational communication strategy affecting organization-public relationships and stakeholder response. *Journalism & Mass Communication Quarterly*, *97*(4), 1026–1053. https://doi.org/10.1177/1077699020916810

CEOs for Gun Safety (2022). 2022 Letter. https://www.ceosforgunsafety.org/pages/2022-letter

Centers for Disease Control and Prevention [CDC] (n.d.). CDC museum COVID-19 timeline. https://www.cdc.gov/museum/timeline/covid19.html

Choi, A., & Cole, D. (2024, March 5). See where abortions are banned and legal – and where it's still in limbo. CNN. https://www.cnn.com/us/abortion-access-restrictions-bans-us-dg/index.html

Collings, R. (2021, September, 3). Walgreens still wants you to get your vaccines. Adweek. https://www.adweek.com/brand-marketing/walgreens-still-wants-you-to-get-your-vaccines/

Cone Communications. (2022). 2017 Cone Communications CSR Study. https://www.cbd.int/doc/case-studies/inc/cs-inc-cone-communications-en.pdf

Cooper, J. N., Macaulay, C., & Rodriguez, S. H. (2019). Race and resistance: A typology of African American sport activism. *International Review for the Sociology of Sport*, *54*(2), 151–181. https://doi.org/10.1177/1012690217718170

Crocs. (n.d.). Free clogs giveaway for healthcare workers. https://www.crocs.com/COVID19-REQUEST.html

Daniels, C. (2022, May 12). The silence is deafening from corporate America on *Roe v. Wade*. Why so many companies are staying quiet. PRWeek. https://www.prweek.com/article/1755864/silence-deafening-corporate-america-roe-v-wade-why-so-companies-staying-quiet

David, P., Kline, S., & Dai, Y. (2005). Corporate social responsibility practices, corporate identity, and purchase intention: A dual-process model. *Journal of Public Relations Research, 17*(3), 291–313. https://doi.org/10.1207/s1532754xjprr1703_4

Dean, G. (2022, January 19). Conservatives lashed out at Carhartt after the company said staff had to get vaccinated. Business Insider. https://www.businessinsider.com/carhartt-covid-vaccine-mandate-conservative-backlash-coronavirus-valade-workplace-boycott-2022-1

Dodd, M.D. (2022, June 3). The American gun violence epidemic: How can companies meaningfully engage? Institute for Public Relations. https://instituteforpr.org/gvp-how-companies-can-engage/

Dodd, M. D., & Supa, D. W. (2014). Conceptualizing and measuring "corporate social advocacy" communication: Examining the impact on corporate financial performance. *Public Relations Journal, 8*(3), 1–23. http://www.prsa.org/Intelligence/PRJournal/Vol8/No3

Dodd, M. D., & Supa, D. (2015). Testing the viability of corporate social advocacy as a predictor of purchase intention. *Communication Research Reports, 32*(4), 287–293. https://doi.org/10.1080/08824096.2015.1089853

Edelman. (2022). 2022 Annual Edelman Trust Barometer. https://www.edelman.com/sites/g/files/aatuss191/files/2022-01/2022%20Edelman%20Trust%20Barometer%20Global%20Report_Final.pdf

ESPN (2022, June 24). Megan Rapinoe, USWNT slam 'cruel' overturning of *Roe v. Wade*. https://www.espn.com/soccer/united-states-usaw/story/4690486/megan-rapinoeuswnt-slam-cruel-overturning-of-roe-v-wade

Gaither, B. M., Austin, L., & Collins, M. (2018). Examining the case of DICK's sporting goods: Realignment of stakeholders through corporate social advocacy. *The Journal of Public Interest Communications, 2*(2), 176–201. https://doi.org/10.32473/jpic.v2.i2.p176

Gerstein, J. & Ward, A. (2022, May 5). Supreme Court has voted to overturn abortion rights, draft opinion shows. *Politico.* https://www.politico.com/news/2022/05/02/supreme-court-abortion-draft-opinion-00029473

Gibson, K. (2022, April 7). House Republicans want to axe Citi contracts over bank's abortion benefits. CBS News. https://www.cbsnews.com/news/abortion-citi-republicans-bank/

Godfrey, P. C. (2009). Corporate social responsibility in sport: An overview and key issues. *Journal of Sport Management, 23*, 698–716. https://doi.org/10.1123/jsm.23.6.698

Goldberg, E. (2022, June 30). These companies will cover travel expenses for employee abortions. *The New York Times.* https://www.nytimes.com/article/abortion-companies-travel-expenses.html

Goldberg, E., Kelley, L., Flitter, E. (2022, June 24). Here are the companies that will cover travel expenses for employee abortions. *The New York Times.* https://www.nytimes.com/2022/06/24/business/abortion-companies-travel-expenses.html

Gun Violence Archive. (2023, March 24). Gun violence archive. https://www.gunviolencearchive.org/

Hodges, L. (2022, July 25). Corporate America reckons with its role in reproductive rights. NPR. https://www.npr.org/2022/07/25/1112599476/abortion-roe-companies-pay-travel-law-ban

Huddleston Jr. T. (2022, June 10). 228 high-powered CEOs—from Lyft to Bain Capital—are calling for 'bold, urgent action' on gun violence. CNBC. https://www.cnbc.com/2022/06/10/ceos-demand-bold-urgent-action-on-gun-reform-in-letter-to-senate.html

Hurley, I. (2017, December). In 2017, the athlete became the activist. Pacific Standard. https://psmag.com/social-justice/in-2017-the-athlete-became-the-activist.

James, L. [@KingJames]. (2022, May 24). My thoughts and prayers goes out to the families of love ones loss & injured at Robb Elementary School in Uvalde, TX! Like when is enough enough man!!! These are kids and we keep putting them in harms way at school. Like seriously "AT SCHOOL" where it's suppose to be the safest! [Tweet]. Twitter. https://twitter.com/KingJames/status/1529201815501299712?ref_src=twsrc%5Etfw%7Ctwcamp%5Etweetembed%7Ctwterm%5E15292018155012 99712%7Ctwgr%5Ee120295e8a872afbe84b7525e57c05f1b4c487eb%7Ctwcon% 5Es1_&ref_url=https%3A%2F%2Fwww.si.com%2Fnba%2F2022%2F05%2F24%2 Flebron-james-expresses-outrage-over-texas-elementary-school-shooting

Kim, J. K., Overton, H., Bhalla, N., & Li, J. Y. (2020). Nike, Colin Kaepernick, and the politicization of sports: Examining perceived organizational motives and public responses. *Public Relations Review*, *46*(2), 1–10. https://doi.org/10.1016/j.pubrev.2019. 101856

Krispy Kreme. (n.d.). Sustainability. https://krispykreme.com/sustainability

Lego (n.d.). #LetsBuildTogether. https://www.lego.com/en-gb/themes/letsbuildtogether/ tips-to-help-families-play-well-at-home

Liptak, A. (2022, January 13). Supreme Court blocks Biden's virus mandate for large employers. *The New York Times*. https://www.nytimes.com/2022/01/13/us/politics/ supreme-court-biden-vaccine-mandate.html

McMillon, D. (2019, September 3). McMillon to associates: Our next steps in response to the tragedies in El Paso and Southaven. Walmart. https://corporate.walmart.com/ newsroom/2019/09/03/mcmillon-to-associates-our-next-steps-in-response-to-the-tragedies-in-el-paso-and-southaven

Miller, S. (2022, May 27). Amid gun violence, Giants manager will not come out for anthem. *The New York Times*. https://www.nytimes.com/2022/05/27/sports/baseball/ giants-gape-kapler-anthem.html

Mombeuil, C., & Zhang, B. (2020). Authentic or cosmetic: stakeholders' attribution of firms' corporate social responsibility claims. *Social Responsibility Journal*, *17*(6), 756–775. https://doi.org/10.1108/SRJ-07-2019-0248

Moran, D., & Albright, A. (2022, May 25). Texas forces companies to be neutral on guns, or lose business. Bloomberg. https://www.bloomberg.com/news/articles/2022-05-25/ texas-forces-companies-to-be-neutral-on-guns-or-lose-business

Morgan, B. (2020, March 17). 50 ways companies are giving back during the coronavirus pandemic. *Forbes*. https://www.forbes.com/sites/blakemorgan/2020/03/17/50-ways-companies-are-giving-back-during-the-corona-pandemic/?sh=2b8704de4723

Nike [@Nike]. (2020, March 21). Now more than ever, we are one team. #playinside #playfortheworld [Tweet]. Twitter. https://twitter.com/Nike/status/124136422055 5354113

Nortey, J. (2022, March 31). Americans skeptical about religious objections to COVID-19 vaccines, but oppose employer mandates. Pew Research Center. https://www.pewre search.org/fact-tank/2022/03/31/americans-skeptical-about-religious-objections-to-covid-19-vaccines-but-oppose-employer-mandates/

Pelak, C. F. (2005). Athletes as agents of change: An examination of shifting race relations within women's netball in post-apartheid South Africa. *Sociology of Sport Journal*, *22*(1), 59–77. https://doi.org/10.1123/ssj.22.1.59

Penning, T. (2022, May 12). I don't shop for social values at corporations. Pier Points. https:// pierpoints.wordpress.com/2022/05/12/i-dont-shop-for-social-values-at-corporations/

Poole, D. (2022, May 24). Angry Kerr rips politicians after Texas elementary school shooting. NBC Sports. https://www.nbcsports.com/bayarea/warriors/emotional-steve-kerr-rips-politicians-after-texas-elementary-school-shooting

Rim, H., Lee, Y., & Yoo, S. (2020). Polarized public opinion responding to corporate social advocacy: Social network analysis of boycotters and advocators. *Public Relations Review, 46*(2), 101869. https://doi.org/10.1016/j.pubrev.2019.101869

Roe v. Wade, 410 U.S. 113 (1973).

Romero, D. (2022, January 25). Starbucks reversal on vaccine mandate sparks customer, barista backlash. Yahoo. https://finance.yahoo.com/news/starbucks-reversal-on-vaccine-mandate-sparks-customer-barista-backlash-191029771.html

Seele, P. and Lock, I. (2015). Instrumental and/or deliberative? A typology of CSR communication tools. *Journal of Business Ethics, 131*(2), 401–414. https://doi.org/10.1007/s10551-014-2282-9

Sheinin, D. (2022, June 2). In athletes' forceful response to Uvalde, advocates see 'a tipping point'. *The Washington Post*. https://www.washingtonpost.com/sports/2022/06/02/uvalde-athletes-gun-reform/

Sonnenfeld, J., Tian, S., Hirsty, G. (2022, June 30). A list of companies supporting abortion rights after the *Roe v. Wade* ruling shows which firms are stepping up, and why. *Fortune*. https://fortune.com/2022/06/30/companies-supporting-abortion-rights-roe-v-wade-first-movers/

Starbucks (2022, January 4). Letter to Starbucks partners: Vaccines, testing and supporting you in the next phase of COVID-19. https://stories.starbucks.com/press/2022/letter-to-starbucks-partners-vaccines-testing-and-supporting-you-in-next-phase-of-covid-19/

Stroman, M. [@STR0]. (2022, July 6). *America continuing to go backwards.* [Tweet]. Twitter. https://twitter.com/STR0/status/1544864951604592640?ref_src=twsrc%5Etfw%7Ctwc mp%5Etweetembed%7Ctwterm%5E1544864951604592640%7Ctwgr%5E80 61a210d976d6496fa8e40578f8531b2acf5fec%7Ctwcon%5Es1_&ref_url=https%3A%2F%2Fsideaction.com%2Fmlb%2Fmarcus-stroman-slams-politicians-gun-violence-social-media-twitter-cubs-bjs%2F

Suciu, P. (2022, January 19). Calls to 'BoycottStarbucks' over coffee chain's vaccine policy. *Forbes*. https://www.forbes.com/sites/petersuciu/2022/01/19/calls-to-boycottstarbucks-over-vaccine-policy/?sh=52c56e3470b1

The Editorial Board. (2022, June 6). DeSantis harpoons the Tampa Bay Rays. *Wall Street Journal*. https://www.wsj.com/articles/ron-desantis-harpoons-the-tampa-bay-rays-florida-budget-veto-progressives-politics-11654543401

The New York Times. (2022a, February 23). Who's requiring workers to be vaccinated? https://www.nytimes.com/interactive/2022/02/23/business/office-vaccine-mandate.html

The New York Times. (2023, May 8). A partial list of U.S. mass shootings in 2023. https://www.nytimes.com/article/mass-shootings-2023.html

USC Center for Public Relations. (2022). Global communication report. https://annenberg.usc.edu/research/center-public-relations/global-communication-report

Vlachos, P. A., Panagopoulos, N. G., Bachrach, D. G., & Morgeson, F. P. (2017). The effects of managerial and employee attributions for corporate social responsibility initiatives. *Journal of Organizational Behavior, 38*(7), 1111–1129. https://doi.org/10.1002/job.2189

World Health Organization (2020, January 5). Pneumonia of unknown cause – China. https://www.who.int/emergencies/disease-outbreak-news/item/2020-DON229

World Health Organization (n.d.). United States of America. https://covid19.who.int/region/amro/country/us

PART 4

Examples from Abroad

PART 4

Examples from Abroad

12

MANAGING DIGITAL STRATEGIC COMMUNICATION DURING THE COVID-19 PANDEMIC

Insights from Italian Ministries and Governmental Institutions[1]

Alessandro Lovari, Francesca Comunello, Alessandra Massa, Francesca Ieracitano, and Alberto Marinelli

Introduction

Italy has been one of the first Western countries to be affected by the COVID-19 pandemic. The total number of people affected by COVID-19 in Italy, at the time of this writing at the beginning of 2023, is 26.090.658, whereas 188.817 people died.[2] News reports showed all around the world the consequences it produced in terms of pressure on the hospitals and medical staff, overwhelmed by the number of patients in severe conditions. Social habits changed in order to cope with the pandemic, therefore using masks and maintaining physical distance from others affected everyday life and social relationships. The lockdown as a preventive measure was perceived initially as an effective strategy by citizens,[3] but it was progressively questioned by citizens and even politicians, polarizing public opinion. In this context (first months of the year 2020), overall, verified COVID-19-related information was often missing, while scientific evidence about the virus, as well as about the strategies to protect individuals and communities, were scarce. While scientists were building their knowledge and studying the virus as it spread and severely hit several Italian areas, citizens were eager for information, to acquire guidelines to better react to the threat, and to build an understanding of the whole situation, which they needed to cope with such a tragic and unprecedented pandemic. In these early months, consequently, a cacophony of unverified and often misleading information started circulating, both in the media and in (mediated) interpersonal communication, rapidly fueling uncertainty and distrust toward governments, politicians, and public institutions (Edelman, 2020; Lovari, 2020; Novelli, 2021). In addition, the Italian government and the ministries on the front lines

DOI: 10.4324/9781003327189-16

of the fight against an unknown virus with unpredictable effects on public health systems (i.e., the Ministry of Health) also found themselves managing a complex communication emergency to reduce possible contagion from the virus, to inform citizens of preventive measures to take and the correct actions to adopt for stimulating prosocial behaviors, even in the face of the emerging spread of disinformation (Agcom, 2020; Brennen et al., 2020). All this has led to a growing interest of citizens and scholars in public sector and public health communication, which have played a key and strategic role during the different phases of the pandemic, on both national and regional levels (Lovari et al., 2021). In this scenario, after reviewing the main scientific literature on public sector communication, and adopting a multimethod approach, this chapter aims to investigate how the Italian institutions addressed and managed the COVID-19 pandemic (2020–2021) from the perspective of strategic communication management and public sector communication (Canel & Luoma-aho, 2019), focusing specifically on the role of social media channels as relational and communicative environments.

Literature Review

Nowadays the relationship management function of public relations is largely acknowledged thanks to many seminal works of major scholars in the field of strategic communication (Grunig, 1992; Grunig et al., 2002; Heide et al., 2018; Hutton, 1999; Kim & Ledingham, 2015; Ledingham & Bruning, 2000; Zerfass et al., 2018). Organization–public relationships can be considered a paradigm for public relations because it shifts the concept of public relations away from manipulation, rhetorical and advocacy practices toward one of dialogue, participation, and engagement (Grunig & White, 1992; Heath, 2000; Kent & Taylor, 2002; Ledingham & Bruning, 2000). The relationship management approach can be applied to different type of entities (corporations, nonprofit and public sector organizations), involved in different fields, markets, and activities (health, tourism, public goods, social issues, products, etc.) (Kim & Ledingham, 2015).

The relationship management approach, and in particular the goal of pursuing the quality of public relations, should play a strategic role in organizational practices. Indeed, organizations vary and change their PR and communication strategies and practices in order to build or nurture favorable relationships with clients, citizens, and other strategic publics (including media and journalists) both in ordinary and crisis situations. The fast diffusion of digital technologies and the rapid penetration of the internet and social media on people's media consumption patterns (We Are Social, 2021) has led organizations to increasingly adopt these new digital tools to relate to their stakeholders. In fact, these participatory platforms can enable and foster more symmetrical communication and dialogical relations (Grunig, 2009), redefining the propensity and expectations for online and offline active and continuous communicative exchanges between organizations and their publics (Lovari & Parisi, 2015; Macnamara, 2010; Solis & Breakenridge, 2009). This approach has also had a strong impact on public administrations' activities and the public sector in general, a sector where a "focus on relationship is urgently needed because recent decades of focusing on productivity have made public sector organizations increasingly dependent on the scientific management paradigm" (Canel & Luoma-aho, 2019, p. 4), based on the principles of efficiency and structure in which the environment remains predictable and post adaptations can be sufficient. This new approach has to permeate and traverse all institutions, and it is mainly visible in PR and communication activities that should not only react to external drivers and exogenous changes, but they should be strategically driven by communicators able to anticipate trends and communicative stakeholders' behaviors, as well as to proactively operate to face societal, organizational, and technological transformations.

Public sector communication in Italy has evolved over the years, for external reasons (i.e., technological revolution), influenced by new national legislation, the evolution of bureaucratical models, and changing organizational cultures (Canel & Luoma-aho, 2019; Graber, 2003). The latter factor is particularly important since public sector organizations have attempted to move from a culture of control to one of citizen engagement. This is particularly complicated because organizational cultures take time to develop, putting together joint practices and learning attitudes, visible and invisible traits, intangible values, beliefs, and assumptions held by organization members (Canel & Luoma-aho, 2019; Schein, 1990). Organizational cultures influence communication and vice versa because they live in a symbiotic relationship. Communication sets the vision and directions in which public sector organizations should move, it makes sense of events and changes, and it shows the organizational culture outside of the institutions to different stakeholders (Canel & Luoma-aho, 2019; Parker & Bradley, 2000). In this context, public sector communications have been shaped by the impact of digitization and by the pervasive role of social media in stakeholders' information seeking practices, as well as in relationship-building among administrations, citizens, and the media (Ducci et al., 2021; Luoma-aho & Canel, 2020).

This process is particularly evident in Italy and in other Western countries (Lovari & Valentini, 2020; Mergel, 2013). Indeed, many scholars have focused their research on social media's impact on communication activities and practices, stressing the speed of communicative flows, the compression of time in reply to citizens' demands, and an increased public expectation of high-paced availability of information. Other researchers have pointed out that despite the participative affordances of these digital platforms, social media are mostly adopted as one-way channels for disseminating messages and propagating information, rather than listening to citizens' needs and nurturing relationships with digital publics (Lovari & Parisi, 2015). Consequently, social media are not strategically managed to enhance interactivity and dialogue, nor to encourage civic engagement or enhance citizens' trust (Haro-de-Rosario et al., 2018; Porumbescu, 2016). This social media adoption seems to promote a rhetoric of technological innovation (Lovari & Valentini, 2020), and to foster a "symbolic participation rather than genuine participation, making people feel a part of the process but giving no one a genuine voice" (Kent, 2013, p. 343).

Moreover, digital communication activities can be affected by unexpected factors and events like organizational emergencies, health epidemics, and natural disasters that rapidly can push institutions to modify their communicative behaviors, reshape organizational routines, and to adopt different relationships' strategies and informative practices. These factors have been particularly evident and disruptive during the COVID-19 pandemic, which saw Italy and Italian public sector organizations be the front runners to deal with communication to citizens, as well as to operate in a new infodemic environment characterized by the quick spread of disinformation, especially on digital avenues (La Rocca et al., 2023; Tasmin et al., 2020).

Italy Confronting the Infodemic

In what has been described as an "infodemic" environment (Colombo, 2022; WHO, 2021), Italian ministries and governmental institutions have faced multi-faceted challenges. While dealing with emergency management processes, being confronted with the unknown and—at the same time—needing to take urgent measures and interventions to counter the emergency, they have also dealt with a communication crisis. On the one hand, they had to deal with the uncertainty that is always attached to scientific knowledge when it is still being elaborated. On the other hand, there was the urgency to provide citizens with state-of-the-art information in order to counter the growing amount of misleading information circulating online (Agcom, 2020), to foster appropriate behavior, to protect public health during this disruptive emergency, and to contribute to citizens' reactions to the pandemic, at an individual and community level. In such a context, furthermore, the pandemic also disrupted the working routines, the internal communications processes, and the decision-making flows of Italian public sector communication and their communication with press offices. In order to effectively deal with the pandemic, indeed, the whole public sector communication ecosystem faced the need to re-organize their working routines, even when dedicated resources (both human and material) were not available (nor increased to face the emergency). In doing so, they adopted different tactics and strategies.

During the pandemic (and especially during the hardest lockdown weeks in March–May 2020), Italy witnessed a sharp increase in digital and social media platforms usage. While Italians were forced to stay at home, digital communication represented essential tools to gather and share information, to continue their work activities, and to stay connected with friends and family (Boccia Artieri & Farci, 2020). Therefore, an increasing number of Italians started using digital and social media on a daily basis, while the time spent online also dramatically increased (We Are Social, 2021).

Before the pandemic, the adoption of social media by Italian institutions had been uneven, in both quantitative and qualitative terms, with different levels of professionalization of PR and communication practitioners (Comunello et al., 2021), as well as the recognition of the strategic importance of these platforms for stakeholders' relationship management (Ducci et al., 2021). The national lockdown (March–May 2020), approved under the so-called "government Conte" (Novelli, 2021) (from the name of the prime minister), was a booster for social media adoption and institutionalization in the Italian public sector, for responding to citizens' needs and requests, as well as to face the impossibility of using traditional paper-based media for public communication. Thus, the increased need for (urgent and verified) information, as well as the increased use of social media by Italian citizens for gathering public health information (Bucchi & Saracino, 2020), represented an additional challenge for Italian public sector communication, impacting especially those institutions involved in health-related topics, particularly the (national) Ministry of Health and local health authorities (Lovari, 2020).

Research Questions and Methods

In this context our research aimed at investigating the transformations in communication management and in public relations strategies and practices during the COVID-19 pandemic, focusing on Italian ministries and governmental institutions. Indeed, Italian central government organizations were immediately put under pressure from a communication perspective, taking actions to quickly update emergency communication strategies and to overcome practices of organizational cultures based on ordinary communication processes tending toward stability and unidirectionality. Considering these premises, we aimed to answer the following research questions:

RQ1) How has the COVID-19 pandemic, and the consequent lockdown, affected the internal communication practices and public relations activities regarding stakeholders' engagement within the Italian ministries and governmental institutions?

RQ2) How have social media been used by Italian ministries and governmental institutions to convey COVID-19 information and to manage external relationships with citizens and strategic stakeholders (such as the media system)?

RQ3) To avoid contagion and mitigate disinformation regarding COVID-19, how did the Italian Ministry of Health use digital communication practices to inform citizens and engage digital publics?

To address these research questions, we used a multimethod approach that mixed qualitative and quantitative techniques, including in-depth interviews with PR and communication professionals working in Italian ministries and governmental institutions, and we discuss the results of a content analysis of the Italian Ministry of Health's Facebook posts conducted previously by one of the authors (Lovari, 2020; Lovari & Righetti, 2020).

More specifically, we interviewed 32 public sector communication professionals in charge as heads of the press and media relations office (n = 16) and social media managers (n = 13), or as high-ranking communication professionals (n = 3) in the Italian ministries and governmental institutions during the term of Prime Minister Giuseppe Conte (2019–2021). The interviewees worked in 23 Italian institutions (11 ministries, 8 ministries "without portfolio,"[4] and 4 governmental central institutions) as PR and communication professionals with leading roles. The high level of information provided by these elite communication professionals was crucial for the objectives of our study (Hertz & Imber, 1995). Interviews were carried out by two researchers (both authors of this chapter), lasted between 30 and 90 minutes, and were conducted online mostly on Skype or Google Meet, according to the preferences and availability of the respondents. An agreement of anonymity was established with the interviewees regarding their names as well as any references to the ministry or institutions they worked for. Therefore, it is not possible to mention in the results which ministries and institutions have adopted different strategies and digital communication practices.

The interviews focused on three main areas: 1) the effect of the pandemic on institutional working routines; 2) the impact of the pandemic on internal processes and decision-making flows; and 3) negotiation processes with both external stakeholders and other ministries. The interviews were digitally recorded, transcribed verbatim, and analyzed with the support of the software NVivo12; additionally, notes taken by two researchers were included in the analysis. The data were analyzed through thematic analysis (Clarke et al., 2015). Two research team members read the corpora three times. They then used an inductive approach to create a coding book. The main codes were related to: a) the approach each ministry or institution takes in managing work routines and communication processes during COVID-19, and b) the role of social media in dialoguing with citizens. The researchers selected excerpts consistent with those codes, identifying terms and discourse that highlights different communicative strategies (subcode) used during COVID-19 by different ministries and institutions, and different roles (subcode) ascribed to social media during the emergency.

The main themes that emerged inductively from the analysis with regard to RQ1 and RQ2 are:

1. the emergence of polarization in communicative strategies during the COVID-19 pandemic;
2. the use of social media as a strategic and ordinary tool for managing external communication during the pandemic.

Data from the interviews were compared with data collected in previous studies, i.e., the content analysis of the Italian Ministry of Health's Facebook posts (Lovari, 2020; Lovari & Righetti, 2020). This content analysis was conducted using a coding book based on inductive variables such as native content or shared content, content focused on COVID-19 or not, and content aimed at contrasting disinformation related to COVID-19.

As a response to RQ3, we combined the results of a previous study's database (Lovari & Righetti, 2020) with the results of the interviews dealing with issues related to using social media for mitigating fake news spreading during the pandemic. The main findings are shown below for the three research questions investigated, and significant excerpts from the interviews are quoted in the text, mentioning the role and typology of the institution of the interviewees. The excerpts have been translated into English by the authors.

Main Findings

In this section, we are presenting the results associating the themes that emerged from the analysis of the interviews with the related Research Questions.

The first research question (RQ1) was aimed at investigating how the COVID-19 pandemic, and the consequent national lockdown, affected the internal communication practices and public relations activities regarding stakeholders' engagement within the Italian ministries and governmental institutions. Therefore, the first step was to analyze what respondents said about the effects of the pandemic on the institutional working routines, the internal communications processes, and the decision-making flows of Italian ministries' communicative and media offices. The first theme emerging from the results is the polarization of internal communicative strategies at the governmental level during the COVID-19 pandemic. It is possible to place Italian ministries and governmental institutions' media and communication offices on a continuum characterized by two extremes: one extreme refers to the invariance of communication practices and working routines, while the other pole represents the tendency to re-engineer skills and work practices due to the COVID-19 lockdown.

FIGURE 12.1   Polarization of institutional communication behaviors with the COVID-19 pandemic.

Media relations and communication offices of Italian ministries and central institutions that were positioned in the pole of invariance followed two different approaches. There were some media relations and communication offices highly affected by the pandemic that were lacking specialized expertise or highly trained personnel, so they were resigned to not being able to reach their communication goals during the pandemic. Because of the emergency situation, the general management of ministries had to accept this attitude from their PR and communication offices, thus only limited activities were carried out to relate with strategic publics. At the same time, there were other media and communication offices still characterized by invariance that adopted "survival" strategies during the pandemic. The lockdown reduced communicative demands related to public events, official ceremonies, or press conferences. Consequently, these offices downsized this content production, making such structures effective in managing communication activities related to the pandemic, although usually the offices were described as understaffed by the interviewees. As one key expert reported:

> Despite the stress of COVID-19, there was a "quieter" working environment. You were able to plan actions, manage the release of content, reports, and regulatory actions of the minister, and better manage the media, citizen, and stakeholder pressure for more information.
>
> *(Head of press office, ministry)*

In the offices that exemplified the re-engineering pole, roles and skills were redefined in response to the COVID-19 pandemic-induced needs. This pole includes even offices that redistributed internal human resources assigning different tasks due to the lockdown. For instance, a social media manager working in a ministry told us that: "After the pandemic happened, due to the reduced number of social offline events, the video makers have specialized in monitoring and managing comments and posts on social networking sites."

The pole of re-engineering refers to managing internal human resources of communication and press offices. Furthermore, this attitude can also be found in the relationship between those offices and the overall internal organization of the ministries they served. Indeed, during the pandemic, some communication and press offices emphasized the strengthening of coordination between press offices and digital or social media departments when they were separate. Additionally, interviewees reported an improved synergy between the press office and the ministry's general management. In some cases, the general management assigned the media relations and communication offices primary responsibility for coordinating the institution's COVID-19 related (internal and external) communication activities, as highlighted in the following declaration of a head of press office in a ministry: "Having instantly operated as a press office should do, we immediately re-engineered our practices based on our strengths by distributing skills and then distributing tasks accordingly."

The second research question (RQ2) was aimed at investigating how social media has been used by Italian ministries and governmental institutions to convey COVID-19 information and to manage external relationships with citizens and strategic stakeholders (such as the media). Therefore, themes that emerged from the thematic analysis pertaining to using social media to manage external communications during the pandemic as a strategic and ordinary tool and also to relate with citizens and other strategic publics are presented.

Governmental institutions and ministries have used social media strategically to convey COVID-19 information in an effective manner, mainly to citizens. Nevertheless, no reference to specific strategies used to manage dialogue with external stakeholders during the pandemic emerged from the interviewees. It highlights how central these institutions have considered the dialogue with citizens during the emergency. Therefore, the strategies adopted to communicate with the digital public are based not only on crafting effective textual messages but also on the selection of new formats and visual strategies for targeting users. With respect to the format, the Italian ministries and institutions have used Facebook live-streaming service many times— the same tool has been frequently used especially by Prime Minister Giuseppe Conte during the early phase of the pandemic (Novelli, 2021)—whereas infographics have become popular tools to convey useful information on official digital channels in a clear and concise manner (Lovari & Righetti, 2020). Furthermore, frequently asked questions (FAQs) were utilized strategically to simulate dialogue with citizens and anticipate their informative needs. As a result of FAQs, press and communication offices were able to respond to citizens' increased requests while reducing the impact on social media management and workflows. This decision was adopted by several ministries to manage the enormous number of user-generated content published by citizens under institutional social media posts or on the occasion of the launch of government COVID-19 campaigns. Indeed, as this social media manager stated: "Using social media, we collected recurrent questions and created specific FAQ pages on the website so that people could find them. FAQs were the most successful content on the site."

At the same time, this government strategy shows how difficult it could be to build and nurture relationships with citizens and other strategic publics on social media, both in ordinary and emergency situations, as other Italian studies have also reported (Lovari & Parisi, 2015; Faccioli et al., 2020). This process highlights how official social media channels are still mostly used for propagating institutional messages (unidirectional, one-way model) instead of actively listening to digital publics and engaging with them (interactive and bidirectional model). Despite the affordances of the platforms and citizens' requests for updated information, Italian ministries prefer to broadcast messages and to limit the dialogical interactions due to the heavy flows of requests during the acute phases of the emergency. Moreover, during the pandemic, some changes occurred in governmental and ministerial social media targeting strategies. Before the COVID-19 pandemic, targetization of users was platform-based. In contrast, further segmentation of the targets within a specific online platform was necessary during the pandemic, to have a more effective digital public sector communication that could inspire social change and favor citizens' prosocial behaviors in specific segments of the population (i.e., youth, young adults, fragile people).

The third research question (RQ3) investigated how the Italian Ministry of Health used digital communication practices to inform citizens about preventive measures, to engage digital publics to avoid contagion and mitigate disinformation regarding COVID-19.

Some interesting strategies emerged from the interviews. First, interviewees reported the importance of having built up strategic partnerships between Italian institutions and digital platforms such as Google, Twitter, and Facebook to raise the visibility of official and institutional information within the cacophony of different voices, and to counteract fake news about COVID-19 (Donovan, 2020; Lovari, 2020). As a social media manager from a governmental institution said: "Both [Facebook and Google] provided a very large budget for free to sponsor our content related to the coronavirus situation that allowed us to develop paid social media campaigns."

Communication professionals noticed that during the first phases of the pandemic, citizens were turning to institutions' social media pages as a tool of dealing with the growing disinformation about COVID-19, and this informative migration was also relevant during the launch of vaccination campaigns in December 2020, showing the presence of interesting paths of trust toward public sector organizations (Lovari, D'Ambrosi & Bowen, 2020). This process is particularly clear in the following interview excerpt:

There is actually a desire, in the midst of all the noise, for citizens to grab what is authentically institutional, so institutional social media channels have had a big boost just in the years of the pandemic.

(High-ranking communication official, institution)

The high volume of reactions and interactions generated by content posted by the Italian Ministry of Health on its official Facebook page also confirms this: the page increased the number of likes from 61,558 to 501,203 followers, with an increase of 714.2 during the early phase of the pandemic. A total of 459 posts were published between January 30 and May 3 of 2020 (from the first Italian case of COVID-19 patients to the end of the national lockdown), reaching 2.511.309 interactions (Lovari & Righetti, 2020). According to interviews, a common protocol, or an official institutional strategy to combat disinformation was not created; it does not exist at the governmental level, despite the launch of a specific task force on fake news in April 2020. Nevertheless, the FAQ format was also used to provide univocal and official information regarding the major issues affected by information disorder. Indeed:

> In the first nine months of the pandemic, the FAQs contained a section called fake news that corrected false information. After that, there is no real protocol, but we make assessments according to the circumstances and sometimes upon the request of some office.
>
> *(High-ranking communication official, ministry)*

An analysis of the posts produced by the Italian Ministry of Health on its official Facebook page shows that infographics were the most commonly used visual format to contain and manage disinformation. As emerged from the study carried out by Lovari and Righetti (2020), two types of infographics can be identified and distinguished: those images aimed at debunking specific fake news (i.e., etiology of the virus; the contagion provoked by animals or by purchasing Chinese products, etc.), and those aimed at raising users' awareness about how to select and identify reliable and official sources of information.

Conclusions

Within the framework of public sector communication (Canel & Luoma-aho, 2019) this chapter shows the importance of strategically managing relations by Italian public institutions with citizens on social media channels, and how this activity can be put under pressure by an external factor—the pandemic—that created a disruption in organizational activities. COVID-19 has affected PR activities and it has impacted the public sector's organizational and communication cultures (Canel & Luoma-aho, 2019; Ducci et al., 2021). In particular governmental social media communication was strategic to enhance and nurture trust between Italian government and citizens, showing control mutuality and a relationship commitment (Grunig et al., 2002), especially during the first and second phase of the pandemic, which was characterized by disinformation, fear, and uncertainty in the population (Lovari, 2020; Novelli, 2021). Indeed, different studies showed this process and highlighted the pivotal role of public sector communication to deal with COVID-19 and to improve public health and social change (Bucchi & Saracino, 2020; Lovari, D'Ambrosi & Bowen, 2020).

The interviews we conducted show how the pandemic accelerated some processes of change in Italian public sector communication at the central government level, with some important distinctions. There has been an increased focus on relationship management within individual ministries and among government communication structures. This was a team effort that, thanks in part to the use of social media and instant messaging platforms, allowed for the creation of new practices, the enhancement of communicators' professionalization, and the reshaping of remote work processes. This resulted in the production of communication flows exerting an impact on the quality of the whole communication process, also from an external perspective. With regard to the relations with citizens and other external publics, managing social media in emergencies has not allowed for the creation and nurturing of two-way relationships (Grunig, 2009). In fact, a few attempts by several ministries and central institutions were stopped due to the large volume of messages from the digital publics, which prompted ministries to find other communication strategies, such as the creation of FAQs on their sites, that also took their cues from user-generated messages in a proactive way. Such a basic form of bidirectionality was positively evaluated by interviewees. Nevertheless, institutions could not meet the demands of numerous publics to satisfy positive expectations about the relationship (Grunig et al., 2002); they were often overwhelmed by the toxicity of digital spaces that was enhanced by the infodemic disorder (Colombo, 2022; Rocca et al., 2023).

Discussion Questions

Considering that there is an increasing need for communicators and public managers "to know how to interact with the public" (Thomas, 2013, p. 786), several questions emerge that are worth discussing and proposing for further research:

1) How can bidirectionality be pursued and dialogic relationships managed within social media managed by public sector organizations? What factors in ordinary and emergency situations hinder the goal of bidirectionality, persisting in unidirectional one-way use despite the affordance of the platforms and citizens' demands?
2) What competencies and skills must communicators have to manage the complexity of relationships that characterize contemporary communicative ecologies in the face of the turbulence of disinformation?
3) How can public sector communication professionals dialogue with citizens through social media platforms, negotiating with social media and algorithmic logics to increase the visibility of institutional content?

Notes

1 This chapter was developed within a research project called "La qualità della comunicazione pubblica social" (The quality of social public sector communication) financed by the Ministero dello Sviluppo Economico – Direzione Generale TSCI-ISCTI, Italian Government.
2 The data are retrieved from the Italian National Health Insitute: https://www.epicentro.iss.it/coronavirus/sars-cov-2-dashboard.
3 A survey conducted by the Italian National Institute of Statistics during the first stage of the pandemic emergency found that 91.2 percent of the interviewed citizens considered the imposed rules to be useful in contrasting the evolution of the pandemic: https://www.istat.it/it/archivio/243357.
4 Ministries without portfolios do not have a complex administrative structure and do not possess autonomous spending capacity or budget to use.

Further Reading

Ducci, G., & Lovari, A., (2021). The challenges of public sector communication in the face of the pandemic crisis: professional roles, competencies and platformization. *Sociologia della Comunicazione*, 61, 9–19, doi 10.3280/SC2021-061002.
Huang, Y.-H. (2001). OPRA: A cross-cultural, multiple-item scale for measuring organization–public relationships. *Journal of Public Relations Research, 13*(1), 61–90.
Solito, L., & Materassi, L. (2021). If a picture is not worth a thousand words: Digital infographics use during the Covid-19 pandemic crisis. *Sociologia della Comunicazione, 61*, 52–70.
van Dijck, J. (2020). Governing digital societies: Private platforms, public values. *Computer Law & Security Review*, 1–4.

References

AGCOM. (2020). Osservatorio sulla disinformazione online. Speciale Coronavirus [Observatory on disinformation. Special on Coronavirus]. AGCOM. Retrieved from https://www.agcom.it/osservatoriosulla-disinformazione-online
Boccia Artieri G., & Farci M. (Eds.) (2020). *Shockdown: Media, cultura, comunicazione e ricerca nel COVID-19*. Roma: Meltemi.
Brennen, J. S., Simon, F. M., Howard, P. N., & Nielsen, R. K. (2020). Types, sources, and claims of COVID-19 misinformation. Reuters Institute, available at http://reutersinstitute.politics.ox.ac.uk/types-sources-and-claims-covid-19-misinformation.
Bucchi, M., & Saracino, B. (2020). Italian citizens and COVID-19, in Public Understanding of Science Blog, 3/21/2020, available at https://sagepus.blogspot.com/2020/03/italian-citizens-and-covid-19.html
Canel, M., & Luoma-aho, V. (2019). *Public sector communication: Closing gaps between citizens and public organizations*. Hoboken, NJ: Wiley & Sons.
Clarke, V., Braun, V., & Hayfield, N. (2015). Thematic analysis. In J. A. Smith (Ed.), *Qualitative psychology: A practical guide to research methods* (222–248), Thousand Oaks, CA: Sage.
Colombo, F. (2022). An ecological approach: The infodemic, pandemic, and COVID-19. In K. Kopecka-Piech & B. Lodzki (Eds.), *The COVID-19 pandemic as a challenge for media and communication studies* (pp. 35–48), London: Routledge.
Comunello, F., Massa, A., Ieracitano, F., & Marinelli, A. (2021). Public sector communication professions in the Twittersphere. *Sociologia della Comunicazione, 61*, 90–108. DOI: 10.3280/SC2021-061007.

Donovan, J. (2020). Social-media companies must flatten the curve of misinformation. *Nature,* April 14. DOI: 10.1038/d41586-020-01107-z.

Ducci, G., Lovari, A., & Rizzuto, F. (2021). The culture of communication in public sector facing the challenge of social media: An explorative research in Italy and France. *Comunicazioni Sociali,* 2, 251–262. DOI: 10.26350/001200_000130.

Edelman. (2020). Trust and the coronavirus. Chicago: Edelman. Retrieved from https://www.edelman.com/sites/g/files/aatuss191/files/202003/2020%20Edelman%20Trust%20Barometer%20Brands%20and%20the%20Coronavirus.pdf

Faccioli, F., D'Ambrosi, Ducci, G., & Lovari, A. (2020). #DistantiMaUniti: la comunicazione pubblica tra innovazioni e fragilità alla ricerca di una ridefinizione. *H-ermes, Journal of Communication,* 17, 27–72. doi:10.1285/i22840753n17p27.

Graber, D. A. (2003). *The power of communication: Managing information in public organizations.* Washington, DC: CQ Press.

Grunig, J. E. (2009). Paradigms of global public relations in an age of digitalization. *PRism,* 6(2), http://www.prismjournal.org/homepage.html.

Grunig, J. E. (1992). *Excellence in public relation and communication management.* Hillsdale, NJ: LEA Publishers.

Grunig, L. A., Grunig, J. E., & Dozier, D. M. (2002). *Excellent public relations and effective organizations.* Mahwah, NJ: Lawrence Erlbaum Associates.

Grunig, J. E., & White J. (1992). The effect of worldviews on public relations theory and practice. In J. E. Grunig (Ed.), *Excellence in public relations and communication management* (pp. 31–64). Hillsdale, NJ: Lawrence Erlbaum.

Haro-de-Rosario, A., Sàez-Martin, A., & Del Carmen Caba-Pérez, M. (2018). Using social media to enhance citizen engagement with local government: Twitter or Facebook? *New Media & Society,* 20, 29–49. DOI: 10.1177/1461444816645652

Heath, R. L. (2000). A rhetorical perspective on the value of public relations: Crossroads and pathways toward concurrence. *Journal of Public Relations Research,* 12(1), 69–91.

Heide, M., von Platen S., Simonsson, C., & Falkheimer, J. (2018). Expanding the scope of strategic communication: Towards a holistic understanding of organizational complexity. *International Journal of Strategic Communication,* 12(4), 452–468.

Hertz, R., & Imber, J. B. (Eds.) (1995). *Studying elites using qualitative methods.* Thousand Oaks, CA: Sage. https://doi.org/10.4135/9781483327341.

Hutton, G. (1999). The definition, dimensions, and domain of public relations. *Public Relations Review,* 25(2), 199–214.

Kent, M. L. (2013). Using social media dialogically: Public relations in the reviving democracy. *Public Relations Review,* 39(4), 337–345.

Kent, M. L., & Taylor, M. (2002). Toward a dialogic theory of public relations. *Public Relations Review,* 28, 21–37. DOI: S036381110200108X

Kim, J.-N., & Ledingham, J. (Eds.) (2015) *Public relations as relationship management: A relational approach to the study and practice of public relations.* New York: Routledge.

La Rocca, G., Carignan W.E., & Boccia Artieri, G. (Eds.) (2023). *Covid-19 and the global crisis of information: Case studies from Europe, Canada and Mexico.* London: Palgrave Macmillan.

Ledingham, S., & Bruning, D. (2000). *Public relations as relationship management: A relational approach to the study and practice of public relations.* New York: Mahwah.

Lovari, A. (2020). Spreading (dis)trust: COVID-19 misinformation and government intervention in Italy. *Media and Communication,* 8(2), 458–461, DOI: 10.17645/mac.v8i2.3219.

Lovari, A., D'Ambrosi, L., & Bowen, S. (2020). Re-connecting voices. The (new) strategic role of public sector communication after Covid-19 crisis, *PACO, Partecipazione e Conflitto, 13*(2), 970–989.

Lovari, A., Ducci, G., & Righetti, N. (2021). Responding to fake news: The use of Facebook for public health communication during the COVID-19 pandemic in Italy. In M. Lewis, E. Govender, & K. Holland (Eds.), *Communicating COVID-19: Interdisciplinary perspectives* (pp. 251–275). Cham: Palgrave Macmillan.

Lovari, A., & Parisi, L. (2015). Listening to digital publics: Investigating citizens' voices and engagement within Italian municipalities' Facebook Pages. *Public Relations Review, 41*, 205–213. DOI:10.1016/j.pubrev.2014.11.013.

Lovari, A., & Righetti, N. (2020). La comunicazione pubblica della salute tra infodemia e fake news: Il ruolo della pagina Facebook del Ministero della Salute nella sfida social al COVID-19. *Mediascapes Journal, 15*, 156–173.

Lovari, A., & Valentini, C. (2020). Public sector communication and social media: Opportunities and limits of current policies, activities, and practices. In V. Luoma-Aho & M. J. Canel (Eds.), *Handbook of public sector communication* (pp. 315–328). New York: Wiley-Blackwell.

Macnamara, J. (2010). Public communication practices in the Web 2.0–3.0 mediascape: The case for PRevolution. *Prism, 7*(3). www.prismjournal.org/homepage.htm.

Mergel, I. (2013). *Social media in the public sector: A guide to participation, collaboration and transparency in a networked world.* San Francisco, CA: Jossey-Bass.

Novelli, E. (2021). Italy: The frontrunner of the Western countries in an unexpected crisis. In D. Lilljer, I. A. Coman, M. Gregor, & E. Novelli (Eds.), *Political communication and COVID-19.* New York: Routledge.

Parker, R., & Bradley, L. (2000). Organisational culture in the public sector: Evidence from six organisations. *International Journal of Public Sector Management, 13*(2), 125–141. doi:10.1108/09513550010338773.

Porumbescu, G. A. (2016), Linking public sector social media and e-government website use to trust in government. *Government Information Quarterly, 33*, 291–304. DOI: 10.1016/j.giq.2016.04.006.

Schein, E. (1990). Organizational culture. *American Psychologist, 45*(2), 109–119. DOI: 10.1037/0003-066X.45.2.109.

Solis, B., & Breakenridge, D. (2009). *Putting the public back in public relations.* Upper Saddle River, NJ: Pearson Education.

Tasmin, S., Hossain. M. M., & Muzumber, H. (2020). Impact on rumors and misinformation on Covid-19 in social media. *Journal of Preventive Medicine and Public Health, 53*(3), 171–174. doi.org/10.3961/jpmph.20.094

Thomas, J. C. (2013). Citizen, customer, partner: rethinking the place of the public in public management. *Public Administration Review, 73*(6), 786–796. doi.org/10.1111/puar.12109

We Are Social (2021). Global digital report, available at: https://wearesocial.com/it/blog/2021/01/digital-2021-i-dati-globali/

World Health Organization. (2021). Infodemic management: An overview of infodemic management during COVID-19, January 2020–May 2021.

Zerfass, A., Vercic, D., Nothhaft H., & Page Werder, K. (2018). Strategic communication: Defining the field and its contribution to research and practice. *International Journal of Strategic Communication, 12*(4) 487–505. doi.org/10.1080/1553118X.2018.1493485

13

A DECADE OF COMMUNICATING ABOUT MENTAL HEALTH AFTER CRISES IN CHRISTCHURCH, NEW ZEALAND

Wan Chi Leung, Georgia Williams, and Kaaren Mathias

Mental Health in Christchurch, New Zealand

Christchurch (Ōtautahi in Māori), New Zealand (Aotearoa in Māori), is well-known worldwide as the "Garden City"; however, in the past decade, life in the city has been challenging. Christchurch has experienced several significant crises that shocked the world: the big earthquake in 2011, the mosque attacks in 2019, and New Zealand's lockdown measures during COVID-19, arguably some of the strictest in the world. While the gardens in the city remain flourishing through these crises, they have significantly impacted residents' daily life and mental health. The government and other organizations in the city have had to respond swiftly to changes in people's concerns after each crisis. The different nature of the crises—natural disasters, terrorist attacks, and a pandemic—pose additional challenges in setting up effective communication messages for residents and providing experiences in communicating mental health after crises, which can be insightful to other cities.

Besides the crises, Christchurch is also a unique case study for communicating mental health because of its diverse culture. The growing ethnically diverse population, including Māori and Pasifika, mean the Western mental health promotion model does not suit all cultures' needs. This chapter starts by analyzing Christchurch's most significant crisis, the 2011 earthquake, and the subsequent mental health campaign "All Right?". We outline in this chapter how Christchurch communities maintained mental health and well-being through these three facets of community mental health competence: first, through their knowledge and skills in mental health, which we illustrate in particular with the mental

DOI: 10.4324/9781003327189-17

health promotion campaign "All Right?"; second, by creating safe social spaces that were both literal (places to meet) and promoting social inclusion and participation; third, we profile how community members promoted well-being and mental health through partnerships for action. This includes communities taking leadership, social aspects of communities such as relationships, leadership, collective efficacy, and place attachment, along with physical dimensions such as resources, services, and preparedness (Aldrich, 2015; Cafer, 2019; Norris et al., 2008; Patel, 2017). Our analysis aims to provide insights into how mental health messages can be more inclusive and equitable for at-risk communities. While we only discuss Christchurch as an example, we believe different countries can learn from each other as issues such as diversity, equity, and inclusion are universal, and the insights from Christchurch can be helpful to communication practitioners when they need to communicate mental health with a culturally diverse public after crises.

Building Knowledge and Skills for Mental Health

Building Psychosocial Well-Being

Strengthening personal psychosocial skills is critical to mental health. Psychosocial skills can include skills such as thinking positively, finding benefits in difficult times, and asking for help or support, as well as skills such as setting boundaries to care for one's well-being, engaging in activities that are restorative or recreational, and sharing one's psychosocial or material resources with others. In order to build psychosocial skills, a sense of self-belief and belonging is critical as a foundation. A robust cultural identity describes the ability of indigenous and all community members to have meaningful access and participation within their cultural framework, acknowledging that each community is diverse and with a range of values and perspectives (Chua et al., 2019; Kenney & Phibbs, 2015). Past research about the All Right? well-being campaign in Christchurch since 2013 suggests that core cultural values are essential for practical disaster recovery efforts and responses (Savage et al., 2018), and the use of appropriate language for translating evidence-based well-being messages into a local setting is one of the factors that contributed to the campaign's success (Calder et al., 2016).

Building individual skills was identified as a critical strategy for mental health during the Christchurch earthquake recovery period (Kenney, 2015; Lambert, 2014; Pfefferbaum et al., 2015). Lambert (2014) described how wider social determinants combined with individual practices for well-being in his analysis of sequelae of the Christchurch earthquake: he found that the combination of attributes of being a member of a large whānau (extended family group in the

Māori language), having no or minimal damage to house and contents, earning high personal income and not moving away from the city was the most robust pathway to resilience (Lambert, 2014). These findings highlight the space and opportunity to build mental health skills, particularly in a crisis.

Physical factors can also strengthen the opportunity to build psychosocial skills. For example, community infrastructure such as marae, schools, churches, and community centers can enable social connectedness and thus increase the opportunity to practice and offer psychosocial support. While the short-term response to disasters or emergencies may require specific skills sets, Vallance and Carlton (2015), in particular, have underlined the value of broad adaptive skills for mental health (general skills like book-keeping, chairing meetings, producing newsletters, finding information, mobilizing people to play a game of sport or a piece of music) can also provide a sense of well-being, social connection, and contribution. An example of a social structure that supported skill building in Lyttelton, Christchurch, was a community time bank, which facilitated skill-sharing of practical skills and provided opportunities to participate between community members (Thornley et al., 2015).

Helping residents build personal psychological skills is one of the essential aims of mental health campaigns. Below we will introduce the relevant campaigns in Christchurch after the crises.

Canterbury Earthquakes and the "All Right?" Campaign

On February 22, 2011, at 12.51 p.m., a shallow 6.3 magnitude earthquake rippled through Christchurch, Canterbury. The physical impact resulted in severe infrastructure, buildings, land damage, and the loss of 185 lives (Christchurch and Canterbury earthquakes, 2022). A natural disaster curates both primary and secondary stressors from the initial devastation of the event and related stressors that stem from the physical and emotional impacts. At its core, a mental health promotion campaign is designed to aid communities to live well and construct through the lens of what matters to them rather than curating assumptions about what people need (Williams, 2022). To assist Canterbury communities in recovering from this disaster, the organization All Right? was instated. All Right? was founded through a grassroots approach by Canterbury health professionals who shared the lived experience of the earthquake with the community.

Disasters can heavily impact the psychosocial well-being of communities. The Christchurch Health and Development Study (CHDS) reported significant depression, other anxiety disorders, and nicotine dependence; the total number of mental disorders increased as exposure to earthquakes increased, with rates of mental disorders 1.4 times higher among those in the highest quartile of earthquake exposure than those not exposed; 13.3 percent of the overall rate of mental disorders among those exposed to the Canterbury earthquakes could be attributed to the disaster (Beaglehole et al., 2019).

To track mental health and well-being over time with Canterbury, the Canterbury Wellbeing Survey reported a significant increase in the self-reported World Health Organization Well-being Index (WHO-5) from 52.4 in 2013 to 60.8 in 2019, showing that recovery from the disaster takes several years (Begg et al., 2021). Recovery literature indicates four key phases communities experience after a disaster; the Heroic Phase, the Honeymoon Phase, the Disillusionment, and the Reconstruction Phase (All Right?, 2022). All Right? commenced in the early stages of the disillusionment phase, where communities feel frustrated and overwhelmed as the length of the recovery process is understood (All Right?, 2022). All Right? communication materials are centered around aiding communities to build emotional literacy to articulate, understand, and validate the emotions they experience. All Right? offers recognition to individuals as experts in their well-being. The application of communication strategies in campaign materials primarily focuses on building community strength instead of dictating what a wellness recovery process should look like (Williams, 2022). This is centered around the notion that individuals do possess the ability to support their recovery. Individuals influence their healing when supplied with the right tools; the conversation does not necessarily require external services and can be held within themselves and their communities.

Resilient and mental health communities can take "deliberate, purposeful, and collective action to alleviate the detrimental effects of adverse events" (Pfefferbaum et al., 2013, p. 251). All Right? structured their communication strategy through input from community voices. This enabled the identification of the community's needs to curate material that directly targets areas that needed support. This was done through conversations with diverse community leaders, drawing many correlations of emotions felt throughout the Canterbury public (Williams, 2022). This created a starting point of insight for the situation, further elaborated through focus groups and surveys with the target communities. It was evident that although there was much emotion in communities, there was a struggle to articulate and name the feeling. The campaign's first year primarily focused on naming emotions reflected through campaign material such as posters. This approach enabled signs around the city, which articulated that it was "all right" for the public to feel how they felt. Some examples of language used are:

- It's all right if you're over it right now
- It's all right to feel a little blue now and then
- It's all right to feel proud of how we've coped
- It's all right if you're feeling pretty stoked

FIGURE 13.1   Posters from All Right? (2022).

This approach showcased that it was okay to feel all emotions; whether they may be deemed as negative or positive, the sentiment is valid. The campaign's next phase was built on how the public could support their well-being by employing the Five Ways to Wellbeing. The Five Ways to Wellbeing highlight simple tasks which can be incorporated into someone's daily routine to promote wellness. All Right? understand that external circumstances, such as socio-economic issues, may hinder someone from living well. The Five Ways to Wellbeing suggests that people can support their well-being by *learning*, *noticing*, *being active*, *giving*, and *connecting* (All Right? 2022). These five ways are things that individuals can do regardless of issues that may not be variables of control.

This concept was reflected by posing questions based on the Five Ways to Wellbeing in communication materials to the public. This design was to provoke thoughts about when they last did an activity to enhance their well-being and to take a moment to reflect on how they were feeling. Some examples of the questions posed are:

- When was your last moment of wonder?
- When did you last get caught up in the moment?
- When did you last catch up?
- When was your last mate date?

All Right? utilized a grassroots approach through discussion with community leaders and the wider public to draw insights into the emotions felt in the Canterbury region in a post-earthquake setting. As Calder et al.'s (2022) evaluation of All Right? finds the success factors of the Facebook page, including the use of appropriate language in a local setting informed by local research; the All Right? messages were not perceived as a government message, and the campaign effectively combined public health and communications expertise. This insight aided

All Right? to craft a campaign strategy to remind communities that they have the power to support well-being and recovery. The initial step was to help communities build their emotional literacy by recognizing emotion and giving it a term. After this, it was about instating simple tasks individuals can do based on the Five Ways to Wellbeing that communities could employ in their daily routines. The All Right? initiative was made for Canterbury by health professionals in Canterbury who had the shared lived experience of the earthquake. Cantabrians were considered at the forefront of campaign development through conversations with community leaders and the wider public. Although the All Right? initiative was initially created for post-earthquake well-being recovery; it has since expanded and led a nationwide campaign to support well-being throughout the COVID-19 pandemic highlighting the success of the strategies used to support Canterbury's well-being.

Moving Digital during and after COVID-19 Lockdowns

After the World Health Organization (WHO) declared COVID-19 a pandemic on March 11, 2020 (WHO, 2020), precautionary measures such as social distancing and lockdowns became part of people's lives. The four-tiered alert level system for COVID-19 was first introduced in New Zealand and set above Alert Level 1 (the lowest alert level) on March 21, 2020. According to this alert level system in New Zealand used until December 2021, most residents could only interact with their tiny bubbles (mostly close family/whānau) at Alert Level 3; at Alert Level 4, the country was in complete lockdown, meaning that almost all businesses were closed except those for necessities and lifeline utilities, and people could only work or study from home and stay with their household bubbles. In 2020, the whole country was in Alert Level 3 and 4 lockdown for around seven weeks from March to May. In August 2021, the entire country was in lockdown again for around three weeks due to positive community cases of COVID-19 identified.

The strict alert systems helped New Zealand achieve relatively low COVID-19 infection numbers during the pandemic, and in 2020 New Zealand was ranked at the top in resilience according to the new Bloomberg COVID-19 resilience ranking (*NZ Herald*, 2019). The government's decisive, swift actions, resources for testing, contact tracing, and a centralized quarantine strategy to limit local transmission have been highly appreciated worldwide. However, the strict lockdown and border control measures meant that human interactions, travel, and family gatherings were highly restricted, posing significant challenges to people's mental health. This was evident in mental health cases at the hospital; for example, while a decrease in mental health presentations to Christchurch Hospital Emergency Department during the five-week COVID-19 lockdown period from March 26, 2020 to April 28, 2020 was recorded, the proportion of overdoses (particularly paracetamol and ibuprofen) and self-harm increased (Joyce et al., 2021).

Given the potential mental health impact, the team that launched the All Right? Campaign (including the Canterbury District Health Board) and Mental Health Foundation of New Zealand launched a nationwide mental health campaign titled "Getting Through Together"/"Whāia E Tātou Te Pae Tawhiti" (in Māori). The campaign made heavy use of the expertise developed in the All Right? campaign. The same website was used as the brand All Right? had been well established over the years (Mental Health Foundation, 2022). Instead of starting an ultimately brand new campaign, building on the successful experience of the All Right? campaign allows ready and effective partnerships formed with critical organizations during the evolving pandemic times and evidence-based psychosocial messaging, including specific messages targeting Māori, which contributed to the success of the Getting Through Together campaign (Canterbury District Health Board, 2021). It has reached 71 percent of the Christchurch population (Canterbury District Health Board, 2020).

With lockdowns and social distancing measures, social media and online resources became the most crucial outlet for mental health campaign messages. The government funding on the All Right? campaign stopped in June 2021 (Gates, 2021); mental health campaign communication strategies were shifted from offline to online spaces in the Getting Through Together campaign. The government-funded more digital tools, like digital apps for mental well-being.

Mental Health for Vulnerable Communities

A key challenge for mental health communication in Christchurch is ensuring that it supports equitable outcomes among diverse cultural and socio-economic groups. The Canterbury Wellbeing Survey shows a significant and sustained disparity in well-being between household income groups, with the lowest household income group scoring lower than wealthier groups in the World Health Organization Well-being Index (WHO-5) at all measured time points (Begg et al., 2021). In Christchurch, Māori people experience structural disadvantage as a result of colonization and racism, which has led to reduced access to mental health services and communications and services that have not adequately engaged with Māori cultural values and frameworks (Agnew et al., 2004; Savage et al., 2018).

In times of crisis, typically multiple minoritized groups have reduced access to information; for example, new migrants to Christchurch did receive messages on a refugee and migrant forum organized by the city council after the Christchurch earthquake and mosque attacks (Anwar & Sumpter, 202n), and further, typically have limited social networks and resources. After an emergency, community members often utilize local resources to seek information and collectively make sense of and reduce uncertainty (Xu, 2018). In the following section, we will discuss the situations of these at-risk communities and the action frameworks for enhancing the mental health of these communities.

Māori and Pasifika

With the persistent advocacy by Māori, the start of the twenty-first century marked mental health services in New Zealand switching from traditionally monocultural service delivery to the deinstitutionalization of mental health services, achieving greater awareness and sensitivity to the significance of culture in mental health (Agnew et al., 2004). Taha hinengaro (mental health in Māori) has been set up by the Ministry of Health as one of the four dimensions of Māori well-being under the Māori Health Models, focusing on "The capacity to communicate, to think and to feel mind and body are inseparable. Thoughts, feelings, and emotions are integral components of the body and soul" (Ministry of Health, 2017).

As Agnew et al.'s (2004) research suggests, culturally safe provision of Māori health services and communications requires culturally safe Māori ethos/kaupapa (values and approaches) and protocols for work, prayer, and healing, as shown by the use of Māori models of health and practices such as "Te Whare Tapa Wha" (four dimensions of Māori well-being) and "Te Wheke" (family health) (Ministry of Health, 2017). After the Canterbury earthquake, the All Right? campaign worked closely with dimensions in a Māori health approach other than Taha tinana (physical health): the inclusion of the wairua (soul), the role of the whānau (family), and the balance of the hinengaro (mind) are as important as the physical manifestations of illness. With the importance of family connections in Māori health, Whānau activities are one of the significant aspects of Māori-focused work. On the other hand, the All Right? campaign also addresses Pasifikas' well-being in terms of spirituality and celebrating cultural heritage. Regular, in-depth research has been conducted to investigate how the campaign supports the resilience and well-being of Māori and Pacifika. While this met the needs of some, a survey of Māori six years after the Canterbury earthquake showed that 34 percent of respondents did not feel they had equal access to post-quake support (Savage et al., 2018).

Mentally healthy and competent communities have been identified as having safe social spaces, knowledge, and partnerships for action (Burgess, 2012). Below, we will introduce two fundamental approaches to communicating mental health for indigenous communities in Christchurch: 1) creating safe social spaces; and 2) building partnerships for action.

Creating Safe Social Spaces

Social connectedness and social capital are necessary for creating safe social spaces for at-risk communities. Social connectedness can be enhanced by providing a space for learning together. For example, during the Christchurch earthquake, a marae (Māori communal gathering place) provided a range of learning opportunities at the marae itself (including room for Māori medicine, Māori language classes, cooking classes, and a community vegetable garden), which promoted relationship building among community members (DeMello, 2020; Phibbs, 2015). Informal support, especially among neighbors, and connectedness can increase awareness; improve preparedness and resilience at individual, family, and organizational (as well as community) levels; create a sense of ownership; build capacity; garner support for action; and foster sustainability (Pfefferbaum et al., 2015; Shimpo, 2019; Thornley, 2015; Uekusa, 2017; Vallance, 2015).

Physical spaces encouraging social interaction and bonding, such as central meetings, lunch places, and communal working areas, increase community well-being (Shimpo, 2019). Community infrastructure across Christchurch that Māori can engage with, such as marae, schools, churches, and community centers, supports and enables social connectedness and increased community well-being and resilience (Kenney, 2015; Kwok, 2016; Thornley, 2015; Vallance, 2015). Identifying essential resources and assets in the community and naming these identifies the existing assets within civil society and facilitates cooperation and trust (Kwok, 2016). For example, after the Canterbury earthquakes, the initiatives of Te Rūnanga o Ngāi Tahu and Papatipu Rūnanga (local Māori tribal council) to mobilize marae-based resources meant they supported community members effectively (Thornley, 2015). Conversely, a lack of community infrastructure was a critical barrier to community well-being in Shirley community in Christchurch, where there were few community meeting spaces and consequently few community organizations and workers before the earthquakes compared with Inner City East and Lyttelton (Thornley, 2015).

Building Partnerships for Action

Increasing participation and building community-based capability helps communities be mentally healthy (DeMello, 2020; Mamula-Seadon, 2015; Vallance, 2015). Two key features of community leadership in the aftermath of the Christchurch earthquake were, first, ensuring key groups are represented at the commissioning and decision-making table (particularly groups that are typically disadvantaged), and, second, using inclusive processes, for example, collective or consensus decision making (Chua, 2019; Kenney, 2015). Multiple studies set in Christchurch identified the Christchurch Earthquake Recovery Authority (CERA)[1] as limiting participation by communities and civil society and described this as a retreat from the decentralized, collaborative democracy which had been prevalent in New Zealand (Mamula-Seadon, 2015; Sovacool, 2018).

Notably, there has been poor and delayed coordination with Māori communities in previous emergencies in New Zealand (DeMello, 2020; Kenney, 2015; Sovacool, 2018), but after the Christchurch earthquakes, this situation changed when the chair of the local tribal authority formed a national Māori Recovery Network which exercised autonomy to address disaster-related emergencies, risks, and recovery concerns by taking collective responsibility for the well-being of others in their tribal region (DeMello, 2020; Kenney, 2015). In the aftermath of the Canterbury earthquakes, the emergence of leaders was crucial to medium to long-term recovery (Kwok, 2016). Civil society was actively involved in the acute phases but seemed less engaged or welcome in the same way in the reconstruction and recovery phases (Spector, 2019). Several community organizations emerged and coalesced around the immediate response to the earthquakes. These groups and others contributed to the recovery through various actions (Cretney, 2018). When Māori communities contribute their experienced-based perspectives in governance to the intersections of science, technology, and policy, work priorities have greater credibility, legitimacy, and relevance and are better able to support mentally healthy communities (Cretney, 2016, 2018; Cretney and Bond, 2017; DeMello, 2020; Kenney, 2015; Kwok, 2016; Lambert, 2014; Mamula-Seadon, 2015; Phibbs, 2015; Sovacool, 2018; Uekusa, 2017; Vallance, 2015).

Impacts of Crises on Non-White and Immigrant Communities

On March 15, 2019, people in Christchurch, New Zealand, experienced an unprecedented terrorist attack in their city. A mass shooter reported as a White supremacist attacked two mosques in Christchurch, killing 51 Muslims and injuring 49 others (Anwar & Sumpter, 2022). Proximate experiences of mass violence can lead to solid traumas and psychological distress in the community (Holman et al., 2008; Jones et al., 2016; Schlenger et al., 2002). In addition, unlike previous mass violence in other parts of the world, the Christchurch mosque shooting involved unprecedented use of social media—the active shooting in one mosque was live-streamed. The video was later shared extensively on social media, which led to great panic in society (Ventura et al., 2019).

The attack strongly impacted particularly non-White and immigrant communities in Christchurch because this group had been a target of this attack. While community members often utilize local resources to seek out information and collectively make sense of and reduce uncertainty after a crisis

(Xu, 2018), it is more difficult for minority ethnic communities like immigrants because they usually have limited local resources. A study of resilience among new migrants to New Zealand and Japan during their natural disasters in 2010–11 showed that these groups were both more vulnerable but also resilient due to their experience already with challenging circumstances, as well as everyday disadvantages, which gave them "earned strength" (Uekusa & Matthewman, 2017). Communities across New Zealand, regardless of ethnicity, have responded to the mosque attack in cognitive and behavioral ways, including public vigils, remembrance events, and marches the week after the attack (*NZ Herald*, 2019). However, non-White and immigrant communities' crisis communication relied heavily on their language channels. Chen & Leung's (2020) focus groups with Chinese people in Christchurch showed that Chinese social media were used extensively for information and emotional support after the crisis. Communication responses in times of crisis need to explicitly shape outputs to meet the needs of minoritized groups who need information in different formats. At crisis times, instead of formal communication channels, digital communication channels in familiar languages are crucial safe social spaces for these immigrants to maintain mental health.

Conclusion

The past decade marks an era of crises and significant challenges in maintaining mental health in Christchurch. Previously, expert advice and national guidance from professionals were often prioritized over local knowledge and practices, which can isolate community members and lead to unhelpful or irrelevant actions (Cretney, 2016, 2018; Spector, 2019; Vallance, 2015). However, the example of the mental health responses in Christchurch after crises supported that local people with knowledge of the local context are best equipped to set priorities for regional development (Anwar & Sumpter, 2022; Uekusa & Matthewman, 2017; Vallance, 2015). Psychosocial skills should be built up with cultural identities; for example, core to cultural identity in New Zealand is the relationship to place: residing in a region includes both mana whenua (referring to the people originating from the region in Māori) and maata waka (meaning pan-tribal in Māori) identities. Notably, creating safe spaces and building partnerships for action have helped enhance mental health among vulnerable communities like the Māori, and the specific kaupapa (Māori approach) has been successful in targeting Māori in campaigns like Getting Through Together during the COVID-19 pandemic. While the All Right? campaign and a collaborative approach with communities had been successful, the switch from in-person and non-digital communications to digital tools suggests more research still needs to be conducted to help engage at-risk communities in communicating mental health.

Acknowledgment

We would like to thank Dr. Zita Joyce (University of Canterbury) for sharing her insights with us at the initial stage of our writing.

Discussion Questions

1. Christchurch has experienced other crises that may affect mental health, such as the wildfires in the Port Hills in 2017, which was New Zealand's most devastating wildfire of recent times (Pearce, 2018). The All Right? campaign has become a well-established brand for communicating mental health through the past decade. What are the main factors for the sustainability of the campaign? What changes in approach might be required in the aftermath of the COVID-19 pandemic?
2. Mental health can be a big concern after a crisis, but there is likely attrition in resources and attention afterward. How should communication and engagement with at-risk communities continue after the initial phase of crises?
3. Safe social spaces (high levels of social inclusion and participation, particularly of groups that typically experience poorer outcomes) were identified as crucial for equitable communications in Christchurch. What were effective forms of practice in the examples of communications after the terrorist attack that ensured that the needs of minoritized groups were addressed through mass communications?
4. Building partnership for actions is essential for communicating mental health with communities, but entering communities can be complex. What is the best initial approach for building partnerships with communities?

Note

1 CERA was a time-limited central government agency tasked with coordination of recovery in Canterbury after the 2010/11 earthquakes

Further Reading

Calder, K., Begg, A., D'Aeth, L., Turner, S., Fox, C., Nobes, B., . . . & Bell, C. (2022). Evaluation of the All Right? Campaign for tangata whaiora/mental health service users in Canterbury, New Zealand. *Health Promotion International*, *37*(1), daab102.

Rawson, E. (2016). Te Waioratanga: Health promotion practice – the importance of Māori cultural values to wellbeing in a disaster context and beyond. *Australasian Journal of Disaster and Trauma Studies*, *20*(2), 81–87.

Reid, P., Paine, S.-J., Curtis, E., Jones, R., & Anderson, A. (n.d.). Achieving health equity in Aotearoa: strengthening responsiveness to Māori in health research. *The New Zealand Medical Journal* (Online), 130, 96–103. Retrieved from https://researchspace.auckland.ac.nz/handle/2292/44418

References

Agnew, F., Pulotu-Endemann, F. K., Robinson, G., Suaalii-Sauni, T., Warren, H., Wheeler, A., & Schmidt-Sopoaga, H. (2004). Pacific models of mental health service delivery in New Zealand ("PMMHSD") project. *Health Research Council of New Zealand.* https://www.leva.co.nz/uploads/files/resources/Pacific-Models-of-Mental-Health-Service-Delivery-in-New-Zealand-PMMHSD-Project.pdf

Aldrich, D. P., & Meyer, M. A. (2015). Social capital and community resilience. *American behavioral scientist, 59*(2), 254–269. DOI: 10.1177/0002764214550299

All Right? (2022). *All Right? recipe: The key ingredients of Canterbury's wellbeing campaign.* Retrieved July 8, 2022, from https://legacy.allright.org.nz/media/documents/ART122_RecipeDocument_A5_2_FINAl_Booklet.pdf

Anwar, N. D., & Sumpter, C. (2022). Societal resilience following terrorism: Community and coordination in Christchurch. *Behavioral Sciences of Terrorism and Political Aggression, 14*(1), 70–95. doi: 10.1080/19434472.2020.1800785

Bakema, M. M., Parra, C., & McCann, P. (2019, April). Learning from the rubble: The case of Christchurch, New Zealand, after the 2010 and 2011 earthquakes. *Disasters, 43*(2), 431–455. DOI: 10.1111/disa.12322

Beaglehole, B., Mulder, R. T., Boden, J. M., & Bell, C. J. (2019). A systematic review of the psychological impacts of the Canterbury earthquakes on mental health. *Australian and New Zealand Journal of Public Health, 43*(3), 274–280. DOI: 10.1111/1753-6405.12894

Begg, A., D'Aeth, L., Kenagy, E., Ambrose, C., Dong, H., & Schluter, P. J. (2021). Wellbeing recovery inequity following the 2010/2011 Canterbury earthquake sequence: Repeated cross-sectional studies. *Australian and New Zealand Journal of Public Health, 45*(2), 158–164. DOI: 10.1111/1753-6405.13054

Bourke, J. A., Hay-Smith, E. J. C., Snell, D. L., & Schluter, P. J. (2017, 2017/08/01/). Community inclusion of wheelchair users during the long-term recovery phase following the 2010/2011 Canterbury earthquakes. *International Journal of Disaster Risk Reduction, 23*, 169–177. DOI: 10.1016/j.ijdrr.2017.05.004

Burgess, R. (2012). Supporting global mental health: Critical community psychology as a potential panacea. *Community psychology and the socio-economics of mental distress: International perspectives* (pp. 108–23). Basingstoke: Palgrave Macmilan.

Cafer, A., Green, J., & Goreham, G. (2019). A Community Resilience Framework for community development practitioners building equity and adaptive capacity. *Community Development, 50*(2), 201–216. DOI: 10.1080/15575330.2019.1575442

Calder, K., D'Aeth, L., Turner, S., Fox, C., & Begg, A. (2016). Evaluation of a wellbeing campaign following a natural disaster in Christchurch, New Zealand. *International Journal of Mental Health Promotion, 18*(4), 222–233. DOI: 10.1080/14623730.2016.1210531

Canterbury District Health Board. (2020). A summary of June 2020 All Right? campaign evaluation findings. Retrieved from: https://www.allright.org.nz/uploads/files/All-RightSummary2020.pdf

Canterbury District Health Board. (2021). Evaluation of the All Right? campaign COVID-19 response – Getting Through Together. Retrieved from: https://www.cph.co.nz/wp-content/uploads/GTTEvaluationReport.pdf

Chambers, R. (1994). The origins and practice of participatory rural appraisal. *Journal of World Development, 22(7)*, 953–969. DOI: 10.1016/0305-750X(94)90141-4

Chen, W., & Leung, W. C. (2020). Uncertainty reduction: Media use and information seeking among Chinese students after mosque shooting in Christchurch. Paper presented in 2020 International Communication Association pre-conference "Rethinking the Relationship between Migration, Media, and Technology in Times of Crises within and beyond the West."

Christchurch and Canterbury earthquakes. (2022). *Christchurch and Canterbury earthquakes*. Retrieved July 7, 2022, from https://my.christchurchcitylibraries.com/christchurch-and-canterbury-earthquakes/

Chua, R. Y., Kadirvelu, A., Yasin, S., Choudhry, F. R., & Park, M. S. A. (2019). The cultural, family and community factors for resilience in southeast Asian indigenous communities: A systematic review. *Journal of Community Psychology, 47*(7), 1750–1771. DOI: 10.1002/jcop.22224

Community and Public Health (2019). Shared programme of action – psychosocial resilience group Canterbury. Retrieve from https://www.cph.co.nz/your-health/community-in-mind/

Cretney, R. M. (2016). Local responses to disaster: The value of community led post disaster response action in a resilience framework. *Disaster Prevention and Management, 25*(1), 27–40.

Cretney, R. M. (2018). Beyond public meetings: Diverse forms of community led recovery following disaster. *International Journal of Disaster Risk Reduction, 28*, 122–130. DOI: 10.1016/j.ijdrr.2018.02.035

Cretney, R. M., & Bond, S. (2017). Shifting relationships to place: A relational place-based perspective on SES resilience. *Urban Geography, 38*(1), 8–24. DOI: 10.1080/02723638.2016.1139865

DeMello, A., Egan, R., & Drew, J. (2020). Resilience-building by community health organizations: a guiding model for practice. *Journal of the Royal Society of New Zealand, 50*(4), 552–571. DOI: 10.1080/03036758.2020.1772324

Environment Canterbury (2020). How many people live in Canterbury? Retrieved from https://www.ecan.govt.nz/your-region/living-here/regional-leadership/population/census-estimates/

Ford, J. D., King, N., Galappaththi, E. K., Pearce, T., McDowell, G., & Harper, S. L. (2020). The resilience of Indigenous Peoples to environmental change. *One Earth, 2*(6), 532–543. DOI: 10.1016/j.oneear.2020.05.014

Gates, C. (2021). Canterbury mental wellbeing campaign All Right? loses government funding. https://www.stuff.co.nz/the-press/news/125656339/canterbury-mental-wellbeing-campaign-all-right-loses-government-funding

Good, G. A., Phibbs, S., & Williamson, K. (2016, Nov.–Dec.). Disoriented and immobile: The experiences of people with visual impairments during and after the Christchurch, New Zealand, 2010 and 2011 earthquakes. *Journal of Visual Impairment & Blindness, 110*(6), 425–435. DOI: 10.1177/0145482X1611000605

Govt NZ (2020). History of the COVID-19 alert system. Retrieved from https://covid19.govt.nz/alert-system/history-of-the-covid-19-alert-system/

Harkins, C. (2020). Supporting community recovery and resilience in response to the COVID-19 pandemic–a rapid review of evidence. Glasgow Centre for Population Health. Retrieved from https://www.gcph.co.uk/publications/938_supporting_community_recovery_and_resilience_in_response_to_covid-19

Health in All Policies Team. (2020). Pandemic supplement. Canterbury District Health Board. https://www.cph.co.nz/wp-content/uploads/IPGPandemicSupplement.pdf

Holman, E. A., Silver, R. C., Poulin, M., Andersen, J., Gil-Rivas, V., & McIntosh, D. N. (2008). Terrorism, acute stress, and cardiovascular health: A 3-year national study following the September 11th attacks. *Archives of General Psychiatry, 65*(1), 73–80. DOI: 10.1001/archgenpsychiatry.2007.6

Horton, R. (2020, Sept. 26). Offline: COVID-19 is not a pandemic. *Lancet, 396*(10255), 874. DOI: 10.1016/S0140-6736(20)32000-6

Jones, N. M., Wojcik, S. P., Sweeting, J., & Silver, R. C. (2016). Tweeting negative emotion: An investigation of Twitter data in the aftermath of violence on college campuses. *Psychological Methods*, *21*(4), 526–541. DOI: 10.1037/met0000099

Joyce, L. R., Richardson, S. K., McCombie, A., Hamilton, G. J., & Ardagh, M. W. (2021). Mental health presentations to Christchurch Hospital Emergency Department during COVID-19 lockdown. *Emergency Medicine Australasia*, *33*(2), 324–330. DOI: 10.1111/1742-6723.13667

Ka'apu, K., & Burnette, C. E. (2019). A culturally informed systematic review of mental health disparities among adult Indigenous men and women of the USA: What is known? *The British Journal of Social Work*, *49*(4), 880–898. DOI: 10.1093/bjsw/bcz009

Kenney, C. M., & Phibbs, S. (2015). A Māori love story: Community-led disaster management in response to the Ōtautahi (Christchurch) earthquakes as a framework for action. *International Journal of Disaster Risk Reduction*, 14, 46–55. DOI: 10.1016/j.ijdrr.2014.12.010

Kwok, A. H., Doyle, E. E. H., Becker, J., Johnston, D., & Paton, D. (2016). What is 'social resilience'? Perspectives of disaster researchers, emergency management practitioners, and policymakers in New Zealand. *International Journal of Disaster Risk Reduction*, *19*, 197–211. DOI: 10.1016/j.ijdrr.2016.08.013

Lambert, S. J. (2014). Māori and the Christchurch earthquakes: The interplay between Indigenous endurance and resilience through urban disaster. Retrieve from https://researcharchive.lincoln.ac.nz/bitstream/handle/10182/7285/MAI_Jrnl_V3_iss2_Lambert.pdf

Lloyd, M. (2020, June 30). *Group tackles isolation and obesity in Christchurch's Pacific community through dance*. Television New Zealand One.

Mallett, R., Hagen-Zanker, J., Slater, R., & Duvendack, M. (2012). The benefits and challenges of using systematic reviews in international development research. *Journal of Development Effectiveness*, *4*(3), 445–455. DOI: 10.1080/19439342.2012.711342

Mamula-Seadon, L., & McLean, I. (2015). Response and early recovery following 4 September 2010 and 22 February 2011 Canterbury earthquakes: Societal resilience and the role of governance. *International Journal of Disaster Risk Reduction*, *14*, 82–95. DOI: 10.1016/j.ijdrr.2015.01.005

Mayer, B. J. (2019). A review of the literature on community resilience and disaster recovery. *Current Environmental Health Reports*, *6*(3), 167–173. DOI: 10.1007/s40572-019-00239-3

McSaveney, E. (2022). Historic earthquakes – The 2011 Christchurch earthquake, Te Ara – the Encyclopedia of New Zealand. Retrieved from http://www.TeAra.govt.nz/en/historic-earthquakes/page-13

Mental Health Foundation (2022). About getting through together. https://mentalhealth.org.nz/getting-through-together/about-getting-through-together

Ministry of Health (2017). *Māori health models – Te Whare Tapa Whā* [Image]. https://www.health.govt.nz/our-work/populations/maori-health/maori-health-models/maori-health-models-te-whare-tapa-wha

National Emergency Management Agency. (2019). National disaster resilience strategy. National Emergency Management Agency. https://www.civildefence.govt.nz/cdem-sector/plans-and-strategies/national-disaster-resilience-strategy/national-disaster-resilience-strategy-summary-version/

Norris, F. H., Stevens, S. P., Pfefferbaum, B., Wyche, K. F., & Pfefferbaum, R. L. (2008). Community resilience as a metaphor, theory, set of capacities, and strategy for disaster readiness. *American Journal of Community Psychology*, *41*(1–2), 127–150. DOI: 10.1007/s10464-007-9156-6

NZ Herald (2019, May 3). Christchurch mosque attacks: 51st victim dies after surgery. https://www.nzherald.co.nz/nz/ news/article.cfm?c_id=1&objectid=12227479

Patel, S. S., Rogers, M. B., Amlôt, R., & Rubin, G. J. (2017). What do we mean by 'community resilience'? A systematic literature review of how it is defined in the literature. *PLoS Currents, 9*. DOI: 10.1371/currents.dis.db775aff25efc5ac4f0660ad9c9f7db2

Pearce, H. G. (2018). The 2017 Port Hills wildfires—A window into New Zealand's fire future. *Australasian Journal of Disaster and Trauma Studies, 22*, 63–73.

Pfefferbaum, B., Pfefferbaum, R. L., & Van Horn, R. L. (2015). Community resilience interventions: participatory, assessment-based, action-oriented processes. *American Behavioral Scientist, 59*(2), 238–253. DOI: 10.1177/0002764214550298

Pfefferbaum, R. L., Pfefferbaum, B., Van Horn, R. L., Klomp, R. W., Norris, F. H., & Reissman, D. B. (2013). The communities advancing resilience toolkit (CART). *Journal of Public Health Management and Practice, 19*(3), 250–258. doi:10.1097/PHH.0b013e318268aed8

Phibbs, S., Good, G., Severinsen, C., Woodbury, E., & Williamson, K. (2015). Emergency preparedness and perceptions of vulnerability among disabled people following the Christchurch earthquakes: Applying lessons learnt to the Hyogo Framework for Action. *Australasian Journal of Disaster Trauma Studies, 19*, 37.

Phibbs, S., Kenney, C., & Solomon, M. (2015). Ngā Mōwaho: An analysis of Māori responses to the Christchurch earthquakes. *Kotuitui: New Zealand Journal of Social Sciences Online, 10*(2), 72–82. DOI: 10.1080/1177083X.2015.1066401

Savage, C., Hynds, A., Leonard, J., Dallas-Katoa, W., Goldsmith, L., & Kuntz, J. (2018). *All Right? An investigation into Māori Resilience*. Ihi Research.

Schlenger, W. E., Caddell, J. M., Ebert, L., Jordan, B. K., Rourke, K. M., Wilson, D., & Kulka, R. A. (2002). Psychological reactions to terrorist attacks: Findings from the National Study of Americans' Reactions to September 11. *Jama, 288*(5), 581–588. doi:10.1001/jama.288.5.581

Shimpo, N., Wesener, A., & McWilliam, W. (2019, Feb). How community gardens may contribute to community resilience following an earthquake. *Urban Forestry & Urban Greening, 38*, 124–132. DOI: 10.1016/j.ufug.2018.12.002

Signal, L., Martin, J., Cram, F., & Robson, B. (2008). *The Health Equity Assessment Tool: A user's guide*. Ministry of Health.

Sovacool, B. K., Tan-Mullins, M., & Abrahamse, W. (2018). Bloated bodies and broken bricks: Power, ecology, and inequality in the political economy of natural disaster recovery. *Journal of World Development, 110*, 243–255. DOI: 10.1016/j.worlddev.2018.05.028

Spector, S., Cradock-Henry, N. A., Beaven, S., & Orchiston, C. (2019). Characterising rural resilience in Aotearoa–New Zealand: A systematic review. *Regional Environmental Change, 19*(2), 543–557. DOI: 10.1007/s10113-018-1418-3

Thornley, L., Ball, J., Signal, L., Lawson-Te Aho, K., & Rawson, E. (2015). Building community resilience: learning from the Canterbury earthquakes. *Kotuitui: New Zealand Journal of Social Sciences Online, 10*(1), 23–35. DOI: 10.1080/1177083X.2014.934846

Uekusa, S., & Matthewman, S. (2017). Vulnerable and resilient? Immigrants and refugees in the 2010–2011 Canterbury and Tohoku disasters. *International Journal of Disaster Risk Reduction, 22*, 355–361. DOI: 10.1016/j.ijdrr.2017.02.006

Vallance, S. (2015). An evaluation of the Waimakariri district council's integrated and community-based recovery framework following the Canterbury earthquakes: Implications for urban resilience. *Journal of Urban Policy, 33*(4), 433–451. DOI: 10.1080/08111146.2014.980401

Vallance, S., & Carlton, S. (2015). First to respond, last to leave: Communities' roles and resilience across the '4Rs'. *International Journal of Disaster Risk Reduction, 14*, 27–36.

Ventura, C., Shannon, J., & May, A. (2019, March 16). 49 dead, 1 suspect charged: What we know about New Zealand Christchurch mosque shootings. *USA Today*.

https://www.usatoday.com/story/news/world/2019/03/15/christchurch-new-zealand-shootings-mosques/3171204002/

Williams, G. (2022). An anlaysis of young adults in New Zealand's engagement with All Right mental health campaigns. University of Canterbury Research Repository. https://ir.canterbury.ac.nz/items/96d3437b-b484-4a96-a7fd-b7a13d963c58

Xu, S. (2018). Crisis communication within a community: Bonding, coping, and making sense together. *Public Relations Review*, *44*(1), 84–97. DOI: 10.1016/j.pubrev.2017.10.004

INDEX

Note: **Bold** page numbers refer to tables and *italic* page numbers refer to figures.

abortion law 172
Abrams, J. 53, 56
acquired immunodeficiency syndrome
    (AIDS) 123
activist communication 89–90
acute lymphoblastic leukemia (ALL)
    138
advocacy: and activism 84–86;
    communication 86–89, 92; and
    fundraising 135–137; social
    responsibility and 167–174
Aghazadeh, Sarah A. 9
Agnew, F. 205
AIDS activism 123–125
AIDS Coalition to Unleash Power (ACT
    UP) 123, 126; organization strategies
    124–125; social movements 125–126
alcohol awareness campaigns 18
Aldoory, L. 50, 51
"All Right?" campaign 200–204, 208
American Beverage Association 25
American Cancer Society (ACS) 137
American Civil Liberties Union of
    Massachusetts 141
American Heart Association 143
American Public Health Association 3,
    38, 140

American Social Hygiene Association
    (ASHA) 123
Anderson, W. B. 152
Anger Activism Model (AAM) 142
Anthony, K. E. 155
anti-venereal disease campaign 123
Argenti, P.A. 175
Argentine Institute of Corporate Social
    Responsibility 36
artificial intelligence (AI) 3
Aspriadis, N. 100
AstroTurf 23
Athlete Activism 172–174
Austin, L. 9, 99

Baker, S. 41
Bardhan, N. R. 48
Bassett, M. T. 122
Bauchner, H. 91
Bernays, Edward L. 16
Biden, Joe 25
Black communities 58, 121, 122
Black Lives Matter (BLM) movement 52,
    83, 86, 122, 126, 166
Black Panther movement 116
Black Panther Party (BPP) 120–123, 122,
    125–126

Boffin, N. 70
Boynton, Lois A. 7
Browning, N. 168
Byerly, C. M. 118

Cajina-Clark, Jeremy 8
Calder, K. 202
Callahan, Mike 38
Campbell, D. M. 34
Canel, M. J. 149
Canterbury Wellbeing Survey 201, 204
Carlton, S. 200
Carroll, Archie 36
Castelli, J. 135
Centers for Disease Control and
    Prevention (CDC) 33, 47, 91, 119, 139
Chang, C. 159
Chen, W. 208
Choi, Minhee 8, 9
Christchurch Earthquake Recovery
    Authority (CERA) 207
Christchurch Health and Development
    Study (CHDS) 200
Civil Rights Act of 1946 121
Civil Rights Movement 118
civil society 207
Clinton, Bill 33
Code of Ethics 32
Coleman, R. 88
Commission on Public Relations
    Education (CPRE) 6, 7
Commission on Training Camp Activities
    (CTCA) 123
communication devices 19–21
community infrastructure 200
community mental health competence 198
Comunello, Francesca 11
conceptual foundation 148–150
Cone Communications CSR Study 166
Conte, Giuseppe 191
controversial social-political issues 168,
    174
convergence framework theory 102
Coombs, W. T. 100
coronavirus disease 2019 (COVID-19)
    pandemic 169–171
Corporate America 172–174
corporate social advocacy (CSA) 10, 37,
    142
corporate social responsibility (CSR) 10,
    35–38, 36, 37, 142, 167, 168

Covello, V. 104
Covid-19 pandemic: digital strategic
    communication during (*see* digital
    strategic communication, during
    Covid-19 pandemic)
COVID-19 vaccines 105
Crenshaw, Kimberlé 48
crisis and emergency risk communication
    (CERC) framework 155
crisis communication: in digital world
    106–107; for social good 98; crisis
    communication theories 99–102;
    public health/social change 102–109
critical health communication 49
critical race theory 50
Culver, John 171

Dallinger, J. M. 85
Davidson, Alex 38
de Beaumont foundation 138
decision-making processes 39
Derville, T. 90
Diani, M. 117
digital communication 187; activities 186;
    environments 110; practices 192
digital crisis communication 108
digital media 159
digital publics 194
digital spaces 194
digital strategic communication, during
    Covid-19 pandemic 183–186,
    189–193; Italy 186–187; research
    questions and methods 187–189
disaster communication 102–103
disaster management processes 103
Dodd, M. D. 168, 175
donor–organization relationship 140

Eaddy, LaShonda 9
Eaves, K. L. 52
Edelman, Richard 59, 174
Edelman Trust Barometer 59, 166
Edrington, Candice L. 9
educational institutions 5
Edwards, L. 51, 118
emergency communication strategies 187
emergency management processes 186
Eng, Nicholas 10
Environmental Protection Agency 155
episodic frame 88
Eriksson, M. 108

ethical decision-making models **40**
ethical public relations 32–33
ethics codes **39**

face-to-face interpersonal communication 156
faith-based organizations 106
Fauci, Anthony 33
FEMA 155
feminist theory projects 50
Fessmann. J. 143
Five Ways to Wellbeing 202, 203
Floyd, George 166
for-profit companies approach 35
for-profit corporate entities 159
framing 87
Franklin, D. 41
Friedman, Milton 35, 36
Frumkin, P. 133
fundraising 135–137, 136–137, 141

Geiling, Natasha 124
Getting, Vlado A. 3
Getting Through Together campaign 204
Gibson, R. 20
Gillett Amendment 1913 148, 150
Golombisky, K. 50
governmental social media communication 193
government campaigns 24–26
government communication 148, 149, 153, 155; strategies 156; trust crisis in 150–152
Government Communication Decision Wheel (GCDW) 149
"government Conte" 187
government crisis communication 156–158
government mismanagement of crisis 155
government–public relationship 148, 152, 155
government social media communication 152–153
grassroots advocacy organization 23
grassroots lobbying 135
Greenville's Black community 25
gun violence 139, 140, 143, 168, 172–174; communication 90–92
Gun Violence Archive 172
Guttman, N. 33

Hample, D. 85
health activism 120–123
health-care companies 167
healthcare industry 136
health communication: campaigns 143; scholarship 58
health crises 104–105
"health disparities" 47
health industry 133
health inequalities 19
health information 21
health partnerships 24
health policy 22–24
Heart Truth Campaign 57, 143
Heath, C. D. 57
Heymann, D. L. 59
high-responsibility crises 100
Hinnant, Amanda 7
Hong, H. 152
human papilloma virus (HPV) 138
Hyland-Wood, B. 156, 158

Ieracitano, Francesca 11
indirect advocacy 135
Infantino, Gianni 106
"infodemic" environment 186–187
Institute for Public Relations 142
institutional communication behaviors *190*
Institutional Review Board process 33
intergovernmental micro-environment 149
Internal Revenue Code, section 501(c)3 of 137
Internal Revenue Service (IRS) 137
intersectionality theory 49, 53
intersectional work 50–52
intra-departmental communication 158
issue framing 87, 88, 90
Italian central government organizations 187
Italian public institutions 193
Italian public sector communication 187, 194
Italian public sector organizations 186
Italy 186–187
Iyengar, S. 88, 91

Jiang, H. 57
Jin, Y. 9, 99, 104
Johnson, C. R. S. 52
Jolly, J. 125

Kaepernick, Colin 168
Kapler, Gabe 173
Kapoor, N. 70
Kass, H, D. 69
Kavanaugh, A. L. 152
Kelly, K. S. 71, 72, 73, 74, 140
Kent, M. L. 150, 151
Kerr, Steve 173
Kim, S. 151
Kiousis, S. 149
Koop, C. Everett 4, 124
Krishna, A. 151

Lambert, S. J. 199
Larson, H. J. 59
Len-Ríos, María E. 7
#LetsBuildTogether campaign 169
Leung, W. C. 11, 208
Levenshus, Abbey Blake 10
Liu, B. F. 99, 108, 156
Liu, W. 103
Logan, N. 34
Long, K. H. 57
Lovari, A. 11, 193
low-responsibility crises 100
Lu, Xuerong 9
Lucas, S. E. 117
Luntz, Frank 138
Lupton, D. 49

Macnamara, J. 100
Manias-Muñoz, I. 99
Marinelli, Alberto 11
Martinson, D. L. 41
Massa, Alessandra 11
mass media campaigns 89
Mathias, Kaaren 11
McCarthy, J. D. 135
McKeever, B. W. 72, 157
McLean, H. 157
McMillon, Doug 173
Mead, Margaret 143
media advocacy 6, 87, 89, 90, 92
media affordances 108–109
media convergence 109
media environments 109
mental disorders 200, 201
mental health: issues 119; in New
    Zealand 198; building knowledge
    and skills 199–204; participation and
    community-based capability 206–208;
    safe social spaces 206; for vulnerable
    communities 204–205

menthol cigarettes 58
Miller, A. H. 151
"misguided essentialism" 35
misinformation 107–108
monkeypox virus 54–56
Morehouse, J. 106
Māori 205
MSM community 54, 55, 56

Nasiri, T. 71
National Institutes of Health (NIH) 34, 119
National Research Act 34
Nelson, A. 122
New Zealand, mental health in see mental
    health, in New Zealand
non-academic organizations 34
nongovernmental organization 137
non-government entities 159
nonprofit crises 105–106
nonprofit fundraising events 141
nonprofit health facilities 133
nonprofit health organizations 133
nonprofit organizational advocacy 135
nonprofit organizations 105, 133–134,
    136, 140, 143; advocacy and
    fundraising 135–137; nonprofits
    benefiting public health 137–139;
    nonprofits benefiting social change
    139–140; research on public relations
    and 140–143; types of 137
nonprofit philanthropic organizations 105
nonprofit philanthropy 136–137
nonprofit PR 141–143
non-white and immigrant communities
    207–208
Nuffield Council on Bioethics 70

online government communication tools
    152
oppositional sensitivities in segmentation
    design 53–54
organizational crisis communication 99
organizational cultures 185, 187
organization–public relationships 153,
    155–156, 184
organization strategies 124–125
Orsini, M. 154
Ortega, F. 154
Overton, Holly 10

Palfrey, J.S. 135
Parran, Thomas Jr. 123
Pasifika 205

Pearl, Monica B. 124
People's Free Medical Clinics (PFMC) 122
Peretti, Jonah 171
"personal responsibility" approach 58
Pfattheicher, S. 59
philanthropic organizations 105
physical spaces 206
Place, K. R. 51
policymaker–public gap 53
political public relations 149
Pompper, D. 50
Ponder, Monica L. 8
population health 49
Post-Katrina Emergency Management
   Reform Act of 2006 155
Power, M. R. 157
practitioner-focused works 51
Pressgrove, G. N. 8, 72
prosocial behaviors 4, 59
PSAs 40, 41
psychosocial skills 199
psychosocial well-being 199–200
public health 49, 79, 116; approach
   90, 91; campaigns 89, 149;
   communication, political economy
   of 58–59; conceptualizing 119–120;
   context 153–156; crises 154, 155, 169;
   crisis communication in digital world
   106–107; disaster communication
   102–103; education campaign 123;
   health crises 104–105; leadership 154;
   media affordances 108–109; media
   convergence 109; messaging 55;
   misinformation 107–108; nonprofit
   crises 105–106; nonprofits benefiting
   137–139; organizations 99; protecting
   169–171; stewardship in 68–71, 73–75,
   76–77; systems 184
public interest communication (PIC) 143
"public interest partnerships" 142–143
public relations: approach 5–7, 6; efforts
   123; relationship management function
   of 184; scholarship 68; stewardship in
   71–73, 73–75, 76–77; strategies 6
public sector communications 149, 185,
   186, 193
public sector organizations 185
publics-focused works 51–52

Quarantelli, E. L. 103

Rabkin, J. G. 125
racial disparities 47, 52

racial justice, health as 122–123
racial minority groups 50
"racial project" 51
racism 60; contextual definitions 48–49;
   intersectional public relations 49–59;
   racial disparities 47–48
relational approach 158–159
relational communication 159
relational government public relations
   approaches 160
relationship management 158; approach
   159, 184; function of public relations
   184; theory 140
relationship nurturing 78
Relay for Life benefiting the American
   Cancer Society 141
reputational threats 105
Righetti, N. 193
Rim, H. 168
Roe v. Wade 171–172

safe social spaces 206
Saltman, R. B. 69
Sanders, K. 148, 149
Schulman, Sarah 124
science communication 17
Seeger, M. W. 108
Sellnow, T. L. 108
Sha, B.-L. 50
situational crisis communication theory
   (SCCT) 100
situational risk awareness 109
situational theory of problem solving
   (STOPS) 141
situational theory of publics 54
SMRT Corporation 37
social advocacy 35–38
social capital 206
social change 42; crisis communication
   in digital world 106–107; disaster
   communication 102–103; health crises
   104–105; media affordances 108–109;
   media convergence 109; misinformation
   107–108; nonprofit crises 105–106;
   nonprofits benefiting 139–140
social connectedness 206
social determinants of health (SDH)
   14–15, 27, 119; communication
   devices 19–21; culture and 16–18;
   government campaigns 24–26; health
   partnerships 24; health policy affecting
   22–24; public relations affects public
   health 21–22

social good: corporate social
    responsibility and social advocacy
    35–38; ethical public relations
    32–33; ethical relationships and
    responsibilities contribute to 31–32;
    ethics 38–41
social habits 183
social marketing 5
social media 101, 153, 156, 157, 159, 186;
    advocacy strategies 140
Social-Mediated Crisis Communication
    (SMCC) Model 100–102, *101*
social movements 116, 117, 120, 126;
    conceptualizing 117–119; strategies
    and tactics 125
social networks 110
social-political issues 168, 174
social responsibility 41, 167–174
social science research 141
societal leadership 166
societal roles and expectations 174–176
Spaulding, C. 106
Stack, Edward 38, 172
Steurer, R. 36
stewardship 78; in public health 68–71,
    73–75, **76–77**; in public relations
    71–73, 73–75, **76–77**
Stewart, C. J. 117
Stroman, Marcus 174
Strömbäck, J. 149
Suffrage and Women's Rights Movements
    118
Supa, D. W. 168, 175
Sustainable Development Goals 2030 69

"Take Winter by Storm" campaign 41
Tan, A. S. L. 57
TARES test 39, 40–41
Tarrow, S. G. 85
Taylor, M. 150, 151
Ten Point Platform and Program 121
thematic frame 88
theory of planned behavior (TPB) 141
theory of reasoned action (TRA) 141
theory of situational support model 141,
    142
Thompkins, Al 35
Tindall, N. T. J. 8, 50, 57
"Torches of Freedom" campaign 16

Torossian, Ronn 32
Toth, E. L. 50, 51
traditional crisis scholarship 102
traditional paper-based media 187
Travis, P. 70
Trump, Donald 25, 141, 142, 157
Trust Barometer Global Report 166
trust crisis in government communication
    150–152
Turpin, T. 51

UK's Public Relations and
    Communication Association code 39
United Nations Millennium Development
    Goals 69
U.S. Food and Drug Administration 2011
    151
U.S. "whole of government" approach
    159

vaccine mandates 169–171
Vallance, S. 200
Valles, S. A. 35
van der Meer, T. G. L. A. 104
Vardeman, J. 8, 52, 56
Vardeman-Winter, J. E. 50, 57
Veil, S. R. 155
Veillard, J. H. M. 71
venereal diseases 123
Vijaykumar, S. 99
virtual environments 18

Wallack, L. 134
Waters, E. A. 35
Waters, R. 8, 140, 141
Williams, Georgia 11
women's rights 171–172
Women's Suffrage Movement 118
World Health Organization (WHO) 67,
    68, 73, 74, 120, 201, 203, 204

Xu, S. 108

Yeomans, L. 60
Young, Rachel 7

Zhao, X. 109
Zhou, X. 108
Zillmann, D. 20